SPARKY
Warrior, Peacemaker, Poet, Patriot

For Fumiko
Who Decorates My Life
and

For the Soldiers of the 100th Infantry Battalion
Whose Courage Has Decorated the Life of America

SPARKY
Warrior, Peacemaker, Poet, Patriot

A Portrait of Senator Spark M. Matsunaga
By Richard Halloran

Watermark Publishing

© 2002 Matsunaga Charitable Foundation

Design by Gonzalez Design Company

Production by Randall Chun Design

Cover photography by Mary Ann Changg

Interior photographs courtesy of the Matsunaga family,
the Senator Spark M. Matsunaga Papers of the Hawai'i
Congressional Papers Collection (University of Hawai'i
at Mānoa Library), *The Honolulu Advertiser*, the
Honolulu Star-Bulletin, *The Garden Island*, the White
House, the U.S. Senate, the Democratic National
Congressional Committee, the U.S. Army, the 100th
Infantry Battalion Veterans, the Hawai'i State Archives,
Alan Takano and Harry Lee

ISBN 0-9720932-1-4

Library of Congress Control Number: 2002108167

Watermark Publishing
1000 Bishop St, Suite 501-A
Honolulu, HI 96813
Telephone: 1-808-587-7766
Toll-free 1-866-900-BOOK
Web site: www.bookshawaii.net
e-mail: sales@bookshawaii.net

Printed in the United States of America

Contents

Foreword

My father always maintained that he was born under a lucky star. But luck alone wouldn't have taken a poor boy from Kaua'i — who earned money for his family by selling tofu with his pet pig Poru — to the United States Senate. It took a commitment to values such as respect, fairness and compassion; the courage to persevere in pursuit of goals such as peace and justice; and a sense of humor to deal with the obstacles and defeats along the way.

He was tireless in his devotion to public service as a calling of the highest order. That made it difficult on my mother, who bore the brunt of the demands of raising us five children. But she admired his dedication and reveled in his accomplishments. With the benefit of hindsight, I can share that admiration and recognize that through both word and example, he instilled his values in us, inspiring me toward a similar journey of commitment and service.

To this day, however, I'm fascinated with his poetry. Year after year, he would introduce a bill to establish the position of poet laureate of the U.S., and year after year he would be ignored, until he finally succeeded. He also persevered in writing poetry himself, and his poems, like most everything else he did in life, came from the heart. In few words, they convey a lifetime of lessons that are his gift and his legacy:

> *Commence your work wherever you can; your major task may be to start.*
> *To seek out the wrong is only half the task; to set it right is the tougher half.*
> *Strike at your foe and be struck in return; befriend your foe and secure your*
> *own peace.*

My family would like to share my father's story in hopes of instilling in others a greater appreciation of his values, courage, sense of humor and devotion to public service.

Matt Matsunaga
Hawai'i State Senator

Introduction

My first meeting with Sparky Matsunaga was at once amusing and mildly disastrous. It was on a chill winter evening in 1972, in the ballroom of a suburban hotel outside of Washington, D.C. at the annual dinner of the Japanese-American Citizens League. I had just returned from a four-month stint for *The New York Times* in Japan and been invited by JACL to talk about U.S.-Japan relations in trade and security. Just before I was to speak, Congressman Matsunaga, then in his tenth year in the House of Representatives, was asked to say a few words. Sparky leapt to the microphone and launched into a vivid tale of Hawai'i in which he mimicked every known accent to perfection — Japanese, Chinese, Hawaiian, Filipino, Caucasian and pidgin — all in good fun and none of it mean. With each new phrase, his audience rippled with laughter, each wave longer and louder than the last. When it was over, sides were splitting and the applause was thunderous.

Then I had to get up to say my piece. The first thing I remember saying was: "Mr. Matsunaga, if you ever want to give up politics, you're going to make a great stand-up comedian." That drew a short chuckle, but from then on it was all downhill as I discussed the implications of the return of the island of Okinawa to Japanese sovereignty, the intricacies of the balance of trade and the various factions of the ruling Liberal Democratic Party. The audience listened politely but I could tell from the glaze in their eyes that they would much rather have been listening to Sparky. When it was over, I stole quietly away into the night.

A little later, I went back to Asia for four years and did not see Sparky until I had returned to Washington and he had been elected to the Senate in 1976. I remember covering a Senate committee hearing in which Max Cleland, who had lost an arm and both legs in the Vietnam War, was up for confirmation as Administrator of the Veterans Administration under President Jimmy Carter. Sparky, who had vacillated over the U.S. involvement in Vietnam but never faltered in his admiration for America's soldiers, said all the right things about Cleland's sacrifices, but without being maudlin. Then he asked Cleland, "You seem to be awfully young for such an important position. Are you really only 35 years old?" Cleland chuckled and nodded over his shoulder, "Yes, Senator, and my mother is sitting right back there if you want proof."

Sometime after that, a correspondent I had known in Tokyo called to invite me to a lunch that Senator Matsunaga was giving for Mary Ushijima, who was visiting Washington after serving for years as a telephone operator and receptionist at the Foreign Correspondent's Club of Japan in Tokyo. I went along to the Senate dining room where Sparky presided over a lively discussion. Then he escorted Mary and the rest of us on a brief tour of the Capitol, pointing out bloodstains that could still be seen in the marble steps where a predecessor had been slain, and then a room off the beaten track where a political deal had been cut or a romantic assignation had taken place in years gone by. I wondered, given the pressures on Senators, how Senator Matsunaga could have found time for this excursion. I learned later that entertaining all sorts of visitors to the Capitol was part of his daily drill.

Over the years, Sparky's path and mine crossed only occasionally as each of us was engaged in different parts of Washington. I took early retirement from *The New York Times* in January 1990 to come to Hawai'i and was saddened only a few months afterward when Sparky died, robbing the nation and Hawai'i of a decent, sunny gentleman who had been well liked in Washington. Several years later, I heard from Harvey Meyerson, a one-time staff aide to Sparky, that the Matsunaga Foundation was looking for someone to write a political portrait of the late Senator. I had considered trying my hand at such a project, and the political life of this happy man seemed intriguing. Thus the focus of this book is on Sparky's political career and touches on his private life only as it affected his politics.

As I got into the research, I gradually became aware of a larger context into which Sparky's political career belonged and began to realize that here was a telling account of America. Sparky Matsunaga, along with Hiram Fong, a Chinese-American, and Daniel K. Inouye, another Japanese-American, were the pioneers who opened the way for Asian-Americans to move into the mainstream of political life in America. They made it possible for later generations of Asian-Americans to be elected to Congress, to win election as governors and state legislators, and to be chosen for senior state and federal government positions.

They were the vanguard who cleared a path for Norman Mineta, the first Japanese-American to become a cabinet officer, initially as Secretary of Commerce in the Clinton administration, then as Secretary of Transportation for President

George W. Bush. Elaine Chao, a Chinese-American, was the second, as Secretary of Labor in the Bush cabinet. Benjamin Cayetano, of Filipino ancestry, became governor of Hawai'i. Robert Matsui, another Japanese-American, was elected a U.S. Representative from California. Gary Locke, of Chinese descent, was chosen to be governor of the state of Washington. General Eric Shinseki rose to be the first Japanese-American to earn four stars as a military officer and become the chief of staff of the United States Army. William Itoh is believed to be the first career diplomat of Asian ancestry to become an ambassador (to Thailand.)

Conducting research for this book has been a rewarding experience in several ways. The first part of the inquiry was detective work. Little beyond newspaper accounts had been written about Sparky's life before he was elected to Congress in 1962. That meant interviewing dozens of people — Sparky's family and friends, aging warriors from World War II, political allies and foes in Hawai'i — and delving into high school and university yearbooks, yellowing newspaper clippings, eye-straining microfilm and a few memoirs. It was all engaging and pulled me into the history of my adopted home state, especially that of the influential Japanese-American community.

The second part of the exploration, into Sparky's life in Congress, included interviews with House and Senate leaders of both political parties and many staff aides, plus rummaging through voluminous Congressional records, newspaper and magazine files, and more than a hundred boxes of Sparky's papers. While I had to cull every nugget of information in the first part of my research, the second part threatened to overwhelm me with paper. My deepest thanks to all who gave of their time and memories to guide me through this endeavor; they are acknowledged on pages 251–253.

A word about sourcing: This is the work of a news correspondent. It is intended for the general reader and not necessarily for the political scientist or other scholar. Therefore, it does not include the footnotes or other provisions of a scholarly study. Where I have thought it necessary to cite a source, it is in the text and in a bibliography of books, newspapers and records that is appended. The approach here is historical narrative; it is often said that the newspaper is the first draft of history. I have long thought that good newspapermen and women should have a sense of history that shows up in their copy. This book is intended to be an extension of that concept.

From this examination of Sparky's political life, I have sought to draw a portrait of Sparky with three interwoven themes:

First, Sparky's life is an all-American story in the finest Horatio Alger tradition — a tale of a boy's rise from a poverty-stricken family in an obscure village on a remote Pacific island to a position of power in the corridors and chambers of the United States Congress. The son of immigrant parents, Sparky grew up on the edge of a plantation on Kaua'i, the most remote of the inhabited Hawaiian Islands, which are themselves 2,500 miles from the American mainland. Hawai'i then was not the resort paradise of girls dancing the hula or visitors sitting under palm trees sipping mai tai cocktails. Rather, the majority of people lived in hovels and earned a pittance for their backbreaking labor on the sugar and pineapple plantations, as did Sparky's father. It was from those impoverished circumstances that Sparky made it all the way to the U.S. Senate. As Senator Daniel K. Inouye, the senior Senator from Hawai'i, once said, "The life story of Spark Matsunaga bears repeating in all American homes as a classic example of the American success story."

Second, this is a Japanese-American story, an account of people who came across the Pacific, just as my Irish forefathers came across the Atlantic two generations earlier, to begin life over again in America. As hard as life was for my great-grandparents, Sparky's parents had it much harder. My folks spoke English, albeit with the Celtic lilt of Ireland, while Sparky's parents spoke Japanese, a language with no connection to the English of America. My folks were Caucasian, the race of the majority; Sparky's parents were Asians, a distinct minority in a land of racial discrimination, both at the time of their arrival and long afterward. The country of my forefathers has never been an enemy of America. In contrast, Japanese-Americans suffered painfully when the land of their ancestors made war on America. Nonetheless, Japanese-Americans and other Asian-Americans have persevered and, led by the likes of Sparky Matsunaga, have made it into the top ranks of American political life. Senator Inouye summarized it well in his book, *Journey to Washington:* "My forbears came from the Orient and it is true that their facial characteristics set them apart from Americans whose roots are in the Western world. But their problems of assimilation were exactly the same: to find work, to maintain a pride in their heritage while adapting to the culture of a strange new land, and slowly, step by painful step, to work their way up the social and economic ladder toward independence and full acceptance by their fellow-countrymen."

Third, Sparky did not fit into any known mold of American politician. The word "unique" is overly used, but Sparky was truly one of a kind. He was an American to the core of his soul, but his political tactics were often Japanese as he operated behind-the-scenes to cultivate support for whatever cause he had taken up. He was immensely popular among his colleagues in Washington, which enabled him to get things done. In Hawai'i, however, he was considered an independent spirit who drew votes from across the political spectrum, yet was disliked by many in the Democratic Party machine for that independence.

There were many other apparent contradictions. Sparky was a skilled, practical politician at the same time he was a dreamer, a visionary with his eyes literally and figuratively fixed on the stars. He mastered the intricacies of tax law and played a critical role in replacing military conscription with a volunteer force. He also persuaded Americans that we needed a poet laureate and should join hands with the Russians to explore space. As a member of Congress, he spurned much committee work, unlike most of his colleagues. Yet he relished the parliamentary machinations of procedure and debate on the floor of the House and Senate and was an acknowledged master of it.

Where some members of Congress, especially Senators, are show horses, Sparky was a work horse. Where some strive incessantly for recognition, Sparky thrived on being the faithful lieutenant who saw that the daily work of Congress got done. Unlike many members of Congress, he cared little for what the so-called national press or television reported about him, but woe be to the staff aide who overlooked a request for help from a voter back home. He seems to have been that rare political animal who understood there were few limits to what could be accomplished if he did not worry about who got the credit. Lastly, Sparky's politics of civility stood in marked contrast to the often bitter personal animosities in American political life today.

Special thanks for help on this book are due to Mrs. Helene Matsunaga, Sparky's widow, who was generous with her time and patient with my questions. Matthew Matsunaga, Sparky's youngest son, a State Senator in Hawai'i and head of the Matsunaga Foundation, kept his word in giving me a free hand to research, write and shape this book. Drusilla Tanaka, then the executive secretary of the 100th Infantry Battalion Veterans Association, pointed me to Sparky's wartime comrades and shared her insights into the world of Americans of Japanese ancestry. Among those to whom Mrs. Tanaka introduced me was Dr. Kenneth Otagaki, Ph.D., the litter bearer who brought the wounded Lt. Matsunaga down off Hill 600 in Italy; he has also shared his insights into Hawai'i as well as his accounts of the war. Having been severely wounded himself later, Dr. Otagaki is among the most courageous men I know in the way he has risen above adversity. Ellen Chapman, an archivist at the University of Hawai'i who has struggled to bring order out of the 1,200 boxes of papers and books in Sparky's Congressional papers, spotted many documents and letters that have added to this narrative. Harvey Meyerson, my friend for 35 years, has been an invaluable guide and source. Martin Tolchin, a trusted colleague from *The New York Times* who has forgotten more about Congress than I will ever know, has given apt advice and criticism. All of them read the draft of the manuscript and offered pertinent and sometimes sharply worded suggestions. I am truly grateful for their efforts but absolve them all from responsibility for errors of omission or commission, as that is my charge alone.

In addition, George Engebretson and Duane Kurisu of Watermark Publishing have been enthusiastic from the outset. I am grateful to Timothy Seldes, my agent and friend, who has given sage advice. I thank those who assisted in the research — Moida Cook, Yoshihisa Amae and Aldona Sendzikas — who consecutively did yeoman work in searching out documents, records and newspaper accounts and then pointed out pertinent facts and vignettes.

Lastly, my wife, Fumiko, born in Japan and naturalized as an American citizen, is an accomplished writer in her mother tongue and in English who has shared her perceptions of America, asked incisive questions, and read and re-read chapters with red pen in hand. This book is dedicated to her with profoundly more gratitude and affection than I care — or dare — to express in public.

Richard Halloran
Honolulu, Hawai'i
March 2002

Sparky

On a dusty road running down to the sea on the remote Hawaiian island of Kaua'i, a group of grade-school boys, mostly Japanese-Americans, raced up and down one day in 1924, then turned to playing dodge ball with a clump of rags knotted together; the boys were too poor to buy a real ball. One lad, younger and smaller than the rest and new to the neighborhood, kept coming in last in the races and was usually the first to be thrown out of the dodge ball games. Finally, one of the older boys laughed, "Hey, you slower than ol' Sparky, the nag." Sparky, or Sparkplug, was a hapless horse in the Fred Lasswell comic strip about two hillbillies, "Barney Google and Snuffy Smith." Google was forever entering Sparky into races in which the nag invariably ran last.

The name stuck. Through his school years, at the University of Hawai'i and during his Army service in World War II, Masayuki Matsunaga was "Sparky" to family, friends, schoolmates and soldiers. After the war, he had his name legally changed to Spark Masayuki Matsunaga because he thought it would be more easily recognized in the political career he planned. Throughout his service in Hawai'i's Legislature, in the United States House of Representatives, and finally in the United States Senate, he was widely referred to as Sparky even if he was addressed as Congressman or Senator. In one instance, during Sparky's first term in the House, President John F. Kennedy either couldn't pronounce or had forgotten the name Matsunaga as he acknowledged dignitaries with whom he shared a welcoming platform in Honolulu. So the President addressed him as "my friend Sparky." Sparky was so pleased he wrote a friend: "The President calls me by my first name."

Sparky's rise in politics began during World War II, when he, Daniel K. Inouye and thousands of other Japanese-Americans fought for America with valor against the Nazi Germans on the battlefields of Italy and France and as intelligence officers against Japan. Having proven their allegiance to America with their blood, they came home no longer willing to be the second-class citizens they had been before the war. In Hawai'i, many Americans of Japanese ancestry, or AJAs, as they called themselves, joined the Democratic Party in the late 1940s, took it over in the mid-1950s, and set out to wrest control of the Territory of Hawai'i from Republican plantation and business owners, mostly Caucasian, who had dominated the islands since they were annexed to the U.S. in 1898.

In what was widely referred to as the "Revolution of 1954," Sparky, Inouye and other Democrats won control of the Territorial Legislature. Inouye immediately became majority leader and Sparky was chosen chairman of the vital Judiciary Committee in 1957. After Inouye was elected to the Territorial Senate in 1959, Sparky succeeded him as majority leader. When Hawai'i became a state in August 1959, Sparky sought to be elected lieutenant governor but lost in the primary, the only electoral setback he experienced in 15 elections over a political career of 35 years. He had recovered by 1962 and was elected to the U.S. House of Representatives. When Hiram Fong retired from the Senate in 1976, the voters in Hawai'i elected Sparky to succeed him. He remained in the Senate until he died on April 15, 1990.

As a politician, Sparky was distinctive. In the summer of 1986, Senator Robert Dole, the Republican from Kansas who was then majority leader and later a presidential candidate, paid tribute to Sparky, at that time in his tenth year in the Senate: "Sparky Matsunaga is very much a Renaissance man. He is a man who thinks about and acts on the issues that shape our country — today and tomorrow." Dole cited Sparky's military service in World War II, his efforts to have established the U.S. Institute of Peace, his long campaign to have the U.S. name a poet laureate and his commitment to the United States. "Senator Matsunaga, perhaps more than any other senator, is a visionary — someone who looks out for this country's long-range future." Dole concluded by saying that Sparky was both "an idealist and a realist....He is a unique and valuable member of this institution."

Being in the first wave of Asian-Americans in national politics, Sparky was sometimes a mentor to those who followed. Early in the second wave was Norman Mineta, a Democrat from California who had been mayor of San Jose before being elected to the House of Representatives in 1974; this was the first class of Congressmen to be elected after President Richard Nixon had resigned to avoid impeachment for his role in the Watergate scandal.

"I came to Congress knowing zilch," Mineta said in an interview. "Sparky was just great. He was my big brother and I used to go to him every day — how do you get recognized on the floor, what should I do about staff, where do I get office supplies, things like that. I considered him my mentor." Sparky had become an authority on the intricate workings of the House rules and one day, as he and Mineta sat together in the House, a swift parliamentary maneuver left Mineta puzzled. "What was that all about?" he asked. Sparky, who had an impish sense of humor, grinned: "If you had looked at Thomas Jefferson's manual on rules, you would have known."

Sparky was a man of many parts, some of them seemingly paradoxical. First and foremost, Spark Matsunaga was an American in every ounce of his being. If scratched, he would bleed red, white and blue. Sparky was enormously proud to be an American and that emotion underlay most of his public life. He was sometimes critical of the United States and his compatriots, notably when he experienced racial discrimination, but that was because he wanted America to live up to its ideals. Fighting discrimination, not only against Japanese-Americans and other Asian-Americans but against every ethnic minority, was a theme that ran through Sparky's entire political life, all in hopes of forging a better nation. As his longtime assistant, Cherry Matano, said, "Sparky was in love with America."

Yet, like many second-generation Americans of whatever origin, Sparky retained a flavor of the land of his ancestors. As a *nisei,* which means second generation in Japanese, he had a facade, what the Japanese call *tatemae,* or "that which stands before," that shielded much of the real man behind. For all of his amiable exterior, his interior, or *honne,* his "true feeling," was hidden and he was a very private man. Part of that facade was vanity about his personal appearance; he would spend a long time in front of the mirror to make sure that his hair was combed over his bald spot.

Like most Japanese, Sparky disliked personal confrontation, which meant that he tried to avoid some of the adversarial aspects of American politics, especially inside the Beltway that circles Washington, D.C. Rather than confront an issue in public, Sparky preferred what the Japanese call *nemawashi,* which loosely translated means "tending the garden" or "thorough preparation;" he would go around to colleagues behind the scenes to explain what he wanted and to seek their support. When he was ready, he would make public his proposal with its support already lined up. In Japan, *nemawashi* is practiced by politicians of every stripe and at all levels. They get together in the evening at a *ryotei,* or geisha house, or in a tea shop or restaurant, to talk informally over dinner and cups of *sake.* This goes on out of the public eye, discreet and off-the-record, but this is where soundings are taken, supporters are reassured and neutrals are persuaded, and even opponents are sometimes committed when a deal is made. It is the lifeblood of Japanese politics, business and social order.

Sparky's Japanese style was perhaps most apparent when he sought legislation intended to redress the grievances of the Japanese-Americans for having been unjustly incarcerated in "relocation centers" during World War II. Shortly after the Japanese attack on Pearl Harbor in Hawai'i on December 7, 1941, President Franklin Delano Roosevelt signed an order under which 120,000 people, about two-thirds of them American citizens and the rest legal resident aliens, were rounded up, torn from their homes and jobs and businesses, and incarcerated in desolate regions in the western U.S. The proposed legislation would have the U.S. government apologize to the AJAs for the violation of their fundamental civil rights and pay each survivor $20,000. In his *nemawashi* to gain support for the bill, Sparky lined up 76 co-sponsors out of 100 members of the Senate; usually two to ten Senators sponsor a bill. When the bill went to the floor, its passage was a foregone conclusion even though the debate over its provisions was rousing and occasionally bitter. The bill was also veto-proof, Sparky having put together enough votes even to override a presidential veto.

Throughout his political career, Sparky did not see a clash or a contradiction between being an American and retaining some attributes of his Japanese ancestry. Over the long run, he believed that Asian immigrants, like those from Europe, were becoming more American all the time. In an address to a national convention of Chinese-Americans in Detroit in 1975, Sparky addressed that issue in light of the national resurgence in ethnic and cultural pride. His conclusion: "We are becoming more American but only because we are developing a keener sense of appreciation of our Asian ethnic heritage....This is what America is all about."

As a politician, Sparky was a visionary, even whimsical at times, but was not a deep political thinker or philosopher. He was pragmatic rather than dogmatic or ideological. He was gregarious to a fault, but made few close friends beyond his family. He loved the limelight of the campaign and the debate in Congress and, like politicians around the world, thrived on the attention and applause of the crowd. At the same time, Sparky was an intensely private person who shared few of his inner thoughts with anyone but his family and friends; he is not known to have kept a diary. He had a truly wide variety of interests, but they were not necessarily connected to a central, organizing theme.

One exception: His unrelenting drive for equality and against discrimination. Sparky was a romanticist who believed profoundly, almost naively, in American democracy. He had taken to heart all that the New England Yankee schoolteachers, who had come to Hawai'i in its Territorial days, had taught him about democracy. In this belief, said George Chaplin, former editor of

The Honolulu Advertiser, "He had a kind of innocence about him." Sparky fervently believed in equality, not just for himself but for all Americans, and insisted that he and every man and woman should be judged for himself or herself and not by the color of his skin or the shape of her eyes. Ordinarily a calm and affable man, the fires of equality burned deep in Sparky's gut and would erupt at whatever he considered to be a slight or an injustice, more to other Asian-Americans or to other races than to himself. Sparky was no "banana"— yellow on the outside and white on the inside. To the contrary, he was comfortable with his Japanese ancestry and knew who he was. Because he saw himself the equal of everyone else, he lacked the instinctive suspicion of Caucasians, better known by the Hawaiian word *haole*, harbored by some AJAs.

"Sparky was a man with a mission," said his daughter, Merle, in a candid essay written for her family. "His religion was politics. He put his faith in politics at age fourteen the way a young person in other circumstances would have chosen to go into the clergy. He absolutely believed that his mission was to fight for the rights of the downtrodden, to relieve the suffering around him....He believed in himself, that he could achieve anything he set his mind to. He often said he was born under a lucky star."

Over time, Sparky fashioned a political creed that combined idealism and realism. He sponsored his share of sweeping, landmark legislation, such as ensuring that the civil rights of all Americans would be preserved and that they would never be incarcerated without due process, as Japanese-Americans had been. Some proposals that he saw come to pass, such as joining with the Russians to explore space, were idealistic. But Sparky's attention was more on the nitty-gritty laws that affected the daily lives of American voters and taxpayers, especially if those proposals were innovative. He was eager, for instance, to promote alternate forms of energy to cut costs and assure supplies to Americans. A proposal to explore the possibilities of sail-assisted technology, intended to reduce the expense of inter-island shipping in the Pacific, illuminated Sparky's realistic approach to problems, his delight in innovation and his pleasure in rhetoric.

In his opening remarks at a 1980 hearing before the Senate Committee on Energy and Natural Resources, Sparky scanned the horizon: "If innovative technologies such as this one are to obtain the legitimacy they deserve, and contribute to the revitalization of the American economy, those at the highest levels of government must cultivate a special kind of receptivity. It is a receptivity to the disparate activities of unique individuals working with day-to-day, down-to-earth problems — such as how to cut the operating costs of a tugboat on the Chesapeake Bay."

"Now if that phrase sounds less ringing, less stimulating and inspiring than phrases such as the reindustrialization of America or business-labor-government partnership or post-industrial technology, then, I submit, it is time for those at the policy-making levels to reach out to the grassroots a bit more. The secret of our historically unequaled capacity for innovation and productivity is there, in the vibrantly curious activities of scattered individualists, whom some would call mavericks, or even tinkerers (and I mean that in a deeply respectful sense), and some of whom are gathered in this room today."

Sparky's creed and his image as a visionary was further refined when he addressed the Senate in January 1985 to propose the exploration of the planet Mars. "Some of my colleagues may wonder: Has the Senator from Hawai'i lost his senses? Here the U.S. Senate convenes to address a veritable avalanche of pressing issues — tax reform, the deficit, defense spending, arms control, unemployment, crime, human rights, environmental regulation, Central America, Afghanistan, the Middle East, farm policy — and the Senator from Hawai'i talks about Mars?

"I believe we also have a duty to try to see beyond the cascading issues that engulf us daily, even while we are considering them. No one likes to be called a reactionary, but if we simply react to problems as they occur, what else are we? Too often, it seems, harried policy makers only have time to consider the future when she has nothing to offer because the encroaching present has already violated her potential.

"I don't accept that…I can't and I won't. I don't believe the American people sent us here only to respond to their immediate needs. I believe our constituents also hope that some day, perhaps, we will respond to their aspirations as well, and not merely by concluding our speeches with misty visions borrowed from greeting cards or uplifting quotes from folklore. The future is neither nostalgia nor a dream, but an unfolding concrete reality, filled with promise, meant to be acted upon pragmatically now, with intelligence and imagination, by those of us who are entrusted with the responsibilities of government."

As Sparky quickly learned when he went to Washington in 1962, Representatives and Senators have two main duties: The first is to serve their constituents back home and to look after the interests of their states in Washington. The second is to work with colleagues from other states and from opposing political parties to promote the national interest and to resolve conflicts on a national level. Some are better at one than the other. In addition, many Senators see the Senate as a launch platform for their aspirations to become cabinet officers or presidential candidates.

Of the two duties, Sparky gave fairly equal weight to both. Former Governor George Ariyoshi of Hawaiʻi said that whenever he needed something for Hawaiʻi done in Washington, "I always called Sparky and he always came through." In the Honolulu office of Gene Ward, a Republican member of the state Legislature until 1998, the most prominent picture was that of Sparky Matsunaga. When asked why he had a picture of a politician from the opposing party on display, Ward replied, "When it came to serving constituents, Sparky Matsunaga was the best. I keep that picture up there to remind myself what democratic politics is all about."

As for his aspirations, Sparky seemed content to be a member of Congress, particularly the Senate, and not to look further. He was also a realist. After he had been in the Senate for ten years, a reporter from the *Washington Post* asked Sparky whether he would like to be President. Sparky said he didn't think the country was ready for a Japanese-American President and anyway, he was quite happy to be a United States Senator. Then he laughed: "When I first went there, I felt very uneasy, very out of place. Everybody else was running for President."

Congressional staff aides divide Senators into two categories, show horses and work horses. "Sparky Matsunaga was definitely a workhorse," said an experienced staffer. "He was an extrovert, like most of them, but he was not an exhibitionist." Some saw Sparky as the faithful lieutenant who was most effective working behind-the-scenes to execute the business of Congress. In the House, he was a member of the powerful Rules Committee, appointed by the Speaker, John McCormack, a Democrat from Massachusetts, who had become Sparky's mentor. Later, in the Senate, Sparky attached himself to Senator Robert Byrd of West Virginia, who was the Democrats' leader through most of Sparky's 14 years in the upper house. Senator Byrd made Sparky chief deputy whip, a position Sparky relished because it engaged him in the everyday parliamentary workings of the Senate as he sought to line up support for whatever bill was at hand, a duty at which he became adept.

In many ways, Sparky was the prototype of the co-leaders analyzed in the 1999 book *Co-Leaders: The Power of Great Partnerships* by David Heenan, a business executive in Hawaii, and Warren Bennis, a professor of business administration at the University of Southern California. "In organizational life," they wrote, "those at the top need exceptional deputies as much as they need fresh air." Co-leadership, they asserted, "is a tough-minded strategy that will unleash the hidden talent in any enterprise…It celebrates those who do the real work, not just a few charismatic leaders."

Sparky differed from many of his Congressional colleagues in at least two ways: He introduced or co-sponsored or supported in debate hundreds of pieces of legislation that never made the newspapers or the six o'clock televised news but which directly affected the everyday lives of American voters and taxpayers. Sparky may never have met a tax break for ordinary Americans that he didn't like. He was a champion of benefits for veterans. He supported several bills intended to reduce crime. He sought to make equitable the immigration laws. He consistently supported food stamps for the poor. Sparky saw weaknesses in the Social Security system long before it became a national issue in the late 1990s.

Second, Sparky believed that the main task of the legislator was to legislate and that was best done on the floor of the House or the Senate. Many of his colleagues believed they had more influence in the committees to which they were assigned and concentrated their political efforts there. With the exception of the Rules Committee, which directly affected the legislative process on the floor of the House, Sparky tended to his committee duties but did not particularly enjoy them.

Sparky rarely drew attention in the press not only because his style and proposals did not attract notice but because he didn't much care what the so-called national press said about him. Members of his staff often despaired because he would not capitalize on a political event to get his name in the paper. Sparky was concerned only about his image and reputation with the voters and taxpayers in Hawai'i because they would decide whether he would be reelected. Stephen Hess, a senior fellow at the Brookings Institution in Washington who has written widely about American politics and the press, wrote in 1987 that Sparky was among the three Senators who received the least attention in the national press and television, the other two being Senators James Abdnor, a Republican from South Dakota, and Alan Dixon, a Democrat from Illinois. Hess found that news reporters were attracted to power and more to potential Presidents than to nonconformists. The late A.A. "Bud" Smyser, at one time editor and later a columnist for the *Honolulu Star-Bulletin*, caught the differences between Sparky and Senator Inouye, who has been notably successful in pulling the levers of power since he was elected to the Senate in 1962. In a succinct assessment in 1989, Smyser wrote: "High national visibility has been a strong element in Inouye's success. Quiet, low visibility seems to serve Matsunaga equally well."

In another facet of his political self, Sparky was an actor and politics was his stage. Like most American politicians, he loved being at the center of attention. As Senator Inouye once said, with a laugh, "We are not humble people." Sparky's thirst was for personal, face-to-face, hand-shaking attention. He relished playing to an audience, whether in the theater, on the campaign trail, on the floor of the House or Senate or with an after-dinner speech, an address on Memorial Day or on the Fourth of July. Sparky fashioned many of his own speeches himself, either working from a blank piece of paper or a draft written by a speechwriter or using material requested from the Congressional Research Service. Even his apparently impromptu remarks on the floor had the mark of having been crafted with an economy of words chosen for effect.

Sparky was an accomplished raconteur with a full repertoire of anecdotes. And like many politicians, he was not above embellishing the facts if that made a better story. In one address, he spoke movingly about a World War II battle as if he had been in it. That fight, however, had taken place after Sparky had been wounded and was far to the rear in a hospital. He could also be earthy. He drew nervous chuckles in a Senate committee hearing room by noting that traveling back and forth between Washington and Honolulu, a ten- to 12-hour flight and a six-hour time change, "made you hungry when you should have been horny and horny when you should be hungry."

Throughout most of his Congressional career, Sparky gave his constituents top priority. He answered every letter that came into his office, except those from people he considered crackpots, and sent small sums of money to families of constituents who had died, what the Japanese call *koden*. He drove his staff to rectify a wrong done to a constituent or to pursue a favor needed. Sparky took nearly every visitor from Hawai'i to Washington, be they bank presidents or sanitation workers to lunch in the House or Senate dining room, sometimes booking two or three tables and hopping between them. When those visitors got back home to Hawai'i, Senator Dole said, "they became walking billboards for Sparky Matsunaga."

A striking paradox lay in the differing perceptions of Sparky in Washington and among the Democratic movers and shakers of Hawai'i. In the Capitol, Sparky was immensely popular on both sides of the aisle; most found him to be a modest man and some even said he was shy. He was the only Asian-American in the House when he took his seat in 1963 and yet was elected president of the freshman class that comprised all newcomers that year. Thomas Foley, former Speaker of the House and later ambassador to Japan, said in an interview, "Sparky was one of the members everybody liked. He didn't have a Congressional enemy. Someone like that can have tremendous influence and he operated across party lines." Senator Robert Byrd, the Democratic Majority Leader who became Sparky's mentor in the Senate, said, "As a public official, he was modest in his manner and bearing. He envied no one, but he was ambitious in the interest of justice and humanity."

Senator Dole said, "Sparky would not make points at your expense in the newspapers, like some in both parties. He could be tough; you couldn't push him around. But he could move the process and not leave blood behind." Representative Don Fuqua, a Democrat from Florida who was elected the same year as Sparky, said, "I don't know of anyone who did not like Sparky Matsunaga. You have to get along with people in Congress and you don't get things done by getting in their faces." Representative Bill Frenzel, a Republican from Minnesota who served with Sparky for six years in the House, echoed that view: "I never heard of anyone in either party who didn't like him. You could trust him."

In Honolulu, however, Sparky was not part of the inner circle of the Democratic establishment that dominated state politics. Tony Kinoshita, who served with Sparky in the Army and later became a political campaign stalwart, said, "The Democrats hated Sparky." The late Sakae Takahashi, who had been in the Reserve Officers Training Corps with Sparky at the University of Hawai'i, then an officer with Sparky in the 100th Infantry Battalion in World War II and later a member of the Democratic inner circle, became a political rival who declined to be interviewed for this book. "Anything I would have to say about Sparky Matsunaga," he said, "would be negative." Former Governor George Ariyoshi noted that both he and Sparky were considered outsiders, at least in the early days of Democratic rule in Hawai'i. Robert Oshiro, who was highly influential in the inner circle, agreed: "Sparky was never part of the mainstream of the party." Representative Patsy Takemoto Mink, whom Sparky defeated in the Democratic primary for U.S. Senator in 1976, was cool in her assessment. Mrs. Mink, who is considered to drive hard bargains in political fights, contended that "Sparky stayed clear of controversial issues." Thomas Gill, a liberal lawyer who served in Congress with Sparky, found him too cautious and unwilling to take stands in certain disputes. According to scholars Dan Boylan and T. Michael Holmes, in *John A. Burns: The Man and His Times,* their book about the governor who led the Democratic Revolution of 1954, Sparky was beyond the pale. In one election, they wrote, "Burns had no leverage with an independent Spark Matsunaga." Judge James Burns, son of the late Governor Burns, summed it up: "Sparky was not a team player. He was on our side but he wasn't on our team."

Part of the criticism of Sparky appears to have been personal. Some complained that he spoke English with what they called a *haole* accent or a "phony Harvard accent." Others thought he had lost touch with his roots in the hard life on the plantations. Still others seemed envious because Sparky had risen to the highest reaches of American politics. In Hawai'i, with its culture based in Polynesia, Japan and other Asian cultures, individuality is often submerged under a group dynamic that operates on consensus. Imagination and innovation are not prized and thus Hawai'i's politics, bureaucracy, educational system, business, and press and television sometimes slip into a mire of mediocrity.

In contrast, Sparky was a maverick with an uncommon style, personal ambition, a strong ego and a touch of braggadocio that irritated some of his peers. A Japanese saying holds: "The nail that sticks up soon gets hammered down." Ted Tsukiyama, a Honolulu prominent attorney and civic leader, added: "And Sparky Matsunaga was a very tall nail." Tsukiyama said in an interview that the Hawaiian concept of 'alamihi might be a better analogy: If several 'alamihi, a common black crab, are thrown in a bucket and one tries to escape by climbing out, the others will reach up to drag him back. Those who would hammer Sparky or would pull him down, and there were repeated efforts to do so, failed for a simple reason: Sparky was immensely popular with the people of Hawai'i and a proven vote-getter with his own political base. In a couple of elections, he won with 82 percent of the vote; in American politics, 55 to 60 percent is considered a landslide. Boylan and Holmes, Governor Burns' biographers, acknowledged that in the 1962 elections, when Sparky was elected to the House and Burns to the governor's chair: "Spark Matsunaga turned out to be a considerable asset to the Democratic Party" even though he was an independent.

In Congress, Sparky was often seen as a dreamer and an idealist who pursued causes that some colleagues considered offbeat. Part of that arose from his otherworldly qualities that were reflected in his love of poetry and fascination with the supernatural. When he sought to persuade Congress to create the post of poet laureate of the United States, he argued that recognizing talented poets "would be further proof of our enlightened commitment to the quality of the arts." In an apolitical plea, he once urged students graduating from the University of Hawai'i to "cultivate a love of beauty."

Perhaps reflecting his love of language and oratory, Sparky began writing poetry as a child and wrote a good bit when he lay wounded in an Army hospital in Italy. He particularly liked the American poet Longfellow and the Briton Wordsworth, as well as the sparse Japanese haiku of 17 syllables. He often recited Shakespeare at Sunday dinner, and even won a $10 prize from the International Poetry Institute in 1970 for this:

Deja Vu
I've been here before, I say —
    That house, that wall, that brook
I've seen them all before;
    Yet I've never been this way
Nor read in any book
    Of what I see, I'm sure.
What strange things
    Our minds must know;
We know not yet our minds.

Sparky was asked in 1982 to donate some of his wartime poems to the military history museum at Fort DeRussy in Honolulu. He agreed, although reluctantly, because he said they were just his personal musings. The Army invited him to read a couple of the poems at a ceremony at which members of the press, radio and television were present. Sparky began reading a poem he hadn't looked at in years. Suddenly, he broke down in tears. A staff aide and former journalist, Harvey Meyerson, knew that Sparky's display of emotion would make the evening news and the front page the next morning, which would be a political coup. But Sparky was embarrassed and apologized for showing his emotions. "Publicity was the last thing on his mind," Meyerson said. "He reacted with spontaneous honesty rather than with a scripted image. That quality had a lot to do with the way he connected with people at a very human level."

Sparky's interest in the supernatural came from his father, Kingoro, who was seen on Kaua'i as a spiritual healer. Sparky related several tales to his daughter, Diane, in which Kingoro had performed a kind of exorcism to rid neighbors of evil spirits. Sparky told Diane, "As an educated man, I have tried to rationalize and scientifically understand these strange occurrences, to look for reasonable explanations. But without logical answers, I am inclined to believe, at this time, that there is something more to life, something more than the sciences have been able to explain. There is an entity called spirit, whether it be good or evil — a spirit with which some of us can communicate. And I am convinced that my father was blessed with the supernatural powers to perceive things one step beyond the rest of us."

At the same time, Sparky was a man of science and technology, especially of energy and space, and the practical benefits they brought to Americans. He kept a scientist on his staff to advise him on technological issues and introduced many bills to advance the evolution of renewable sources of energy such as solar power and hydrogen fuel. He took particular interest in space, and an international award for space science is named for him. To Sparky, science and the supernatural were no more contradictory than they were to Leonardo Da Vinci, the 15th-Century Renaissance man whom Sparky sometimes quoted in speeches.

Like some American and many Japanese politicians, Sparky kept his wife and children mostly out of the public eye while the children were young. Sparky's wife, Helene, said in several interviews that she didn't know much about what went on in Sparky's office because she was home raising their five children. "He didn't bring his problems home," Helene said. "He just went to work and came home late, tired." Sparky often worked into the night, going out in the early evening to a political or diplomatic gathering at which he was a teetotaler, then returning to his office where a pot of tea awaited him. He sipped the tea, often laced with honey, as he scrawled answers to letters, frequently into the early morning; staffers noted the time and date he always put on his memos. When he left the office, his inbox was empty. As this became ritual, Sparky's children resented the amount of time he spent on politics and not with them, a common complaint in families of modern-day politicians.

While preferring that his children not appear in the press, Sparky included them in parts of his political life. Daughter Merle said, "All of us participated in his campaigns. I can remember going door-to-door to pass out brochures at a very young age, going to *lūʻau* (a Hawaiian feast), pancake breakfasts, churches, parades. We all worked as summer volunteers in his offices, in Hawaiʻi during campaign years and on the Hill otherwise." She noted that she and her sister, Diane, went from Washington to Hawaiʻi to help with their father's first campaign for the Senate. "I can remember how serious Sparky was about that campaign, and that he even consulted us as to what he should focus on if he won the race." Merle said she urged him to get onto the Energy Committee: "You can't imagine how thrilled I was when he did get on the committee and became a proponent of alternative energy sources." Sparky took his oldest son, Keene, to the 1968 Democratic National Conventional in Chicago, when dissidents took to the street in rage as Vice President Hubert Humphrey was being nominated for the presidency inside. He took Merle to the 1972 convention in Miami Beach, where Senator George McGovern was nominated for the presidency.

In her essay on Matsunaga family life, Merle said, "Sunday dinners were the most important ritual at our house. It was the only day of the week he was sure to be home at dinner time. We had assigned seats at the table — arranged so certain children were separated so they would not fight. Sparky said grace and we were all required to say the Lord's prayer. Toward the end of dinner, he would either have riddles or quizzes for us, or he would recite Shakespeare, or some poem he had memorized in his childhood. Or he would try out his latest jokes on us. Often we had already heard them and would groan when he started — he did not appreciate that but would continue anyway.

"As his political career took off, his private life, already subsumed to his public life, became more non-existent and he spent more hours at his office than at home, or anywhere. He grew more and more out of touch not only with his family but with mundane things: the price of a loaf of bread or current trends." She said, "Sparky had to have the last word on everything that went on in the house. Even the dogs were named exclusively by him. It all had to fit into some order of the universe that had to do with perfection, symmetry, with a little superstition thrown in.

"Sparky loved children and loved to play with us," Merle said. She continued: "His standards were extremely high; good grades in school and achievement in sports were of paramount importance. He also insisted that we be properly groomed, had perfect table manners, and knew how to shake hands properly. We had individual lessons on handshaking (very important in politics)....Success was everything to him. It was also very important that we knew how to stand up for our rights and fight back if provoked." Later, Merle added: "The message to us children was never to turn away in shame or disgust at someone else's racial slurs but to challenge him or her to change.

"Progressive as he was in politics, at home he was a traditionalist and kept the old double standards he grew up with. Boys and girls had different rules and expectations of them. Girls did dishes, cleaned the house, and learned how to cook; boys collected the garbage and did yard work. When we were teenagers and wanted to date, girls were given warnings and limits, boys had no limits placed on them."

Sparky, who had been a boxer as a lad on Kaua'i and later in the Army, made a point of keeping physically fit and could jump rope and hit a punching bag well into late middle age. He even installed a punching bag in the basement at home. "We all knew when he arrived home from work," Merle said, "because of the sound of the punching bag reverberating through the house, often very late at night. He did calisthenics every morning and boasted to us that he weighed the same as in his Army days." Sparky was stunned when he had health problems late in life. Merle said, "He thought because he was fit it would never happen to him."

Merle pointed out one of Sparky's idiosyncrasies — speeding. "He loved to drive," she said. "Rather, he loved to *speed*. He used to boast how long it took him to get to work each day, or to Chevy Chase Circle, from our house (I believe 11 minutes was his best time), or to Dulles Airport. And he had every traffic light from our house to the Capitol timed to the point which, if he approached certain lights, he knew whether to take a detour or wait for the green, to shave however many seconds off his commute. He was unabashed about using his privileged status as a Congressman to avoid speeding tickets. He was also very conscious of his image in his car, never buying a luxury make, and never accepting Cadillacs from the local dealers. Of course, he always owned American cars. When he knew he was dying, he decided he could finally treat himself to the luxury of owning a Cadillac."

After he got pulled over by a policeman one day, Sparky scribbled this piece of doggerel:

"Impartial traffic cop
That blushingly speeding cars to stop
Or, greening, let them go
What equality thine acts do show,
   Man, thy maker, needs to know."

When one looks back over the half-century of Sparky Matsunaga's public service, his legacy might be called the politics of civility. On the floor of the Senate or House or in committee, Sparky was as civil to his political adversaries as he was to his allies. He could be fierce in debate and occasionally testy, but always ended a parliamentary battle, as Senator Dole said, without blood on the floor. Sparky was equally civil to a working man from Hawai'i who had spent his savings for a once-in-a-lifetime trip to Washington to have lunch with him as he was to the President of the United States. He was as civil to Caucasians and African-Americans as he was to Asian-Americans and as civil to foreigners as he was to Americans. His public trademark was courtesy and respect. It stood in some contrast to the antagonism and cynicism that mar so much of American political life today.

One day in late 1982, as the Senate closed a lame-duck session, Senator Byrd said during an exchange on the floor: "I do not know of any Senator who exemplifies civility and friendliness more than does the Senator from Hawai'i. I think we can use more civility around here." Later, after Sparky had passed away, Senator Byrd continued in the same vein: "We remember him as a quiet, unassuming man, a man who was brave on the far-flung battlefields of his nation, but who was persistent in the pursuit of peace." The Republican floor leader, Senator Dole, added: "He was a genuine hero to the country and to the people of his state that he loved so much. He also brought dignity and fairness to the business of this body."

Senator David Boren, a Democrat from Oklahoma, recalled that when the two young Boren children came to the Senate dining room to meet him while the

Senate was in a late session, "Sparky Matsunaga was one of those people who always took the time to come over and visit with the children, to share a story with them, tell them some story about his home state of Hawai'i that both entertained and educated them....He was the kind of man who, in the midst of all of his responsibilities, took the time to be kind to a seven-year-old boy. He took the time to be kind to members of the staff in the Senate dining room or the Capitol policemen on the beat or anyone else who needed his help or his advice."

Citing Sparky's achievements after he had passed away, Senator Boren concluded: "We will miss him most of all because he was an example of human possibility, of kindness, of courage, of love and compassion for others, that stands as an example of moral courage and kindness for all of us. He was a great Senator but, above all, he was a great human being." ❖

Hanapēpē to Mānoa
1916–1941

Sometime in 1902, the young man who would be Sparky's father, Kingoro Matsunaga, ran away from home in Kumamoto Prefecture in Kyushu, Japan's southern island, after his stepmother had forced him into a seminary to train as a priest in Shinto, the pantheistic religion of Japan. Kingoro, then 22, sailed first to the island of Maui and later took a packet boat to Kaua'i in search of work. He got work on a sugar plantation owned by the McBryde family, immigrants from Scotland, on the south coast of Kaua'i, where he was a guard at a water pump in Kukui'ula.

Kingoro was befriended there by another Japanese plantation worker, Takuji Ikeda, who was 35 years older. From time to time, Takuji invited Kingoro to his tiny home for a meal or a beer with his family. Takuji's wife, Chiyono, was a picture bride, as were many on the plantation. After a Japanese immigrant had worked for awhile and saved a small sum of money, a broker came around with pictures of girls from poor families in Japan who were willing to come to Hawai'i to marry for the adventure, or to escape poverty, or to avoid being sold into a geisha house or worse. Sometimes, a Japanese laborer in Hawai'i wrote to someone in his hometown to ask for pictures of eligible women. From them, he selected a bride and invited her to Hawai'i. Altogether, those marriages were really not much different from marriages at that time in Japan, where parents of young men and women, with the help of go-betweens, arranged unions with little say from the young people involved. Except, of course, that the picture brides sailed across a wide ocean to a strange country and a life of hardship.

In this case, Chiyono Fukushima's older sister had been chosen as the picture bride, but she had taken one look at Takuji Ikeda's photograph and refused to leave her home in Hiroshima Prefecture, arguing that he was much too old to be her husband. It fell to Chiyono to accept the marriage, since to back out after having promised the marriage broker would have dishonored the family. Chiyono was thus officially married to Takuji while still in Japan, emigrated to join him in Kaua'i in 1903 at the age of 23, and bore him two sons and two daughters. In the natural course of events, Takuji died in 1914 at the age of 68.

A year later, Chiyono married Kingoro. Whether Kingoro married her out of affection for a woman the same age, or from a sense of obligation to his friend Takuji, or out of concern for an impoverished young widow with four children, or because it was a convenient way to acquire a wife is unclear. It may have been some of each. In any case, Masayuki Matsunaga was born a year later on October 8, 1916, in the Kukui'ula camp of the McBryde plantation. A sister, Dorothy, and a brother, Andrew, came along later, two years apart. From all accounts, Kingoro was a good stepfather to Chiyono's children, perhaps remembering his own unhappiness at the hands of his stepmother. Even so, he doted on his firstborn son in the manner of many Japanese fathers. Sparky credited Kingoro as perhaps the biggest influence in his life, sometimes quoting lessons his father had taught him: *"Kuro ga atte fukai jinsei ga wakaru,"* meaning, "Understanding the deep meaning of life comes from hardship." (Sparky may have misquoted his father in Japanese as this probably should have read: *"Kuro ga atte jinsei no fukasa ga wakaru."*)

Hardship was no stranger to the Japanese who came to Hawai'i in the late 19th and early 20th Centuries. The first Japanese immigrants arrived in 1868, shortly after the American Civil War and the year in which the Tokugawa Shogunate in Japan was overthrown in the Meiji Restoration. As Japan headed into its modern period, it was a time of economic and political turmoil, and 142 men and six women were recruited by advertisements for a paradise of easy work and high wages. Artisans, unemployed bureaucrats and soldiers, and a few convicts signed on to come to Hawai'i, but none were farmers accustomed to hard labor in the fields; 38 soon gave up and returned to Japan. Another 13 left when their three-year contracts were completed.

In 1888, King Kalākaua, of the independent Hawaiian monarchy, visited Japan to suggest a union through a marriage between the royal Hawaiian rulers and the imperial family of Japan. The Japanese politely declined but did agree to Kalākaua's plea for more workers to help overcome a labor shortage in Hawai'i. Contracts were drawn up in which the Hawaiian government would pay for passage to Hawai'i and provide free housing, in return for which laborers would work for 26 days a month — ten hours a day in the fields or 12 hours in the sugar mills. Wages and subsistence came to $15 a month for men and $10 for women. The Japanese government recruited sturdy farmers from depressed areas in central Japan, notably Hiroshima Prefecture, and sent 945 workers in 1893. The governor of the prefecture,

Miki Nabeshima, instructed them to remember that they would be "crossing 3,000 miles of ocean to that faraway foreign country with the sole purpose of earning and saving money in order to return home some day to live comfortably."

The early Japanese immigrants to Hawai'i came mostly from poor prefectures — Hiroshima, Kumamoto, Yamaguchi and Okinawa — after hearing about Hawai'i from recruiters or by word of mouth. Unlike most European immigrants who came to America to start life anew, those Japanese expected to return after they had completed their stints in Hawai'i. Most, however, were unable to make it back home because wages were so low that they could not save enough to pay for the passage. They were stuck in miserable living quarters working under often brutal foremen. The Japanese government, as a party to this arrangement, sent officials to remedy the situation but to little avail, and immigration slowed to a trickle. In 1898, Hawai'i was annexed to the United States, and in 1900 the immigration of labor under the contracts was ended. That opened the gates and, from 1900 through 1907, Kingoro Matsunaga and 68,300 other Japanese came to Hawai'i, this time mostly to escape poverty in a Japan struggling to catch up with the West.

These later Japanese immigrants differed from the earlier ones in that they resembled Irish and Eastern European immigrants who came across the Atlantic to break away from poverty and to start life over again. In the same way, the Japanese planned to build new lives in Hawai'i without returning to Japan. Of those Japanese, 35,000 left Hawai'i for the West Coast, where wages and working conditions were better. The so-called Gentlemen's Agreement between the Japanese and U.S. governments in 1908, a racist pact intended to stop the flow of Orientals into an America dominated by white Anglo-Saxon Protestants, ended almost all immigration from Japan and Asia. Even so, 75,000 Japanese lived in Hawai'i in 1910, where they comprised about 40 percent of the population of 190,000. Hawaiians or part-Hawaiians made up a quarter of the population, while Chinese, some of whom had arrived as early as 1802, comprised one-sixth. A smattering of other Asians, Polynesians and Caucasians — called *haole* — were among the rest.

Although Sparky was too young to remember life in Kukui'ula before 1920, he heard enough about it from his family to say later: "At that time, the plantation paid only a dollar a day. With seven children to support and my mother unable to work because my kid brother still needed attention, ours was a poverty-stricken family." That monthly income, he said, "was not sufficient to pay for the food and the necessities of life which we bought at the plantation store." Workers were permitted to charge purchases and have the price deducted from their pay. If there was an unpaid balance for more than two months, the company cut off the worker's credit until the debt had been paid out of his wages. "My father would get empty envelopes," Sparky said. "It got to the point where we couldn't even have food in the house." He told his children later that his mother sometimes skipped a meal if there was not enough food to go around, saying she was not hungry or had already eaten.

Sparky recorded his impressions of plantation life in a free-verse poem apparently written as he recovered from wounds during World War II; it is rendered here as written, including misspellings:

How well I remember having seen
Manuel, the luna*, crack his whip
From atop his kalakou** horse
To drive the laborers out to toil.

I recall old Kaneshige, aged & ill of health
Kicked out of bed, a mat upon the floor
Out of his shack, to him a home
To harvest more essential sugar cane.

If Manuel should ever do that to my pop
I'd kill him, then I thought,
But Pop is strong, as all men know,
And never shys from work.

Besides he's a religious man, and Manuel
    respects him well.
Despite his brutal beastly way
Manuel is grateful Pop saved his
Daughter Mary from haluscinations
With a few magic words of prayer.

   * Foreman
 ** Sparky probably meant "kalakoa," which is a pinto spotted with several
    colors and may be derived from the English word *calico*.

On the brink of abject poverty but not contracted to any plantation, Kingoro moved his family a few miles west to Hanapēpē in the early 1920s.

Hanapēpē was an independent town, one of the few on Kauaʻi that did not belong to a sugar plantation. Raising sugar cane and milling it into raw sugar dominated the life, economy and politics of the island from before Sparky's birth until well after World War II. (McBryde Sugar Company remained in business until 1996, closing after 97 years of operation.) Built on the edge of rice fields that stretched up a valley on either side of a stream, Hanapēpē then was home mainly to Japanese and Chinese immigrants. The rice, unlike the sugar, was for local consumption and not for export. Kingoro found a better job as a stevedore in Port Allen, just down the road from Hanapēpē, while Chiyono brought in extra cash by setting up a kitchen to make tofu, or soybean curd, which Sparky delivered in his wagon with his pet pig, Poru, tagging along. Kingoro and Chiyono also erected a public bathhouse for which Sparky and his sister and brother gathered firewood to heat water.

Sparky was a year late entering school but did well and skipped the fourth and seventh grades as he went to the Kōloa and ʻEleʻele grammar schools nearby and the Waimea Intermediate School, five miles west of Hanapēpē. Life continued to be hard but Kingoro imposed strict standards. "Regardless of how poor we were," Sparky later told the *Hawaii Herald*, "we'd never steal and we'd never beg. And if there were times when one of the children would receive food of some kind, he would raise holy hell with us for getting food from others. He thought that would be tantamount to begging." Kingoro had a softer side and loved to tell stories, to sing and to dance the old Japanese dances, most of which Sparky learned from him.

Moreover, Sparky told his daughter, Diane, "my father was recognized on Kauaʻi as a sort of spiritual healer." Sparky said he was an eyewitness to an exorcism his father performed on a man possessed of an evil dog spirit. In another incident, a young mother was about to slay her baby boy with a kitchen knife when her husband stopped her and someone called the police. They wanted to send her to a sanitarium but her parents persuaded the police to take her to Kingoro. He chanted prayers in another exorcism that lasted for more than an hour, until the young woman snapped awake and wondered where she was. The police considered her cured and returned her to her husband and parents. "These stories which I have related seem impossible, almost incredible to be believed," Sparky said. "I perhaps would not have believed them myself if they had been told to me by others. But I have actually witnessed with my own eyes these happenings."

In those days on Kauaʻi, there was only one high school, in the town of Līhuʻe on the east coast of the island, 30 miles from Hanapēpē. To earn bus fare, Sparky worked part-time as a stevedore on the dock in Port Allen and as a yardboy, weeding the flower bed and vegetable garden for 20 cents an hour. Gladys Brandt, wife of the superintendent at the pier in Port Allen and a teacher, remembered that Sparky did his work quietly. "He was kind of a precise young man, very polite, even back then," Mrs. Brandt said. "You always knew he would do his work."

Kauai High School reflected the social order on Kauaʻi in the 1930s. All of the faculty and staff, 14 women and 7 men, were Caucasians, mostly recruited from the mainland by the business establishment in Honolulu to teach democracy and the American way to the children of immigrants. The majority of the 109 students who graduated from the high school in 1933 were AJAs, and the rest were sprinklings of youths of Chinese, Korean, Filipino, Portuguese, Hawaiian and *haole* ancestry. Sparky fit in easily, becoming chief justice of the student court, sports editor of *Ke Kehiau*, the school yearbook, and a reporter for the school newspaper. The yearbook's sketch of Sparky said: "His prowess in math and science has never been questioned but it is chiefly his personality that makes him famous."

Two teachers, Isabel Anderson in English and Robert Clopton in civics, left particularly strong marks on Sparky. Mrs. Anderson taught English in a school where 90 percent of the students grew up speaking the singsong pidgin of the plantation, a jumble of English, Hawaiian, Portuguese, Japanese, Chinese and made-up words, all of which made it possible for the many ethnic groups to talk to each other. For instance, "Hey, I t'ink da kine food so good it broke da mout' awready" meant "I think that kind of food is really good."

Mrs. Anderson, better known as Ma Anderson, persuaded her students that they must speak standard English if they were to escape from the plantation into college or decent jobs. "Mrs. Anderson was a stately lady who made you speak good English," said Kazuo Senda of Kauaʻi, who served with Sparky in the 100th Battalion. For Sparky, it was the beginning of a lifelong love affair with the English language. Rather than resent Mrs. Anderson's insistence, most of the other students took her advice to heart. The 1933 high school yearbook is dedicated: "To Mrs. Anderson, we shall ever feel a debt of gratitude for helping us to master the English language." (In Hawaiʻi today, an argument occasionally erupts about whether children should be permitted to speak pidgin in school or should be required to speak standard English. There is little doubt where Sparky would have come down in that dispute.)

Sparky credited Clopton with guiding him toward politics. He remembered challenging the civics teacher, who had recently arrived from the mainland: "Is it the objective of American democracy to pay a Caucasian three times what is paid an Oriental even though they work side by side doing the same kind of work?" Sparky asked. Clopton replied, "Why, of course not. Are you trying to tell me such a situation prevails in Hawai'i?" Sparky shot back: "Yes, sir." Clopton, who later became dean of the College of Education at the University of Hawai'i, checked out Sparky's allegation, then called him aside after class one day. "Sparky, the only way you're going to change the social and economic system in Hawai'i is to change the laws. And how do you do that? You must became a legislator, a lawmaker — get into politics, run for public office." Clopton said he expected Hawai'i to become a state someday and that Sparky should seek to become a United States Senator. "Boy," Sparky said later, "he really put the bug in my ear."

While Sparky was in high school, the town of Hanapēpē suffered two economic setbacks. First, the port of Nāwiliwili, near Līhu'e, was chosen over Port Allen to be developed as Kaua'i's main outlet for shipping sugar to O'ahu and the world. Then a new highway passed between Hanapēpē and the sea, diverting business away from the merchants in the town. Shortly after that, just as Sparky graduated from high school, the Great Depression of the 1930s reached Kaua'i from the mainland. Sparky desperately wanted to go to Honolulu to the University of Hawai'i, where the tuition was only $120 a year, and was quietly envious of classmates who entered in the fall of 1933. But even with his older half-sister married, his family's finances didn't allow such a move, with other children still at home.

Moreover, Kingoro had been badly injured when several 100-pound sacks of sugar fell on him in the course of his stevedore job. As a result, Sparky's parents needed him to stay home to help provide for his brothers and sisters. He started working full time as a stevedore, then got a job at the Mikado store where he delivered groceries, kept track of stock and helped to keep the books. To earn a little extra money in the evenings, he went to the camps on the sugar plantations, set up a projector and showed movies on a bedsheet hung on the side of a shack.

Somewhere in that period, Kingoro, evidently seeing no contradiction with his own Shinto and Buddhist religious beliefs, advised Sparky to become a Christian. "This is America," he told his son. "You should be like other Americans and become a Christian." Sparky joined the Methodist Church and later became an Episcopalian. Andrew Matsunaga, Sparky's younger brother, explained that for his father, "any god was good." When Kingoro suffered his accident, he experienced his own rebirth of religious belief, promising the gods that he would return to his Shinto studies if he was healed. When his health returned, he became a part-time Shinto priest, building a small shrine near his home and ministering to his neighbors.

After working for four years at the Mikado store, Sparky caught a break. *The Garden Island* weekly newspaper announced in March 1937 that it was holding a contest to see who could sell the most subscriptions over the next four months.

First prize would be $1,000, second $750, and third $250, plus cash prizes and commissions of 50 cents a subscription each Saturday. How a newspaper on an island of 30,000 people that sold for five cents a copy—or $2.50 a year—could put up more than $2,000 in prize money defies explanation, but microfilmed copies of the paper in the Kaua'i Community College library today prove it was so. The newspaper reported that $1,000 would buy a new car with money left over, pay for a small business or make a large down payment on a home. What Sparky realized, he recalled later: "It would buy a lot of education at the University of Hawai'i." In year 2002 dollars, that $1,000 would be worth approximately $23,250.

By early April, Sparky and 15 other men and women had entered the contest even as they pursued their regular jobs. At the end of the month, he was in fourth place, and the newspaper carried front-page stories to promote the contest. In mid-May, Sparky was in third place, then in second in early June. The newspaper moved the goalposts in mid-June, extending the race to August 24. Spark fell to third place where he stayed until the Fourth of July, when he jumped into first. He slipped back to second in early August, took the lead with a week to go and finally held on to win. The August 31 issue of *The Garden Island* printed a picture of a shirtsleeved Sparky on the front page accepting a check from the newspaper's publisher, C.J. Fern.

As a mainstay in the family finances, Sparky gave his parents $600 and begged them to let him go to the University of Hawai'i. They agreed. He put $400 in his pocket and, since time was short to get to the university before the school year opened, threw his rather meager belongings into a suitcase and caught the weekly overnight packet boat *Waialeale* from Nāwiliwili to Honolulu. He rode on the deck with the cargo after paying a fare of $4. It seems to have been the first time Sparky was off the island of Kaua'i and, though he did not know it then, he would never go back there to live. "When I sailed on the old inter-island steamship from Kaua'i to Honolulu," Sparky said years later, "I felt like Columbus embarking for the New World."

When Sparky enrolled in the university, he was just a month shy of his 21st birthday and thus older than most of his classmates, although there is no evidence that his tardy arrival in college fazed him or caused any resentment among his peers. Through the next four years, three currents flowed through Sparky's life. The first was living in the Okumura Home, a dormitory run by a Christian minister, Reverend Takie Okumura, who, Sparky said, "other than my parents and immediate members of my family, had the greatest role in shaping the course of my life." The second current was the university itself, where Sparky studied to be a high school teacher but spent more time in dramatics, debate and public speaking to prepare himself for a career in politics. The third was the Reserve Officers Training Corps (ROTC) that began his grounding for military service in World War II. Just two months before Sparky entered the university, Japan had invaded northern China from Manchuria, launching what would become World War II in Asia and the Pacific. The war had started in Europe in September 1939, when Nazi Germany attacked Poland; Sparky was then entering his junior year in college.

Reverend Okumura, who had become a convert to Christianity in Japan at the age of 23, was a graduate of Doshisha University in Kyoto, which was allied with several New England churches and colleges, notably Amherst. After he was ordained, Reverend Okumura sailed to Honolulu in 1894 to serve as a missionary among the Japanese immigrants. Among his ministries, he built the Okumura Home as a haven for orphans and a boarding school for Christian youths from the outlying islands. Reverend Okumura was soon caught up in a long-running quarrel within the Japanese community, in which members of one faction were advocates of Christianity who believed Americanizing themselves and their children, and learning the English language. Their motto: "One language under one flag." On the other side were advocates of Buddhism who espoused being Americans but retained Japanese culture and values, and maintained Japanese language schools for their children after classes in the public schools.

As the most persuasive leader of the Christian faction, Reverend Okumura preached what scholar Dennis Ogawa calls in his book *Kodomo no tame ni* (*For the sake of the children*) "a sophisticated recognition that the Japanese population of Hawaii should embody a mixture of both Japanese and American elements." Among his listeners was a rapt Sparky Matsunaga. Ogawa sums up Reverend Okumura's philosophy: "He found traditional Japanese values of filial piety embedded in Christianity; he compared the age-old Japanese warrior with the Christian soldier; he stressed the similarities between Confucianism and Christianity." The preacher's concepts were epitomized in the Makiki Christian Church that he designed and built in what is now midtown Honolulu. It was fashioned after the Himeji Castle in central Japan, with a white tower soaring 100 feet into the air and topped with upswept eaves. "In style and purpose," Ogawa writes, "the intention was to combine Christianity with Japanese culture."

Reverend Okumura emphasized two thoughts: "Forget the idea 'Japanese' and always think and act from the point of view of the American people as long as you live under the protection of America." As for the next generation, he said, "You should educate and build them up into good and loyal American citizens." Halfway measures would not do, he said; parents should train their children "into not half-and-half but 100 percent American citizens." Sparky absorbed much of Reverend Okumura's thinking, some of it in private conversations in the preacher's Lincoln library that Reverend Okumura permitted him to enter, a rare privilege not given to most others at the home.

There was a practical side to Sparky's stay in the Okumura Home, where his age gave him an advantage over most of the other students. Reverend Okumura gave him room and board in exchange for teaching Sunday school and supervising the boys in chopping wood to heat water and in other chores. "I had worked as a stevedore," Sparky told a newspaper writer, "and was strong as hell. I could command the respect of the boys." The minister let Sparky use the home's station wagon to drive students to the university, charging them a dime instead of the 15 cents on the city bus. He had to pay for oil and gas but cleared $12 to $13 a month. Sparky was also allowed to use Reverend Okumura's roadster for social occasions, which must have caused a splash in a day when few college students had cars. Sparky made another $16 a month feeding white mice in an experimental lab under a National Youth Administration program. He even sent money home to his family, although his mother refused to spend it and presented it to Sparky as a savings fund when he graduated.

The University of Hawai'i, whose campus sprawled across the entrance of Mānoa Valley at the foot of the mountains behind Honolulu, reflected the realities of Hawai'i's social order in the 1930s. The administration and senior faculty were predominantly white and male while many of the elected student leaders were Asian-Americans, mostly male but with a sprinkling of women. The fraternities, sororities and clubs were segregated by ethnic group for Caucasians, AJAs, Chinese, Hawaiians and Koreans, and further divided into those for men and those for women. The Hakuba Kai, or White Horse Association, was a club for Japanese-American men and Sparky was its president during his senior year. Even the school's annual beauty pageant was segregated into contests for Caucasians, Japanese, Chinese, Korean and Hawaiian women, plus a category for women of mixed race that was called "cosmopolitan."

Segregation in Honolulu's two public high schools was imposed by a language test. Every child entering high school was given an examination to see whether he or she could speak standard English. Those who passed went to Roosevelt High, which was filled with the sons and daughters of haoles and a few upper-class Asian families. Those who failed because they spoke pidgin went to McKinley High, known as "Little Tokyo." Sam Mukaida, who came from the

Big Island and lived in the Okumura Home with Sparky, said that he, Sparky and others from the outer islands had trouble adjusting to the segregation at the university: "We didn't know what discrimination was because we went to high school with all kinds of kids — Japanese, Chinese, Filipinos. Koreans, Hawaiians. Most of the haole plantation managers sent their kids away to the mainland to go to school."

Sparky studied to become a high-school teacher not because he had any burning desire to be an educator but because it might give him a platform from which to jump into politics. He told the *Hawai'i Herald* that the first AJA to be elected to the Territorial Legislature from Kaua'i had been a schoolteacher. "The way he worked it," Sparky said, "was that he had his former students working for him. That was one of the ways I thought I'd get to be a legislator — become a schoolteacher and build my support among my students. It was all planned." Even so, Sparky's grades, plus his extracurricular activities, were good enough to earn him a place on the honor roll of "Real Deans."

A teacher of speech, Lucinda Bukeley, carried on the work begun by Ma Anderson at Kauai High School. All freshmen were required to take a speech class to reduce their reliance on pidgin and to improve their standard English. Sparky later told a writer from the *Honolulu Star-Bulletin* that a visiting professor of speech, a Mrs. Larrie, thought that Orientals in Hawai'i could not learn to speak proper English because there was "a difference in the voice mechanism." Sparky went on: "Mrs. Bukeley was aghast. She would challenge this, and she picked me as her guinea pig. I spoke pidgin — I'm from Kaua'i. I couldn't sound 'th' or distinguish between the long 'i' and the short 'i' (*teek* for *thick*). She became my Pygmalion. She took me to her house on Diamond Head and had me listen to her collection of Shakespeare by Maurice Evans and Lionel Barrymore. She let me sit there and listen to the recordings, and then asked me to repeat the sounds, reading from Shakespeare. She really worked with me."

Outside of class, Sparky was in a Theater Guild play in his sophomore year and won the award for best diction. "When it was announced that I was the winner, I went onstage to get my award. Mrs. Bukeley ran up on the stage, she hugged me and she said, 'We did it, Sparky, we did it!' She proved that an Oriental could be taught to speak English." Sam Mukaida said that even with this help, Sparky "struggled a bit because he had grown up on Kaua'i where he had had little opportunity to speak standard English with other people." Before going to speech class, Mukaida said, Sparky practiced before a mirror not only to get pronunciation right but to make sure his facial expressions fit with his speech. For those in the *nisei* or second generation like Sparky and Sam, it was all part of what Mukaida called the move "to be American, to speak American, to be patriotic." On the basis of his performances, Sparky was chosen as part of an eight-person team that toured outer-island schools. The team talked with high school students about the importance of staying in school and aiming for a university education.

Marjorie Carter Midkiff, who was in the drama club with Sparky, recalled his acting prowess, especially in comedies. "He liked to perform," she said. "He loved to give a speech and he was just plain funny whether he was acting or with his friends." The university theater put on a variety of plays in keeping with the social order, with actors playing roles of their own ethnic group — Japanese playing Japanese parts, Chinese playing Chinese, Caucasians playing Caucasians. *The Missouri Legend*, about the famed outlaw Jesse James, featured an all-white cast. A play entitled *Namu Amida Butsu*, which is a Buddhist chant, had Japanese-Americans playing all roles in a drama about universal loneliness. For Chinese-Americans, there was *The Delightful Perfidy of Yen Ming*, a comedy.

In his junior year, Sparky added debate to his activities, first in intramural competition, then on the varsity team. Within the university, Sparky and Nat Logan Smith defeated Walter Goto and Keichiro Yamato in a match over Japanese language schools in Hawai'i, arguing that they should be abolished so that young AJAs might put their full attention toward learning standard English and becoming good Americans. The varsity debates were carried on long distance with teams at Stanford, the University of Redlands east of Los Angeles and Washington State University. The affirmative and negative debaters on each team recorded their opening arguments, which were then exchanged by mail with the opposing team. After listening to those arguments, each team recorded its rebuttals and sent them off. This was competition for the experience only, with no winners or losers declared.

Sparky was active in the Oriental Literature Society and on the staff of the yearbook, *Ka Palapala*, but, curiously, not in university politics. The yearbook shows no record of Sparky being elected to class office or of having been an officer in the student government. He told an interviewer for the *Honolulu Star-Bulletin* that he had stood for office once but had been defeated. "We had a very heated student-body election," he said, "but Walter Chuck beat me by six or seven votes." After the election, a friend who knew him as Sparky asked whether Masayuki Matsunaga, as he was listed on the ballot, was his brother. "The votes I missed," Sparky said, "were those who didn't know that Masayuki was Sparky."

In the meantime, war clouds were gathering in Asia as Japan's aggression expanded; in July 1937 the Japanese Imperial Army invaded China from Manchuria. Six months later, Sparky wrote a freshman English essay that might have seemed naive at the time. Entitled "Let Us Teach Our People to Want Peace," the essay said: "What makes Americans so pugnacious? What in America makes it so easy for the recruiting officer and so hard for the pacifist? My answer is this: 'Because the feelings of the people are with the recruiting officer.' Why? Because the process by which we are educated, in the home, in the church, in the school and in the community at large, results in attitudes favorable to war." The essay continued: "Other agencies in the community serve their share. War trophies in museums and parks, parades, over-emphasis of the sensational by newspapers and magazines, all tend to bring out the warlike feelings of the people. We are living in a society based too largely on a militaristic foundation. The peace-loving emotions of the people have not been cultivated. Wants are the drives of all human action. If we want peace we must educate people to want peace. We must replace attitudes favorable to war with attitudes opposed to war."

Those sentiments did not stop Sparky from joining ROTC and doing well as a cadet. Here again Reverend Okumura influenced Sparky, persuading him to enlist in ROTC and to secure a commission in the Army when he graduated. The yearbook noted that ROTC had been in the background of college life until 1941: "Now the ROTC plays a vital part in the nation's preparedness and the University's unit has been swept into the foreground." The start of the military draft in 1939 caused a surge of enlistments in ROTC, which grew from a handful of cadets to more than 600 within a year. In training, Sparky scored well enough on the rifle range to earn a sharpshooter's badge and, for his leadership, was promoted to cadet major and battalion commander in his senior year. Of the six senior ROTC officers that year, four were haoles and two were AJAs. Sparky was elected to Saber and Chain, the ROTC honor society, and when graduation rolled around, was one of 16 cadets who received commissions.

Major Maurice Kerr, ROTC professor of military science and tactics at the university, called Sparky in just before he pinned on his gold bars as a second lieu-tenant to advise him: "If I am not mistaken, within six months Japan and the United States will be at war. If I were you, in order to erase any suspicions, I would volunteer for service so they wouldn't be able to question my loyalty." Besides, the major said, "you would have the advantage of being in before the others." Sparky would soon take the advice.

About the same time, the president of the University of Hawai'i, David L. Crawford, published a thoughtful essay in the school yearbook about the coming conflict. It was both a plea for patriotism and a warning to AJAs about what might be in store for them. "The most important service which all students can and must perform is to help preserve the principles of democracy, even in the time of crisis." Crawford stretched the point when he said, "Our ancestors fought and died for the freedom that we enjoy." Naturally, that did not apply to latecomers like the AJAs who, moreover, had been treated as second-class citizens. But Crawford was right when he further wrote: "It appears to be our turn to do some more fighting for the same cause."

"Our freedom, of course, is never absolute but always relative," he continued, "relative to natural laws and to the rights of other humans. It is not guaranteed to us, except as we fight for it, and once won, it does not remain with us, except by struggle." Then came the warning apparently directed at the AJAs: "Freedom is not constant. There are times when its exercise must be restricted temporarily. There are times and occasions when one does not feel as free as usual to speak his thoughts. There are times and occasions when freedom of action must be curbed for the common good. War, whether actual or prospective, makes a situation in which some customary manifestations of freedom have to be laid aside for the sake of national unity and efficiency." While Crawford may not have foreseen the detention of AJAs, he surely saw something unpleasant lying ahead for them.

Outside the university, suspicions of Japanese-American loyalty rumbled in an undercurrent as World War II approached. AJAs were caught in the middle, suspected by Americans of being spies for Japan and suspected by Japanese as being spies for America. In addition, some middle-class haoles resented competition from AJAs who had moved off the plantations to set up small businesses, enter the professions and participate in local politics. The reality, according to scholar Yukiko Kimura, was that the *issei*, or first generation of AJAs, either didn't believe Japan was guilty of aggression or deliberately kept themselves ill-informed, the better to avoid confronting the situation. About the American-born generation, however, Kimura wrote: "Because of their intimate participation in the larger community, *nisei* tended to hold the same critical view of Japan's increasing military aggression as that of the general public." Nonetheless, Kimura said, "As war with Japan became imminent, apprehension grew in the larger community concerning the Japanese residents."

Robert Shivers, the Federal Bureau of Investigation's agent in charge of its Honolulu office, started inquiries 18 months before the Japanese attack on Pearl Harbor. By mid-1940, he concluded: "There was no reason to question the loyalty of the citizens of Japanese ancestry." A Chinese-American, Hung Wai Ching, led the way in organizing The Committee for Racial Unity in December 1940, with Shivers as chairman, to combat suspicions of Japanese-Americans. Another committee, also chaired by Shivers, was constituted in early 1941 with trusted AJA leaders as members. This committee held a "Patriotic Rally" in June 1941 at McKinley High School that was addressed by an Army intelligence officer, Colonel M.W. Marston. He asked the 2,000 AJAs there to avoid actions that might cause the Army to assume responsibility for enforcing peace and order among civilians. Shivers reported later that the meeting "provided some definite and clear-cut criteria to guide the behavior of the Japanese."

Even so, the fearful reverberations concerning Japanese-Americans continued, and it was against this background that Sparky was commissioned on June 17, 1941. He enjoyed a few weeks off after graduation and on July 27 reported for duty with Company K of the Hawaii National Guard's 299th Infantry Regiment, stationed on the island of Moloka'i, 25 miles southeast of O'ahu. He was a platoon leader for three months, then was promoted to executive officer of the company in October, also serving occasionally as acting company commander when the company commander, George Cooper, was away.

While being an executive officer as a brand-new second lieutenant was heady stuff, Sparky evidently got off to a good start in his military service. Cooper rated him "superior" as a platoon leader and "excellent" as executive officer. Satoru Okamura, who had known Sparky when they were grammar school students at the 'Ele'ele school, had been drafted earlier in 1941 and arrived on Moloka'i in September, serving as a clerk at the airfield near Ho'olehua that Company K was assigned to guard. Okamura recalled that life was fairly routine and that he didn't see much of Sparky, since the lieutenant was so often in the field training his platoon or in the company office in his capacity as executive officer.

For Sparky, and Satoru and the other soldiers on Moloka'i, that autumn was the calm before the thunderstorm and the last quiet days they would know for a long time. ❖

One Puka Puka
1941–1945

At 7:55 a.m. on Sunday, December 7, 1941, the date that President Franklin Delano Roosevelt declared would "live in infamy," Sparky's life and that of every other American of Japanese Ancestry changed beyond comprehension. That morning, 181 Japanese warplanes launched from six aircraft carriers 220 miles northwest of Honolulu swept through a saddle between the Koʻolau and Waiʻanae mountain ranges or around Barbers Point to mount a surprise attack on the U.S. naval base at Pearl Harbor. Some of the attacking planes struck Hickam Army Air Field adjacent to Pearl Harbor, the Army posts at Schofield Barracks and Wheeler Army Air Field in the middle of Oʻahu, and Kāneʻohe Marine Base on the windward, or opposite, side of the island.

A second wave of 168 warplanes came an hour later. When the Japanese had withdrawn, they left Pearl Harbor in towering flames and billowing smoke: 12 warships sunk or crippled, 164 aircraft destroyed and another 159 damaged. Most devastating, 2,395 Americans had been killed, nearly half of them in the battleship *U.S.S. Arizona*. She sank in nine minutes after a Japanese bomb penetrated her forward powder magazine, which exploded in a thunderous roar. It was the worst naval defeat in American history. In a bitter irony, at least 29 of the dead were civilian Americans of Japanese Ancestry, including five small children. Nancy Masako Arakaki, eight years old, was killed while she was walking to Sunday school in downtown Honolulu, possibly by falling shrapnel from anti-aircraft guns fired at the attacking Japanese aircraft.

Sparky was acting company commander on Molokaʻi that Sunday as his unit had finished a seven-day alert the day before and the company commander was away. He and First Sergeant Francis Ching, Sergeant Walter Judd and Sergeant C. Mokuau were about to leave camp to hunt deer when a plane, evidently an observation plane, flew overhead. Looking up, Sparky said, "The maneuvers are getting realistic. Look at that! They have the Rising Sun painted on the wings and fuselage."

Over the radio a few minutes later came the word: "This is the real McCoy; Pearl Harbor is being bombed by the Japanese!" Sparky said he could see clouds of smoke from 60 miles away. Many others on Moloka'i heard about the attack from radio station KGMB, where Webley Edwards, a disc jockey who usually played Hawaiian music, reported, "This is the real thing! This is not a maneuver!" Joseph Dowson, a high-school boy who grew up on Moloka'i, wrote later: "Everybody was standing around outside, looking around in the sky."

Panic broke out as the Japanese were expected to invade. Francis Kudo, a company clerk who was home on a weekend pass from Company K, remembered getting the news on the radio and having his brother drive him five miles to the company headquarters near the airport. There he found men scurrying about, mostly picking up .30-caliber ammunition for their rifles. "We did not have time to talk," he said.

Satoru Okamura, the company clerk from Kaua'i, remembers seeing Sparky briefly in the supply room handing out rifles and telling the 117 soldiers in the company where to take up guard posts on the beach and near the airfield. Later, Sparky went out to see that the soldiers were where they were supposed to be. When a Japanese submarine surfaced and fired at fuel tanks, Sparky's outfit returned fire and drove the submarine away. Few anywhere in Hawai'i got much sleep for the next few days because of the expected Japanese invasion. "When invasion of the Hawaiian Islands was believed imminent," Sparky told author Bill Hosokawa, "all Americans regardless of race stood side by side in beach dugouts and trenches, fully prepared to repel the enemy."

Japanese-Americans were stunned and dismayed by the surprise attack from the land of their forefathers even though the threat of war had been increasingly evident since 1937. AJAs were frightened and angry that Japan had attacked their country, all the more because the Japanese had mounted the assault without warning or declaration of war. Daniel Inouye, then a senior in high school and eventually a U.S senator, wrote years later: "It came to me that any one of the men in that armada of planes flaunting the Rising Sun could be my cousin, and to this day I do not know but what it might have been so, for I have never wanted to find out."

AJAs were frightened because they knew their allegiance would be suspect. As a 1999 article in the *Hawaii Tribune-Herald* recalled, "Radios and newspapers screamed, 'A Jap is a Jap! The only good Jap is a dead Jap!'" (The pejorative "Jap" is as insulting to a Japanese-American as "nigger" is to an African-American.)

With an ugly mood billowing up, AJAs were all the more frightened because they did not know what would happen to them. What followed was a swift and bewildering sequence of events. Even before the smoke had cleared at Pearl Harbor, the Territorial governor, John Poindexter, declared martial law and suspended the writ of *habeas corpus*, which gives Americans fundamental protection against illegal or arbitrary imprisonment. He was quickly upstaged by the Army commander, Lieutenant General Walter Short, who proclaimed himself military governor.

The FBI rounded up Japanese language school principals, Buddhist priests, civic leaders, martial arts instructors and anyone else suspected of sympathizing with Japan. Most were released after interrogation but some were interned on Sand Island, not far from Pearl Harbor. Albert Oki and Ken Otagaki, soldiers in the Army's 65th Combat Engineers, were taken at gunpoint by haole soldiers of the same outfit and strip searched. "We drank together, we bunked together, but all of a sudden we became enemies after December 7," Otagaki recalled in Thelma Chang's book *I Can Never Forget*. At sea, two fishing boats with AJA crews were mistaken for Japanese by the pilots of U.S. fighter planes on December 8 while returning to harbor. The planes strafed the boats, killing six fishermen.

The next day, as President Roosevelt appeared before Congress to ask for a declaration of war, 317 young AJA men at the University of Hawai'i were sworn in as soldiers in the Hawaii Territorial Guard. General Short, who had been cautioned that the young men were of Japanese ancestry, said, "I think they are perfectly loyal." A morning newspaper had reported with alarm that saboteurs had landed on O'ahu; the report turned out to be erroneous. Another rumor had Japanese paratroopers dropping on St. Louis Heights, then on the edge of Honolulu; the new recruits in the Territorial guard were rushed off to investigate.

Barbed wire was thrown up everywhere, machine guns mounted, sandbags placed, trenches dug. A curfew and blackout were imposed. The Secretary of the Navy, Frank Knox, arrived by plane from Washington on December 11 for a personal inspection and left convinced that Hawai'i was seething with a fifth column of Japanese spies and saboteurs. The situation was so confused that Army recruits at Schofield Barracks in central O'ahu were disarmed and segregated for a day by ethnic groups — Japanese, Filipino, *haole* — then rearmed and sent back to training.

Ten days after the attack, General Short was relieved of his command, as was the naval commanding officer, Admiral Husband Kimmel. Short was replaced by Lieutenant General Delos Emmons who, in the chaos, was besieged on all sides about what to do with Japanese-Americans, particularly those in uniform. His first reaction was to have them all arrested. When Colonel Kendall Fielder, the senior intelligence officer, reported that there was no place to put them, General Emmons relented.

Moreover, it soon became evident that AJAs were critical to the labor force and to running the wartime economy. Emmons rejected a suggestion from Washington on December 19 that all AJAs be interned. Some businessmen of other ethnic groups, seeking to be rid of competition from AJA small businesses, turned against the Japanese-Americans. On the other side, J. Garner Anthony, the most prominent haole lawyer in Hawai'i, defended the Japanese-Americans as loyal Americans. So did the Chinese civic leader, Hung Wai Ching. That did not prevent General Emmons from disbanding the Hawaii Territorial Guard in January 1942. The AJAs responded by forming the Varsity Victory Volunteers to build defenses and provide labor on other projects in the war effort.

By mid-January, the chaos had subsided, as had the threat of an immediate Japanese invasion. *The Honolulu Advertiser* reported there had been no cases of espionage by AJAs. Nonetheless, all Japanese-Americans were issued identification badges bordered in black; four different ratings determined where the wearer could and could not go, such as the naval station at Pearl Harbor. About 250 AJA men were interned at Sand Island as were 25 Germans. Ken Otagaki was transferred from the 65th Combat Engineers to an Army veterinary unit, that still being the day of a horse-mounted army, while Albert Oki was sent from the engineers to the 298th Infantry where large numbers of the soldiers were AJAs. A general at Schofield Barracks told them, "Boys, you are going overseas. You're going to be a combat outfit." Oki said, "You could hear a pin drop."

While O'ahu was in a swirl, the neighbor islands apparently escaped much of the confusion. Sparky and the other soldiers in Company K on Moloka'i went about training, building defenses, stringing barbed wire, and guarding the airfield and the beaches. Even so, Yuzuru Morita was quoted in *I Can Never Forget*, "Rumors were going around that soldiers of Japanese ancestry were going to be interned on Molokai." Images of the 18th Century popped up among the AJAs who remembered how Hawaiians afflicted with leprosy had been isolated under miserable conditions on that island's Kalaupapa peninsula, where Father Joseph Damien de Veuster, the Belgian Roman Catholic priest, had come in 1873 to help care for them.

The War Department, the forerunner of today's Department of the Army, questioned General Emmons again on February 1, 1942, as to whether Japanese-Americans were loyal and urged that the AJAs in the 298th and 299th Infantry Regiments be discharged. Colonel Fielder, the intelligence chief, said he had no evidence that Japanese-Americans were anything but loyal and Emmons said he needed the soldiers until reinforcements arrived from the mainland. Unswayed, the authorities in Washington again told Emmons to fire all AJAs from government offices and bases. He again declined because that would have slowed Hawai'i's economy, which was was being geared into the war effort.

On February 19, President Roosevelt signed the infamous Executive Order 9066 that directed the Army to exclude anyone considered a danger from any areas it designated, and to provide food and shelter for them elsewhere. The words "Japanese" or "Japanese-American" did not appear in the order but there was no doubt as to its intent. The Army proceeded to intern 120,000 Japanese-Americans from the West Coast in makeshift "relocation centers" in desolate areas of the western U.S. The AJAs, the majority of them from California, were rounded up; stripped of homes, farms and property; and herded into the concentration camps. Two-thirds of those incarcerated were native-born American citizens, the rest legal resident aliens.

During four years of detention, 5,981 of the internees were babies born in the camps and were American citizens by constitutional right. The exclusion order did not immediately apply to Hawai'i, but eventually about 1,100 AJAs from Hawai'i were sent to the camps. Most Japanese-Americans in Hawai'i escaped that nightmare because Caucasian, Chinese and other ethnic leaders spoke up for them.

In Hawai'i, the AJA soldiers remained suspect through the rest of that winter, with President Roosevelt and Secretary of the Navy Knox continuing to favor internment of Japanese-Americans from Hawai'i and dismissing AJAs from the National Guard. Secretary of War Henry Stimson and Assistant Secretary John McCloy, plus the Army staff, were opposed on grounds that the internment was unconstitutional or impractical. Stimson and McCloy were reinforced in early April when General Emmons reported that AJA soldiers wanted to serve in combat to prove their patriotism. As an apparent compromise, the War Department suggested sending them to the mainland to be labor troops.

Twice more in May, General Emmons urged the War Department to permit him to send the AJAs to the mainland. Finally, General George C. Marshall, the chief of staff, stepped in to order that the Japanese-Americans in the 298th and 299th Infantry Regiments, which were far below strength in numbers, be formed into a provisional battalion, the next smaller sized unit, and shipped to the mainland for training. Part of the reason was that enough replacements had arrived from the mainland that the AJA soldiers were no longer considered necessary for the defense of Hawai'i.

That order from the Operations Division of the War Department General Staff, dated May 28, 1942, was decisive in its effect on Sparky's life and those of other AJAs. Many misunderstandings grew up around it, some that Sparky held at the time and some that are still held today. One was that the provisional battalion was being shipped to the mainland either to be incarcerated like the civilian AJAs from the West Coast or to be used as a labor battalion. In fact, the battalion was intended from the outset to be trained for combat. The second misunderstanding was that the weapons of the AJAs had been taken away because they were not trusted. In fact, the weapons were turned in to save on transport costs and because they were needed for replacements arriving in Hawai'i. The AJA soldiers were to draw new weapons on the mainland as soon as the supply lines, strained by the sudden onslaught of the war, could deliver them.

In its critical provisions, the May 28 order stated:

1. Commanding General, Hawaiian Department, has been directed to organize a provisional infantry battalion to consist of all officers and enlisted men of Japanese ancestry in the 298th and 299th Infantry Regiments in Hawaii, and to transfer this provisional unit to the mainland at the earliest practicable date.

2. This unit will pass to the control of the Commanding General, Army Ground Forces, at Port of Debarkation. It will be dispatched therefrom promptly to a training area in the Central Defense Command to be designed [sic] by the Commanding General, Army Ground Forces. On arrival there, it will *be reorganized, equipped, and trained for future use as an infantry combat unit* to be ready for field service on 10 days notice after September 30, 1942. (Italics added.)

3. Instructions have been issued to the Commanding General, Hawaiian Department, to dispatch this unit to the mainland *less weapons and motor transportation, which will be replaced on arrival of the unit in the designated training area.* (Italics added.)

Paragraphs 4 and 5 of the order concerned logistic details. The order concluded: "The need for secrecy regarding the nature, origin, destination, and other matters regarding this unit will be brought to the attention of all concerned." That appeared to be an order included in many wartime instructions, not just for this particular battalion.

In a subsequent order, dated June 19, 1942, the Army Ground Forces headquarters in Washington laid out the details for rearming and reequipping the battalion in phases, noting that its complete equipment was to be issued by August 31, 1942. It repeated the order that "the battalion will be organized, equipped, and trained as an infantry combat battalion." One paragraph applied only to this battalion and is worth noting in light of subsequent misunderstandings: "Every effort must be made to maintain morale and esprit de corps in the unit at a high level. So far as is possible, officers and men must be made to feel that their unit is an honored element of the Army and that it is being trained with a view to its ultimate employment in combat."

Even so, the Army appears not to have explained any of that to Sparky and his fellow soldiers. The AJAs, in the raw emotional climate of the day, assumed the worst. A combination of a failure in Army leadership and the taut sensitivities of Japanese-Americans, compounded by the confusion in Hawai'i, on the West Coast and in Washington, made for a festering sore that could have been avoided with some thought and candor.

Sparky later told the *Hawai'i Herald* that May 29, 1942, the day after the decisive order was given, was hard. "What a day that was," he said with indignation. "We were given orders to turn in all our arms and ammunition — those of us of Japanese ancestry. It was an emotional jerker for me to be forced into turning in my side arms to my commanding officer after having stood ready to defend my country." Many AJAs still resent the way they were treated with suspicion in those early days even though the facts showed they were not suspect.

Once the May 28 order had been given, the Army wasted little time in executing it. The soldiers posted on the outlying islands were shipped to O'ahu and assembled within several days at Schofield Barracks. Francis Shinohara remembered that during a formation at Schofield, Army leaders apologized to the AJAs for confiscating their rifles. On June 4, Sparky was promoted to first lieutenant and the next day, he and the rest of the troops were loaded aboard a train bound for Honolulu Harbor. The troop movement was supposed to be secret but many members of the soldiers' families lined the tracks to say goodbye and to deliver a message that, summed up in the 100th Battalion's 50th-anniversary volume, *Remembrances*, said: "Do your duty. America is your country. Go and do your best. Do not bring shame to the family." In pidgin, the poignant send-off was: "No make shame."

The troops boarded a converted troop transport, the *S.S. Maui*, along with civilians being evacuated and set sail for a destination unknown to them. Ed Harada remembers, "I recall seeing a lone girl run to the railing at Pier 11 and wave to us." Francis Shinohara said later, "Our 'Aloha 'Oe' to Hawai'i was very lonely as we secretly sailed on the old ship."

The next day, U.S. military leaders announced that the Japanese navy had suffered a severe defeat at the battle of Midway; the threat of an invasion of Hawai'i had passed. A week after sailing from Honolulu, the *S.S. Maui* passed under the Golden Gate Bridge at the entrance to San Francisco Bay and docked across the bay in Oakland. The civilian passengers disembarked during the day but the AJAs were told that, with anti-Japanese-American feelings running high, they were to keep out of sight until nightfall so as not to cause an incident.

After dark, the troops were led off the ship into three waiting trains and told to keep the window shades down lest bystanders think they were Japanese prisoners of war. Ken Otagaki, who liked to shake things up a bit, kept inching the shades up to see where they were and had a running argument with a sergeant who kept making him pull them down. The trains slipped out of Oakland separately, one taking a southern route, the second a central route and the third a northern route, all headed for Camp McCoy, Wisconsin, although that was not then known to the soldiers.

At this time, what had been the Hawaii Provisional Battalion was designated the 100th Infantry Battalion (Separate), the "separate" indicating that it was not part of a regiment, which usually comprised three battalions and supporting units. The soldiers from Hawai'i soon nicknamed their unit "One Puka Puka," a *puka* in the Hawaiian language meaning a zero or a hole.

The battalion was not the first in the U.S. Army to be based on ethnic or racial composition. An Irish brigade served in the Union Army during the Civil War as did African-American units, perhaps the most notable of which was the 54th Massachusetts Regiment. Four regiments of African-American soldiers, the 9th and 10th Cavalry and the 24th and 25th Infantry, served in the West during the post-Civil War expansion there. They were called "Buffalo Soldiers" by the Indians for their curly hair. African-American units fought in France during World War I and again in Europe in World War II. The 99th Infantry Battalion (Separate) was composed of soldiers of Norwegian ancestry, the 101st Infantry Battalion (Separate) was of Austrian ancestry and the 122nd Infantry Battalion (Separate) was of Greek ancestry in World War II.

Nor were the soldiers of the 100th Battalion the first Japanese-Americans to enter military service or to die for America. Seven Japanese-Americans were killed in the explosion of the *U.S.S. Maine* in 1898 in the harbor at Havana that triggered the Spanish-American War. Japanese-Americans served in a segregated Company D of the Hawaii National Guard during World War I but did not go overseas.

What made the 100th Battalion distinctive was that it was the first unit since the Revolution to serve in the U.S. Army when the land of their fathers and mothers was the enemy. The Irish, African-Americans, Norwegians, Austrians and Greeks did not face the prospect of shooting at their cousins or even their brothers; a few brothers of the *nisei* had returned to Japan before the war and were subsequently drafted into the Japanese armed forces. Nor did members of the other ethnic units feel the need to prove their loyalty to America. The soldiers of the 100th Battalion were to do so well in training that a larger unit, the 442nd Regimental Combat Team (RCT), was formed in 1943 and reached Italy in June 1944, just after the battle at Anzio. The 100th was melded into the 442nd RCT as the first of its three infantry battalions but retained its own identity and colors. As Martin Tohara, first sergeant of D Company in the 100th, said, "They joined us, we didn't join them." Given this singular background, One Puka Puka became a brotherhood that has endured for six decades even as its veterans have entered their 80s.

When the trains reached Camp McCoy on June 16, 1942, and pulled into a siding, the first sight was a high fence topped with barbed wire. Some of the soldiers thought the worst, that they were going to be incarcerated or, almost as bad, become guards at a prison camp. "Oh, oh, here we go — concentration camp," Sparky said later. "Some of the pessimists were right." He told scholar Gary Okihiro, in his book *Cane Fires*, "We pictured ourselves as a battalion of forced laborers." After 30 minutes, the trains moved on to disgorge the troops near a tent area.

Once again, the Army had failed to tell the *nisei* troops what had been planned for them, and the *nisei*, with their sensitivities overwrought, assumed calamity had struck. Sparky related a story about Camp McCoy to author Bill Hosokawa: "We were put through close-order drill and trained with wooden guns." So were thousands of other soldiers elsewhere in America because the arsenals had not yet caught up with the demand for rifles and other weapons. The AJAs were evidently not told that. "We wrote home of our great desire for combat duty to prove our loyalty to the United States," Sparky continued. "It was not known then that our letters were being censored by higher authority. We learned subsequently that because of the tenor of our letters, the War Department decided to give us our chance. Our guns were returned to us, and we were told that we were going to be prepared for combat duty as the 100th Infantry Battalion. Grown men leaped with joy on learning that they were finally going to be given the chance on the field of battle to prove their loyalty to the land of their birth." In fact, the decision to send the AJAs into battle had been made long before and a little candor on the part of the Army leaders could have avoided that misunderstanding.

For the next few weeks, life was turbulent as the battalion got organized. The unit was commanded by Lieutenant Colonel Farrant Turner, a haole reserve officer from Hawai'i who was friends with many Japanese-Americans. His second in command and executive officer was Major James Lovell, a haole teacher who lived in Hawai'i and who was also a friend of many AJAs. The battalion of 1,406 soldiers and 38 officers, 22 of whom were haoles, was oversized, a normal battalion having 800 to 1,000 soldiers and 40 officers organized into a headquarters company, a heavy weapons company and three rifle companies. The 100th Battalion comprised five rifle companies that would be trimmed down to three companies as the battalion suffered casualties. Unlike other battalions that drew replacements for casualties from a replacement unit, the 100th in effect trained and carried its replacements with it.

Like almost everyone else, Sparky was shuffled around. Even though he was only a first lieutenant, he commanded C Company, a rifle company, for a month, then became the company's executive officer when a haole, Captain Andrew Fraser, was assigned as company commander. After nearly six months, Sparky was reassigned to D Company as executive officer under the command of Captain Jack Mizuha, who later became a prominent judge in Hawai'i. D Company was the heavy weapons company armed with machine guns and mortars that would provide supporting fire for the rifle companies. As second in command, Sparky was responsible for administration, supply, food and medical support, freeing the company commander for training, operations and combat leadership. In combat, Sparky would bring up the rear of the company with the cooks, supply sergeants, clerks and any other support the company needed.

As any Army executive officer could attest, it was a thankless but essential task. Captain Mizuha, the company commander, was an aggressive, take-charge, fiery leader, far different from the mild-mannered, humorous, gregarious Matsunaga. Even so, they got along, said Martin Tohara, the first sergeant who served directly under both, because "Sparky listened to Jack." Mizuha responded by giving Sparky the top mark of "superior" in his efficiency reports.

Major Lovell, the battalion executive officer, said in an interview that Sparky was a good officer. "There was never any trouble with him," Lovell said. "He was highly respected by the men and he saw that they were fairly treated. He would keep the boys out of trouble. Jack Mizuha was a hard-charger and Sparky was a cooling influence. Sparky knew when to talk and what to say and he had a leveling influence. He was an intelligent person."

Some of the soldiers thought Sparky was a "sissy" and snickered because he had taught Sunday school while living in the Okumura Home in Honolulu. If they were goofing off, one said, they might say, "Look out, here comes the Sunday school teacher." Later, when they went into combat in Italy, Lovell said, "All references to his conduct were A-plus. He was well-equipped to handle most combat situations." Lovell added, however, that Sparky was not flashy. "Nothing stands out about Sparky Matsunaga in combat," Lovell said. "You might not have known he was there."

The basic training at Camp McCoy went well during the summer and early fall, but the men from tropical Hawai'i had mixed feelings about the first snowfall as they felt the cold more than the hardy Scandinavians of Wisconsin. Even so, they soon got the knack of a snowball fight. People in the nearby towns of Sparta, Tomah and LaCrosse went out of their way to welcome the *nisei*, inviting them to their homes, churches and social halls. A few romances even blossomed between blonde, blue-eyed girls and black-haired, dark-eyed young men, and to this day, men of the 100th Battalion have retained ties to that community. On the post, the *nisei* sometimes got into fights with white soldiers from a Texas division until Colonel Turner told them, "Don't try to take on a whole division — save your fights for the battlefield."

When Sparky delivered a commencement address at Wisconsin State University in 1966, he recalled the pleasant reception the *nisei* had received in 1942, saying, "The entire battalion paraded through the streets of your capital city." He noted, however, that "one elderly gentleman remarked after viewing the parade that although he did not see any feathers on our caps, he thought for a moment that the Indians had modernized and gone back on the warpath. We didn't blame him one bit, for it was the first time that he or most of the others had seen anyone of Japanese ancestry."

It was different when the battalion moved south to Camp Shelby, Mississippi, in January 1943 for advanced training. Again, things went well with the commanding general singling out the 100th after an especially difficult field exercise, saying the troops "played the game well despite the rotten weather."

Off post, the Deep South was still in the grip of rigid segregation and the Japanese-Americans resented the racism as much as the whites of Mississippi resented their presence. More than one fistfight broke out either with white soldiers or local citizens. Happily, the battalion did not stay long at Camp Shelby but was shipped to Louisiana in April for two months of maneuvers. The One Puka Puka returned briefly to Camp Shelby in June to receive its colors. The Army had selected an insipid slogan for a motto to be inscribed on the flag, "Be of Good Cheer," at which the *nisei* soldiers scoffed. To remind themselves and all other Americans why they wanted to go into combat, the battalion asked for and got a new motto: "Remember Pearl Harbor." The soldiers were also issued mattress bags. Shinohara said, "Later, we were to realize its grim use." On August 11, the battalion left by train for Camp Kilmer, New Jersey, to board the troopship *James Parker* in New York on August 20 bound for North Africa.

The Atlantic crossing was uneventful and filled with card and dice games. The ship passed the Rock of Gibraltar, which one of the soldiers said looked "just like the Prudential ad," and arrived on September 2 in Oran, Algeria in northern Africa and on the southern coast of the Mediterranean. At that time, the famous German general, Field Marshal Erwin Rommel, and his Afrika Corps had been defeated and the allies were preparing to invade Italy. The 100th Battalion was given a choice of guarding supply depots and trains in North Africa or going to combat in Italy. Major Lovell, the battalion executive officer, said, "We told them we were there to go to combat."

The battalion was assigned to the 34th "Red Bull" Division, commanded by Major General Charles Ryder. In an early meeting with the battalion's officers, General Ryder made a wise promise: "No matter how easy the first battle is," he said, "the morale of the troops will never fail afterwards if you win it. I won't take special care of you otherwise, but I will let you win the first battle." The general put out word that the 100th Battalion had joined the division and would be assigned to the 133rd Infantry Regiment. He particularly instructed all in his command that the new arrivals were not to be called or referred to as "Japs," which they would not tolerate.

Colonel Ray Fountain, commanding the 133rd Infantry, made the same point to his regiment. "They are not Japanese but Americans born in Hawai'i. They don't ask any special consideration and we won't give them anything that isn't given to all other units. The battalion will be fighting with the rest of us, taking its regular turns." The colonel turned out the band to welcome the 100th, and their first night camped in bivouac, soldiers from other battalions wandered into the 100th's area to share bottles of wine and to learn Hawaiian songs. In training, several teams from the battalion went to school to learn about mines that German soldiers deployed extensively in their defensive positions.

Then, in rapid succession, the Italians dropped out of the war on September 8, Allied Forces landed at Salerno on September 9, and the 34th Division loaded aboard ship on September 19 and landed at Salerno on September 22. The 100th Battalion, with more than 1,300 soldiers, went ashore and began to push inland against the formidable German Wehrmacht. The corps commander, Major General John Lucas, sent instructions to the three divisions under his command: "There has recently arrived in this theater a battalion of American soldiers of Japanese ancestry. The troops take particular pride in their American origin. Your command should be so informed in order that during the stress and confusion of combat, cases of mistaken identity may be avoided."

The cold autumn rains had begun and mud became a constant obstacle. The battalion pushed ahead, at one point covering more than 15 miles in a day's fighting when four or five miles was a good average. Conrad Tsukayama became the first casualty when he suffered a face wound from shrapnel on September 28 when a passing jeep triggered a mine. He was sent back to a hospital but walked away to rejoin the 100th because, he said later, "I didn't want them to send me to another outfit after I recovered." The next day, Shigeo "Joe" Takata, a popular baseball player, and Keichi Tanaka were the first of the battalion to be killed in action, taking out a German machine gun nest. Takata won the battalion's first Distinguished Service Cross, the Army's second-highest decoration for valor.

The battalion captured the town of Benevento to win their first battle, as General Ryder had promised, and in doing so rescued 22 American paratroopers who had been trapped behind enemy lines for two weeks. There followed two waded crossings of the ice-cold Volturno River. During one of them, Sparky's only clean underwear somehow got loose from his backpack and floated down the river to the amusement of his troops. The 100th Battalion captured its first German prisoners during these firefights and some of the Japanese-American soldiers took mischievous pleasure in finding ways to communicate with the Germans that Japan had switched sides and was now fighting against Germany. The Germans, never having seen AJAs, were often taken in. By the end of October, the battalion was poised for one more crossing of the Volturno and pushing into the hills on the way to the fierce battle of Monte Cassino.

A memorandum from the War Department reviewed the battalion's performance after its first month in battle: "The combat record of an infantry battalion composed of Japanese-American personnel emphasizes the fact that these people have earned the respect, admiration, confidence and friendliness of <u>all</u> members of our armed forces. [Underlined in original]" After reciting several AJA accomplishments, the memo directed that those facts "be brought to the attention of appropriate units and installations under your command and that all military personnel serving in units or installations to which Japanese-Americans are assigned be informed accordingly."

About this time, a mysterious Private Thompson entered the scene. As the 100th Battalion moved along a road preparing to attack into the hills, Thompson appeared saying he was AWOL, or absent without official leave, from his paratroop unit. He had been over the ground and offered to guide the battalion through the minefields and into the hills. His offer was quickly accepted and the mile-long column headed into the hills.

Captain Mizuha of D Company was up front with the battalion command group about three-quarters of the way to the top of Hill 600, the objective south of

Monte Cassino, when he discovered that most of his company had stopped at the bottom of the hill. Sparky, bringing up the rear, apparently had misunderstood a garbled radio message and stopped to await orders. With them were the mortars that would be needed to take and hold the top of the hill. Thompson offered to go down the hill to bring Sparky and the rest of the company up to the front. He reached Sparky and, about 45 minutes later, Sparky led the soldiers through the minefield but not without tripping mines and losing several men. On the way up the hill, Thompson himself tripped a mine and was blown to pieces. No dog tags, letters or distinguishing marks were ever found and his identity is still unknown.

After dark a short time later, Sparky and his troops stumbled into another minefield. When a soldier tripped a mine, Sparky was slightly injured in the neck but Yasuo Kawano, Sparky's radioman, was mortally wounded by shrapnel in the temple. Sparky wrote to a friend in Wisconsin that he and a runner tried to give Kawano first aid and prayed that he would not die. "Never in my life had I prayed so fervently as I did that night for the life of one who had served me so loyally," Sparky wrote. Fifty minutes later, Kawano died. Sparky recalled later that Kawano had said he knew his death would mean a better life for Japanese-Americans back home.

Another soldier, Yoshinao "Turtle" Omiya, was blinded by the same burst. Ken Otagaki, a stretcher bearer, came by a little while later and said, "Sparky, you are not hurt so bad. I got other guys up front with severe wounds. I'll come back to get you later." Sparky agreed but an hour later someone else stepped on another mine and this time Sparky was badly wounded in the right leg. At dawn, Otagaki and his litter crew came back and carried Sparky off Hill 600. He was taken to an aid station in the nearby village of Pozzilli to be patched up then shipped to the 17th General Hospital in Naples. (Otagaki himself was gravely wounded by a mortar burst two months later, losing his right leg, two fingers from his right hand and the sight of his right eye.)

The 100th Battalion went on to fight in the battle of Monte Cassino, which was among the bloodiest of the war. When it was over, only 521 of 1,300 soldiers remained standing. After the battle at Anzio, the battalion became part of the 442nd Regimental Combat Team and went on to fight in northern Italy, in southern France where it rescued the "Lost Battalion" of Texans who had been surrounded by the Germans and again in northern Italy where it helped to crack the last of the German resistance on the Gothic Line before the Nazis surrendered. Altogether in three years of service, 3,147 men served in the battalion, of whom 338 were killed in action and 1,703 Purple Hearts were awarded for wounds received in battle. In U.S. military parlance, a ten percent loss in dead and wounded is considered an excessive rate of casualties; the 100th Battalion suffered a 65 percent loss.

Private Sadao Munemori won the nation's highest military decoration, the Congressional Medal of Honor, awarded posthumously. The Distinguished Service Cross, the second highest, went to 24 soldiers; 147 Silver Stars were awarded as were 238 Bronze Stars for valor. More than a half-century later, the U.S. acknowledged that prejudice had prevented even more decorations from being awarded. On June 21, 2000, seven veterans of the 100th Battalion were decorated with the Medal of Honor for "gallantry in action above and beyond the call of duty." At the same time, another 12 veterans of the other two infantry battalions of the 442nd RCT, including Senator Daniel Inouye, were decorated with the Medal of Honor, as were two more Asian-Americans from other units. Rarely in U.S. history has an American military unit compiled such an extraordinary record as the 100th Battalion/442nd RCT. None has surpassed it.

Bill Mauldin, the combat cartoonist and correspondent, explained why the AJAs fought as bravely as they did. As quoted in Thomas Murphy's book, *Ambassadors in Arms,* Mauldin said, "If these *nisei* in Italy didn't get fed right, they raised hell just like any other American soldier. They liked to come to town on passes and make whoopee as much as anyone else, and they certainly wanted to survive the war as much as their fellow soldiers in other units. But when they were in the line, they worked harder than anybody else because they wanted to prove something. They were willing to take extra chances and do extra jobs in hopes that a grateful nation would maybe give their families, many of whom were in concentration camps formally known as 'relocation centers,' a few breaks that were long overdue."

After three months in the hospital, Sparky was well enough to do office work and to write poetry. In a letter to a friend in Wisconsin, Sparky said he felt he hadn't done his full share for the men at the front and wished he could go back. "Oft times I feel like cursing my fate," he wrote. "Yet, in the light of deeper thought, I console myself with the belief that things are better as they are and that the Almighty meant them to be as they are. Besides, as a fellow office worker remarked, 'It's better to be a live lieutenant than a dead captain.'"

Some of Sparky's poetry written at this time was serious, some whimsical. On the serious side was "On Being Wounded."

> When in the light of thought I ask
>   Myself; Just who am I and what,
> What lasting imprints good or ill,
>   Have I for future mortals wrought?

'Tis then my pride in vainness cries,
   My ego ebbs to naught from high,
And sadly do I realize
   The plight of many a soul as I:

Be born to live, to suffer, die,
   Unseen, unheard, unknown, unknelled;
Like chips upon a checkerboard
   No choice, no will, resigned, compelled.

Let patriots wave and sing and shout,
   Let politicians treaties seal.
Our souls which rise from wounded, maimed,
   Are dead to things untrue, unreal.

A bit more whimsical was this piece of doggerel entitled "O.R. Nurse (or Oops, Doc!)"

I wonder what's behind that mask,
Below those lovely eyes;
(Oops, doc, that hurts!)

Her lash curled, her brows trimmed neat
Do match her white disguise
(Oops, doc, that hurts!)

I wouldn't mind those scissor-cuts
And needle pokes one bit,
(Oops, doc, that hurts!)

If only she would hold my hand
And squeeze it just a bit;
(Oops, doc, did it hurt?)

And look at me the way she does,
(Although she is no flirt)
I don't care what's behind that mask.
(Oops, doc, just let it hurt.)

At the end of April 1944, Sparky was discharged from the hospital but was not fit for combat. He was assigned to the 7th Replacement Battalion that operated in Naples and in North Africa, first as a motor transport officer and then as company commander in a battalion that received replacements from the U.S., issued them weapons and field gear, briefed them on the fighting, assigned them to units and transported them to the front. Veterans of D Company said they remembered seeing Sparky come up to the front in a truck to deliver replacements or supplies but the war, in effect, was over for him. He left Italy in mid-August 1944 to return to the U.S. by ship.

On board, Sparky got into a conversation with a white officer who, not knowing him, said, "I don't like the Japs, even the Japanese-Americans. Once a Jap, always a Jap." Sparky bristled but kept his cool, asking the white officer if he had ever met a Japanese-American. "No," the other officer said, "but my friends told me." Sparky said the white officer "looked hard at me and said, 'You're Chinese, aren't you?'" Sparky said no, he was Japanese-American and had been twice wounded in combat. At the end of the voyage, he concluded, the white officer "came to me and said he had changed his mind." Sparky credited that episode with making him "resolve to contact as many people as possible like him and tell them that we Japanese-Americans are like any other Americans."

After landing in New York on September 1, Sparky was interviewed by Richard Yaffe of *PM*, a daily newspaper, and asked why the 100th Battalion had fought so hard. "The men in the battalion," Sparky was quoted, "feel they have something extra to fight for, more than the average soldier. That is, they have their loyalty to prove ever since Dec. 7, 1941."

Sparky and three other officers from the 100th Battalion headed toward Hawai'i via Chicago and Wisconsin to see friends from Camp McCoy days, evidently at a leisurely pace. In late September, the Nisei Council of Milwaukee threw a banquet for them at which they related their experiences, Sparky dwelling on soldiers being willing to give up their lives for the sake of their parents and other AJAs. "They meant," Sparky said, "a world free of racial discrimination."

In the audience was an official from the War Relocation Authority (WRA), a government agency responsible for resettling AJAs throughout the country when they were released from the internment camps after the war. He came up to Sparky and suggested that he could do much good for Japanese-Americans by speaking along the lines he had that evening. He particularly wanted Sparky to talk to business executives in a position to hire *nisei*. Sparky agreed. The WRA official, Sparky said, "picked up the phone and called the Pentagon and had my orders changed."

He was to report to Fort Snelling, near Minneapolis-St. Paul in Minnesota, home of the language school of the Military Intelligence Service, or MIS.

The Japanese-Americans who served in the MIS were among the most unsung of unsung warriors in World War II. Where the 100th Battalion and the 442nd RCT were sent to Europe to preclude racial mix-ups on the battlefield, the AJAs in the MIS were sent to the Pacific to translate captured documents, interrogate Japanese prisoners, and most dangerous of all, go into caves and bunkers to persuade Japanese soldiers to surrender. Most of the MIS soldiers spoke some Japanese, having learned it from their parents, and were sent to the school at Fort Snelling to sharpen it up and especially to learn military terms that would be useful in gathering intelligence. Sparky reported to Fort Snelling on October 3, 1944, and was soon assigned as company commander of I Company in the School Battalion, which was primarily an administrative job looking after the language students.

That position was really a parking place as Sparky's main assignment was to give speeches throughout the Midwest on behalf of AJAs, as suggested by the WRA. Sparky was in his element, given his love of the English language, his increasing command of rhetoric, and his convictions about the loyalty of Japanese-Americans and why they deserved to be treated as Americans, not as second-class, hyphenated Americans. Over the next eight months, Sparky claimed he gave 800 speeches, including those to soldiers and officers at Fort Snelling. No doubt that was excellent training for the political career on which he had set his sights. One report said that 700 businesses later hired *nisei*, although there was no way to prove a direct connection between Sparky's campaign and those jobs.

At a Kiwanis Club luncheon in Milwaukee on December 6, 1944, for instance, Sparky asked his listeners to tell their friends "that there are thousands of us Americans of Japanese descent fighting over there, side by side, with their own sons." He particularly noted that many of those incarcerated in the internment camps would have become American citizens except for the immigration laws that prevented them from doing so. He said, "In the Heart Mountain relocation camp in Wyoming there is a mother who has given six sons to the service and whose seventh son has volunteered and is ready to be called up. Yet she can never become one of us." He reiterated a main theme, that the men of the 100th Battalion fought "because they had to prove that they were worthy to be called American."

Captain George Grandstaff, a much-respected white officer from the 100th Battalion, asked to make similar appearances while he was on leave in his home state of California in June 1945. "My main interest is to see that the splendid work they [Japanese-American soldiers] have done in combat is called to the attention of the people of the Pacific Coast in order that Japanese-Americans who desire to return here may receive fair treatment," he wrote to the War Department. "A white officer who had lived in California most of his life could emphasize their splendid combat record as no Japanese-American could."

In his talks in California, Grandstaff said that on his return home, "One of the first shocks that stabbed me in the stomach like a cold bayonet was to find racial prejudice and discrimination against the fathers, mothers, sisters and kid brothers of the men in my outfit." He urged a fundamental change in attitude among Californians.

Sparky's sense of humor often bubbled up in these sessions but on one occasion misfired. He said that "I found myself addressing audiences consisting of nothing but white faces. It was not until I spoke in Hibbing, Minnesota, that I spotted an Oriental face in the audience. I made a special request of the master of ceremonies to be introduced to this person, and as I approached him I stuck out my open right hand and said, 'Dr. Livingston, I presume.' In all seriousness and in complete puzzlement, he looked at me and responded, 'I am so sorry, I am Dr. Tanaka.'"

Sometime in the spring of 1945, Sparky was promoted to captain even though his military record said that did not happen until November. Pictures of him at Fort Snelling kept in a tattered scrapbook clearly show the "railroad tracks" of two silver bars worn by a captain. Germany surrendered in May and it was only a matter of time before Japan did the same. Sparky was ordered to Hawai'i, leaving Fort Snelling in late June and arriving in Honolulu in early July. He went home to see his family in Hanapēpē, then returned to Honolulu with no specific military assignment. The war ended on August 15, after the atomic bombings of Hiroshima and Nagasaki, and Sparky was assigned to a separation center in September to process soldiers out of the Army as the U.S. demobilized. Two months later, he began his own terminal leave, and received the Bronze Star "for exemplary conduct in ground combat against the armed enemy during the Rome-Arno campaign."

Sparky was honorably discharged two days after Christmas 1945, happy to put his military service behind him. Even so, the war and his Army experience had had a penetrating effect. He had learned firsthand the suffering of war, having been wounded himself and seeing friends being maimed for life or killed in action. Much of his strenuous efforts for peace later could be traced to his brief encounter with war. The Army experience sharpened Sparky's abhorrence of discrimination. Further, his military service ingrained in him a lasting interest in veterans' affairs that he pursued throughout his political career.

After the troops came home from Europe, President Harry S Truman invited units from the 442nd RCT and 100th Battalion to a formation on the lawn of the White House where he presented them with a Presidential Unit Citation. Perhaps the most poignant of the President's remarks was: "You fought not only the enemy, you fought prejudice — and you won."

Looking back during a memorial service at Arlington National Cemetery in June 1963, Representative Matsunaga, by then a new member of Congress, echoed President Truman's thought but went on to say, "We must undertake to carry on the unfinished work which they so nobly advanced. The fight against prejudice is not confined to the battlefield alone. It is still here and with us now. So long as a single member of our citizenry is denied the use of public facilities and denied the right to earn a decent living because, and solely because of the color of his skin, we who 'fought against prejudice and won' ought not to sit idly by and tolerate the perpetuation of injustices." ❖

Peaceful Revolution
1946-1962

Sparky and other Americans of Japanese Ancestry came home from World War II to embark on a political and social revolution in Hawai'i, though not many of them would have couched it in those terms then. They had proven their loyalty to America. They had seen the world on the mainland of the U.S., in North Africa and in Europe. They had gained access to more education through the G.I. Bill and to other benefits to launch businesses. They had jobs and careers to start, marriages to make and families to form. Perhaps most important, the *nisei* were no longer willing to accept second-class citizenship nor to return to a dreary life on the plantation.

Daniel K. Inouye, who was to become Hawai'i's most powerful politician, summed it up: "We had played a small but vital part in the great war, and now that it was won we were not about to go back to the plantation. We wanted our place in the sun, the right to participate in decisions that affected us." His concluding punch: "There must be no more second-class citizens in the Hawai'i of tomorrow."

While the *nisei* soldiers were off fighting, Hawai'i itself had begun to change. As a scholar at the University of Hawai'i, Dennis Ogawa, wrote in *Kodomo no tame ni*: "The war had turned Honolulu and its environment into a modern city. The war economy had provided what seemed limitless jobs in the urban areas, making impossible the 'return to the plantation' which prewar sugar interests had hoped to instill in the unemployed young. New small industries, independent small businesses, the economic ramifications of the blossoming tourist industry — all developments stemming from the wartime boom — were sources of new wealth which undermined the monopolistic control of the Merchant Street powers." (Merchant Street in Honolulu was the headquarters site of most of Hawai'i's big corporations.)

Nonetheless, Hawai'i was still feudal in many ways and only a peaceful revolution could change it. Among the leaders of that revolution was an Irish-American police captain, John Burns, who had defended the AJAs during the dark days of suspicion. He had helped to organize an "Americanization" program in which Japanese-Americans were urged to behave like Americans in public and in private, including an effort to "Speak American." That campaign was hard on the *issei*, or first-generation Japanese-Americans, some of whom spoke little English and retained many of the traditions, habits and diet of Japan. That sometimes caused a cultural clash and misunderstandings with the *nisei* when they came home committed to an American way of life.

After the war, Burns was quick to recognize the potential political power of the returning AJA soldiers and drew in a small group to discuss how AJAs and other non-haole communities could take an active part in the political life of the Islands. That circle included Daniel Inouye, but not George Ariyoshi, who was to become governor of Hawai'i, nor Sparky Matsunaga, the independent. The revolution had three defining moments:

- The Territorial election campaign of 1954. The Democratic Party, having taken in most of the AJAs home from the war, took control of the Territorial Legislature for the first time and ended the Republican rule that had controlled it since the annexation of Hawai'i to the U.S. in 1898. It was in this campaign that Sparky launched his political career.
- Statehood in 1959, culminating a drive that had started three years after Sparky was born. In 1919, Prince Jonah Kūhiō Kalaniana'ole, who had been elected Hawai'i's non-voting delegate to Congress, introduced the first bill intended to have the Territory of Hawai'i admitted to the Union. It took Hawai'i 40 years, longer than any other state, to gain admission but Sparky was among those who made crucial contributions to attaining statehood.
- The gubernatorial election of 1974, when George Ariyoshi was elected to be the first Asian-American in the nation to sit in a governor's chair. Hawai'i's first two governors, William Quinn, a Republican, and John Burns, a Democrat, were both haoles. Ariyoshi's election marked the culmination of the 20-year revolution.

At the same time on the mainland, the civil rights movement was surging ahead. President Truman had stimulated it in 1948 by ordering the armed forces to break up segregated units and integrate African-Americans, then referred to as Negroes, into what had been all-white units. During the Korean War of 1950–1953, black soldiers earned the "right to fight" by serving in integrated units. The second critical juncture was in 1954, when the Supreme Court ruled that segregated schools were inherently unequal and ordered that states begin integrating schools "with all deliberate speed."

That was followed in 1955 by the sit-ins led by the Reverend Martin Luther King, Jr. that succeeded in integrating buses in Montgomery, Alabama. Two years later, the first modern Civil Rights Act established a commission to investigate denial of voting rights, and in 1960 a subsequent act made a federal offense of obstruction of court orders by a threat of violence. The civil rights movement had little direct effect on Hawai'i, which was caught up in its own battles, but surely had a subtle influence on the islands.

On New Year's Day in 1946, Sparky was out of uniform and like most ex-G.I.s everywhere, was eager to get on with his life. That was especially true for him because he was older than most of the returning veterans, having just passed his 29th birthday. He decided not to go back to Kaua'i because jobs were more plentiful in Honolulu and the capital city was the political heart of the islands. On January 30, he legally changed his name to Spark Masayuki Matsunaga because, given his political ambitions, it would be much easier to remember. It cost him $1.20 to register the change. "With a name like Masayuki," he said many years later, "I couldn't have been elected dogcatcher."

Curiously, however, Sparky did not leap into action. Perhaps he needed time to decompress and to think things through or he wanted to save some money as he planned to go on with his education, although he was not sure where or in what — maybe a master's degree in education so that he could teach. He took what must have been for him a couple of mundane jobs, first as a veterans counselor with the Department of the Interior, then as executive staff assistant to the regional director of the War Assets Administration, whose job was to get rid of surplus military equipment that could be used in civilian life. He did start building a political network by becoming adjutant of the O'ahu chapter of the Disabled American Veterans, then commander for a year in 1947. He wangled seats on the governor's Commission on Housing and on the Territorial War Memorial Commission.

By 1947, Sparky had gotten his act together and made two decisions that affected the course of his life. While still in the Army, he had been giving orientation lectures at Fort Kamehameha, near the Hickam Air Base, to returning G.I.s on what their rights would be under the G.I. Bill or with the Veterans Administration. There he met Helene Tokunaga, a secretary who had been forced to drop out of the University of Hawai'i because her father had passed away. Sparky began courting Helene, who soon accepted his proposal of marriage. They were married on August 6, 1948 in Reverend Okumura's Makiki Christian Church. Sparky was dressed in a white dinner jacket while Helene wore a traditional Western white silk wedding gown with a veil and a long train and carried a large bouquet of flowers. In contrast, many of the brides in the older *issei* generation those days wore the traditional Japanese heavy brocade kimono complete with wide *tsuno-kakushi* headgear to hide the horns of jealousy. The Matsunaga newlyweds went to Kona, a resort area on the Big Island, for a two-week honeymoon.

Second, Sparky decided sometime in 1947 to apply for admission to both Harvard and Yale law schools, a time-consuming process even if not so complicated as today. He pulled together his high school, university and Army records, and got recommendations from a prominent judge, Bernard Levinson, and the president of the University of Hawai'i, Gregory Sinclair. Why Harvard and Yale? "Because," said Helene, "they were the best and Sparky wanted the best." Sparky was accepted at both but chose Harvard because he thought it the nation's most prestigious law school.

After their honeymoon, Sparky and Helene left for Cambridge. Helene said those were happy years. Sparky threw himself into his studies even though he was less interested in law than in politics, and saw law as a political stepping-stone. His grades were passable but not outstanding. Helen Kim, a Korean-American from Hawai'i and a student at nearby Boston University, occasionally visited Helene and Sparky and found him "really focused to succeed." Even with their wartime service behind them, Kim said, "that was an era when it was terribly necessary for Japanese-Americans to prove themselves. They had to continue proving themselves because society had not yet accepted them."

Sparky was not the first Asian-American at Harvard Law — Hiram Fong had been there in the 1930s — but he was one of a few in the late 1940s. Helene said she was a "little apprehensive" because she had never been to the mainland. Her anxiety didn't last long as they were not confronted with discrimination and had no trouble finding a place to live. "I just loved it there," Helene said. "Everyone was so friendly. They did ask, though, are you Chinese or Japanese?" Their apartment became a bit cramped after their first child, Karen, was born in 1949 and they had to scrimp on Sparky's monthly allowance on the G.I. Bill, but generally, Helene said, they had fond memories of those years.

There was one exception. Each year, the law school sponsored the Ames Moot Court in which students argued cases before a panel of experienced judges. It was an honor to take part in the competition and Sparky was pleased to be paired on December 5, 1950 with Philip Erwin Silberberg, a bright classmate, in arguing for the defense. They worked hard to prepare, and their argument, they thought, went well before Vincent MacDonald, a judge on the Supreme Court of Nova Scotia, John H.C. Morris of the British bar and Warren F. Farr of the Boston bar. Sparky and Silberberg, however, were defeated at the semifinal level, which obviously disappointed them. It also puzzled them because they thought they had had the better of the advocacy, as did others who witnessed the mock trial. Later, Judge Morris quietly told Sparky that he and Silberberg lost because Judge Farr had made it clear that he would not vote for a Jew to win. Sparky was so angry that his biography forever after carried the notation that he had been a semifinalist in the competition. Even after he had risen to the Senate, the biographical sketch he submitted to the Congressional Directory noted, as if in protest, his semifinal place in the moot court.

In contrast was a triumph that enhanced Sparky's political prospects. In the spring of his second year in law school, he received a phone call from Joseph Farrington, Hawai'i's non-voting delegate to Congress, asking him to come to Washington to testify before a Senate committee and to meet with the formidable Senator Henry Cabot Lodge, a Republican from Massachusetts. The issue was statehood for Hawai'i and Farrington wanted a Japanese-American who could explain what the 100th Infantry Battalion and the 442nd Regimental Combat Team had done during the war and why that service, among other things, entitled Hawai'i to be admitted to the Union. Sparky was the closest in distance and, Farrington thought, the most articulate. Sparky pleaded that he had a tough exam for which he had to study but Farrington persisted and Sparky found a way to go, with veterans associations of the 100th Battalion and the 442nd RCT helping to pay his fare.

Hawai'i had sought for years to become a state. There were several objections from the mainland: The population of Hawai'i then was only 20 percent white; the rest were Asian or Polynesian. Hawai'i was not contiguous with the 48 states on the Mainland; Manifest Destiny in the 19th Century had driven the U.S. to acquire Hawai'i but making it a state would be something else. The Revolution of 1954 was on the horizon; statehood would mean two more Democratic Senators and another Democratic Representative, the prospect of which did not please Republicans. Lastly, conservatives feared communist influence in Hawai'i, particularly in the labor unions.

Sparky appeared before the Senate Committee on Interior and Insular Affairs on May 3, 1950 to plead Hawai'i's case on a bill known as H.R. 49 because it would bring Alaska in as the 49th state, with Hawai'i being admitted as the 50th. After introducing himself and noting he had been wounded twice in the war that had ended only five years earlier, Sparky launched into an emotional appeal, evoking images of combat: "I have had the unforgettable experience of having watched fellow Americans die on the field of battle — men with whom I had played as kids, men with whom I had attended school, men with whom I had lived and fought through mud and snow, and men whom I had learned to love and respect."

Sparky continued, "It is often said, even by men with combat experience, that while at the front, a soldier forgets about ideals and fights only for self-preservation. I can truthfully state, however, that those men whom I watched die did die for ideals — died so that those whom they left behind might have a better life through enjoying the full rights and privileges of American citizenship, despite their racial ancestry." A little further on, Sparky said, "Most of the men expressed great hopes for the future. They were hopeful because they felt deep within themselves that as a result of their sacrifices at the front, Americans back home would come to recognize them as plain Americans and not hyphenated Americans.

"Above all," Sparky said, "we found greatest hope in the fact that men of other units were willingly risking their lives for us. On one occasion, when our battalion ran into some difficulty and was about to be enveloped by the enemy, a regimental commander of the 34th Division [which was Caucasian except for the 100th Battalion], in issuing attack orders to his command, said, 'Men, the 100th is in trouble up there; we must get to them.' The men of the regiment fought as they had never fought before, and did get to us."

Sparky noted that skeptics "feel that Hawai'i will never be granted statehood and consequently they will never be granted the full status of American citizenship." He countered, "We who are optimistic by nature, on the other hand, look with encouragement to the fact than an overwhelming majority of the American people have already expressed through the various public opinion polls, the press, the radio, and through their local and national organizations that they do favor the immediate grant of statehood to Hawai'i."

Finally, Sparky implored the committee: "I am confident I speak for all veterans of World War II who reside in Hawai'i when I say that the granting of immediate statehood to Hawai'i will mean the full and final recognition of the great sacrifices we made in answer to our country's call. I beseech you, therefore, to report H.R. 49 favorably onto the Senate floor so that we might be granted an opportunity to plead for our just due — a single star on Old Glory which we can call our own. We know you will not let us down."

The Associated Press reported, "When Matsunaga finished, Senator Glen H. Taylor, (D-Idaho), presiding at the afternoon session of the statehood hearing, said he had never in his six years in the Senate heard more moving testimony. Many in the audience were in tears." Several days later, Sparky replied to a congratulatory letter from Colonel Farrant Turner, the former commander of the 100th Battalion: "My talk was designed for emotional appeal. When men refuse to be moved by convincing cold facts, we felt that an appeal to their emotions might do the trick."

Politically, Sparky's testimony brought him much attention back in Hawai'i, where *The Honolulu Advertiser* printed his remarks verbatim and in full over four days.

In addition, Farrington had asked Sparky to see Senator Lodge, whom Farrington had learned was preparing a letter to other Senators opposing statehood for Hawai'i. Given Lodge's prominent position, that could have become a huge obstacle to statehood. Farrington knew that Lodge respected the soldiers of the 100th Battalion because the Senator had seen them in action during the war. As Sparky related the encounter to *The Honolulu Advertiser*: "I went to Lodge's office and his secretary said his schedule was full. He couldn't see me. I told her that Lodge had come to the front when we were in combat, expressed great admiration for what we were doing and told me to drop by if I ever came to Washington." The secretary went into Lodge's office and came back to say the Senator would see him for five minutes.

"The five minutes went by and I was still telling him why Hawai'i should be a state," Sparky said. He reiterated what he had said in the committee hearing, emphasizing the reasons the AJAs in the 100th Battalion and the 442nd RCT had fought and died for America. After 45 minutes, according to Sparky, Lodge relented, saying, "For you and the 100th and the 442nd, I can do at least this much," and dropped the "Dear Colleague" letter into the wastebasket.

Farrington also asked Sparky to see Senator Russell Long, a Democrat from Louisiana who was then a rising star in Congress but a Southerner not disposed to bringing multiracial Hawai'i into the Union. Sparky presented his case for statehood after which, he told the Senate years later, Senator Long "gave me some advice I have always remembered: 'Young man, you must remember that a U.S. Senator is primarily interested in two things — first, to be elected, and second, to be reelected. So don't come to me, go to my constituents. If my constituents tell me that I should support Hawaiian statehood, I will.'"

Sparky said, "I took his advice and enlisted the support of one of his staunchest supporters, a prominent businessman and civic leader of New Orleans, George Lelightner. Eventually, we were successful in convincing Russell Long to visit Hawai'i. He did so and became a statehood champion and his conversion to the cause was instrumental."

A month after Sparky's visit to Washington, the Korean War broke out and statehood for Hawai'i was shelved. Sparky spent some of that summer in Washington walking the corridors of the Capitol, meeting with as many Senators as he could to persuade them to support statehood for Hawai'i, but to no immediate avail. Not until after the Korean War ended in 1953 was the drive for statehood revived. Another delegation from Honolulu, led by Governor Samuel Wilder King, went to Washington in 1954 with Sparky wearing his Army uniform and talking about the sacrifices of the soldiers in the 100th Battalion and the 442nd RCT.

In 1950-51, during his third and final year at Harvard Law, Sparky and a classmate, Samuel Freed, worked together on a long paper, presented in April 1951, entitled "Two Thousand Delinquents," in which they searched for the causes of crime among young people. While perhaps not surprising that a student of law should delve into the causes of crime, this appears to have been the start of a long-lasting interest in legislation on crime that showed up in Sparky's Congressional career, notably in the House of Representatives. Sparky and Freed said they were looking for indicators that "might be used by schools, guidance clinics, and other social agencies and organizations in predicting delinquency before it starts." They hoped to find something that could be useful in "administering preventive treatment."

They came up with a "Prognostic Table" that has been largely validated by experience. Their research showed that delinquents often came from families in which the parents had little formal education, the father was an unskilled laborer and the family was on the economic margin. Sparky and Freed found delinquents more likely to come from families that had already spawned delinquents, and from homes broken either by divorce or death. Delinquents often had no more than an eighth-grade education, had been held back in school, had faltering work habits, had left home and did not belong to constructive organizations such as the Boy Scouts.

Sparky and Freed concluded that those closer to the immigrant experience were less likely to become juvenile delinquents. In family background, they said, "native-born children of foreign-born parents accounted for but 21.4 percent of the total delinquents." Further, "foreign-born children of foreign-born parents contributed far less than their proportionate share to the criminal ranks," only 19.4 percent. They concluded in 1951 what seems still to be true: "The lack of trained personnel has been and is one of the greatest, if not the greatest, handicaps with which society is faced in its struggle to combat delinquency." Years later, Senator Daniel Patrick Moynihan, a Democrat from New York and an erudite politician, was astonished to find that the work of Sparky and Freed had contributed to pioneering studies of juvenile delinquency conducted by Drs. Sheldon and Eleanor Glueck.

After Sparky graduated from Harvard Law in the spring of 1951, he and Helene returned to Honolulu where he had two immediate tasks: Get a job to support his growing family and resume building a political base. New family responsibilities came Sparky's way. Not only were there young children but Sparky brought his elderly father and mother over from Kaua'i to live with them, along with

Helene's mother and her brother, John Tokunaga. Sparky passed the bar exam on the second try in 1952 and went to work as an assistant public prosecutor for the city of Honolulu. Another assistant prosecutor was Daniel Inouye. Among Sparky's assignments was to prosecute alleged violators of the wartime controls that still applied to rental housing. It was a losing cause after an appeals court judge, Ronald B. Jameson, found the rent control law to be unconstitutional. He ruled that the wartime housing emergency no longer existed and even Honolulu's high cost of living did not warrant rent controls.

Sparky had better luck in politics. Personal contacts are important in politics everywhere; in Hawai'i, with its Asian and Polynesian culture, they are vital. Sparky concentrated on veterans associations, a natural constituency. He became a member of the board of directors of Club 100, which continued the brotherhood rooted in the 100th Battalion's experience in the war, and was elected president for a year in 1953. He rejoined the Disabled American Veterans, became a trustee and was their judge advocate in 1953-54. In turn, the DAV awarded Sparky a Certificate of Merit in 1954 for his "unselfish devotion to the cause of statehood for Hawai'i." He was elected chairman of the United Veterans Legislative Committee, a lobbying group, in 1953 and chairman of the AJA Veterans Council in the same year, which marked the start of his support for veterans throughout his political career. Sparky served on the Relocation Advisory Committee, continuing the advocacy of equality he had begun in his military service. He joined the Brotherhood of St. Andrew, an Episcopal service group, and indulged in his love of acting by becoming a member of the board of directors of the Honolulu Community Theater.

Meantime, while Sparky had been away at Harvard Law, Jack Burns, the leader of the peaceful revolution, had been meeting with a small circle of mostly Japanese-Americans to persuade them to enter politics. Burns read the demographics and could see the rise of Japanese-Americans in Hawai'i's population, which was 40 percent after the war. Gavan Daws, a historian of Hawai'i, wrote in *Shoal of Time*: "Immigrants were taking out citizenship in ever-increasing numbers, and their sons and daughters were citizens by birth. The party that could harness this force and turn it into votes could carry everything before it."

Daws continued, "Jack Burns could see victory ahead, and his deepest convictions told him at the same time that the rise of a party able to cross racial lines would bring about a profound and irreversible change for the better in the life of the territory." The Democrats came close in 1947 when they split the Territorial House of Representatives with the Republicans, 15 seats each, and were close in the Territorial Senate, where they had seven of the 15 seats. But they slipped back after that.

Burns, who had resigned from the police force to enter politics, believed that an AJA conquest of the Democratic Party should be founded on the veterans of the 442nd RCT. Daniel Inouye was an early recruit. Then came Dan Aoki, the president of the 442nd club. The three of them sought to persuade other veterans of the 442nd RCT that they should help build a strong Democratic Party. In addition, they sought some ethnic balance by bringing in Chuck Mau, a Chinese-American, and William Richardson, a part Hawaiian-American.

Sparky, having been in the 100th Battalion, was not part of this group, even after his return from Harvard. Nor was George Ariyoshi who, unlike many *nisei*, spoke excellent Japanese and enlisted in the Military Intelligence Service rather than the 442nd. After Ariyoshi had served as governor, he lamented the divisions within the Democratic Party that stemmed from the way Burns and the AJAs operated. "From the beginning, we were plagued by factionalism within the Democratic Party," he wrote in his book, *With Obligation to All.* "Factions sprang up around strong individuals and around labor unions as well. A schism between the Neighbor Islands and Oʻahu played a part. To some extent, issues divided people into factions but beneath the surface there often was raw grasping for power." The governor's assessment sounded remarkably like the factional politics of Japan, so maybe some of it had been inherited.

When Sparky announced in August 1954 that he would be a candidate for a seat in the Territorial House of Representatives, Burns tried to dissuade him from running so as not to weaken support for other candidates he favored. Even so, Sparky's announcement echoed Robert Clopton, the high-school teacher on Kauaʻi who had told him that the best way to improve things was to win elective office and change the laws. "I believe," Sparky said, "that our American way of life can be best preserved by active and intelligent participation in government by honest men."

Sparky won a place on the ballot by running neck and neck with Daniel Inouye in the primary, each getting about 10,660 votes, and then launching into the main event in which there were 12 candidates for six seats at large in the Fourth District on Oʻahu. The Democrats put up four Japanese-Americans, plus a Hawaiian woman and a *haole* man. All six of the Republicans were white men. The racial overtones were unmistakable and the campaign was hard fought and sometimes bitter, with each side accusing the other of racist appeals.

In *Shoal of Time*, historian Daws noted that ethnic politics were not new in Hawaiʻi but that "the question was merely redefined." Former Governor Ariyoshi differed: "The controlling group often has been described as a white oligarchy, but such a description is too simplistic. It was a plantation-based society, which did not exist for the common man but for the benefit of the owners. It excluded the great majority of the people of talent and dedication from its rewards, merely because of the circumstances of birth and economics. This great majority included virtually all non-white people. Caucasians who were outside the controlling group — who were not well-connected — were often kept from advancing as well."

Beyond that, the main Democratic theme of the campaign was that Republicans represented the past, Democrats the future. Statehood was an issue as some Republicans were opposed to it because they feared it would upset the status quo. Republicans charged that the Democrats were in the pocket of the International Longshoremen's and Warehousemen's Union (ILWU), which was led by Harry Bridges and Jack Hall. They had been accused of being communists. The Democrats accepted the union's support but vehemently denied the communist charge.

In his campaign, Sparky adamantly opposed legalized gambling, a debate that continued in Hawai'i through the rest of the 20th Century and into the next. Sparky contended that experience in other states had shown that when "gambling in any form is legalized, social evils within the community multiply and the coping with those evils invariably means more tax dollars." He asserted, "Any legislator who proposes any measure to legalize gambling would be performing a definite disservice to his electors."

As the election on November 2 approached, Inouye said, "There was a certain promise in the air, a secret and contagious spirit." Ariyoshi was less optimistic, saying there was "no great sense of change in the making."

After the votes had been counted, the Democrats had swept almost everything to the stunning surprise of themselves, the Republicans and nearly everyone in Hawai'i. Democrats had won 22 of 30 seats in the State House of Representatives and nine of 15 in the Senate. In the Fourth District, five of six Democrats had won in what the *Honolulu Star-Bulletin* called the biggest upset of all as that district had not elected a Democrat to the House of Representatives since 1946. Inouye led with 29,393 votes and Sparky ran second with 27,531.

"The defeat of the Republicans was so complete," the *Star-Bulletin* said, "that it wiped out almost the entire leadership of the 1953 House." That included Hiram Fong, the Chinese-American Republican who had been the Speaker of the House. Only one Republican incumbent in the Fourth District, Hebden Porteus, who had been majority floor leader, had survived and only one Democrat, the haole Willie Crozier, was defeated. A Senate race was poignant: Sakae Takahashi, who had been a company commander in the 100th Battalion, was elected as a Democrat while James Lovell, the former battalion executive officer running as a Republican, was defeated. And in another poignant result, John Burns, the mastermind of the Democratic victory, was narrowly defeated for the post of Hawai'i's non-voting delegate to Congress, a position vital to the continuing effort to have Hawai'i admitted to the Union. It went to Mrs. Elizabeth Farrington, widow of the Joseph Farrington who had invited Sparky to Washington. Just as Burns had not supported Sparky, so Sparky had not supported Burns, he disclosed later. That may have affected the outcome of Burns's campaign somewhat because he lost by only 890 votes out of 138,000 cast.

The jubilation of the Democrats carried over into their inaugural in the Legislature in February — and almost proved to be their undoing. On the morning of February 16, a *kahuna*, or priest, clad in the scarlet-and-yellow feathered cape of the ancient Polynesian chiefs, chanted a Hawaiian prayer as he led the legislators in to take their oaths of office. Sparky marched in with the delegation from O'ahu. After singing the state anthem, *Hawai'i Pono'i* ("Hawai'i the Righteous"), the Democrats started to take control of the House and to organize committees. Within ten minutes, they found themselves embroiled in a debate with Republicans over a point of order. The ensuing argument was heated until Inouye, the new majority leader, rose to say pointedly, "We are here. We have the majority. I suggest you let us proceed."

Proceed they did but more like carpetbaggers in the South after the Civil War than as a responsible governing majority. Nearly 300 bills, many of them tax-and-spend proposals that were clearly pork barrel, were introduced. One bill would have exempted the ILWU from taxes. Many bills never got out of committee and of those that did and were approved on the floor, 71 were vetoed by Governor King, the Republican appointed by President Dwight Eisenhower. (Hawai'i would not have an elected governor until statehood.) The Legislature was able to muster enough votes to override the veto in only two instances. The *Honolulu Star-Bulletin* admonished in an editorial: "The people of Hawai'i are interested primarily in good government at a reasonable cost. There are certain minimum services they expect and should get. They do not need and do not want radical proposals of visionaries." In an interview, Inouye conceded, "None of us knew what this business was all about."

Inouye said that "once Sparky got into the Legislature, he really involved himself. There was no question that he was a mover and shaker with political skills." In fiscal matters, Sparky indicated that he was a conservative. "During my terms as a member of the Hawaiian Legislature," he said later, "I considered it almost an article of religion that income must equal outgo, and that a governmental unit has no business spending money that it doesn't have." As a state legislator and a member of Congress, he showed that only compelling reasons would change that fundamental view.

By the end of the session, Sparky was so frustrated by what he had seen as the bickering, lack of competence and self-serving outlook of many colleagues that he announced he would not stand for reelection in the fall of 1956. It was an astonishing decision for a man who had planned a political career from the time he was in high school. Asked if he would seek reelection, Sparky let loose a blast: "I will not run. I am thoroughly disillusioned with people and government. I have found myself being forced to compromise myself against principles, a thing in private life I would never do. I am disgusted."

By the summer of 1956, however, the call of the campaign and the excitement of the Legislature was too much and Sparky changed his mind. He said friends "have convinced me that I am under an obligation to the public to seek re-election, that the experience I gained in the last Legislature must be used for the public benefit." He could not resist taking a poke at other Democrats, asserting, "Unless competent men of goodwill choose to assume the responsibilities of government, we will permit ourselves to be governed by incompetent, self-seeking politicians."

He elaborated to a student assembly at the University of Hawai'i, recalling that "I was so disillusioned with men in government that I made a statement that I would not seek reelection." Sparky continued, "Then I read an article, 'The Necessity of Being Unprincipled in Politics.' I finally came to realize that legislation is a matter of compromise." He added, "If you go on the basic principle that it is a matter of compromise, then you won't feel unhappy or that you're violating basic principles."

About this time, Sparky and Eichi Oki, who had graduated from Harvard Law two years after Sparky, set up a law practice. Sparky needed to make a living because the Legislature met only 30 to 60 days and both he and Inouye had been required to resign as assistant public prosecutors when they ran for office in 1954. Oki and Sparky had met through their wives, who had been classmates and friends at the University of Hawai'i. Oki helped Sparky in his 1954 campaign for the Legislature and was on the legislative staff for awhile. He said their law practice was "a kind of chop suey" in clients and lasted only two years because Sparky was becoming a full-time politician and was not attending to the law practice. Oki said Sparky was a good lawyer "because he could think and he could write well and he had that never-give-up determination."

Sparky stood for reelection to the Legislature in November 1956, won handily and persuaded his colleagues to elect him chairman of the Judiciary

Committee, which was considered to be a major post, even though he was still an outsider to the dominant Burns faction. Inouye said part of Sparky's appeal was that "he was a lawyer of some competence." The Democratic Party lost four seats in the Territorial House, down to 18 of 30, but picked up three in the Territorial Senate to hold 12 of 15. John Burns was elected by a large margin over Mrs. Farrington to become Hawai'i's delegate to the Congress in Washington. By this time, Sparky had made his peace with Burns, he said, "because during the last two years, I realized that he was a man of his word." As this took place, Republicans led by President Dwight D. Eisenhower, won 41 of 48 states in the presidential election but left control of Congress in Democratic hands.

Sparky's major accomplishment in the 1957 legislative session was to abolish the death penalty for criminals, even those convicted of violent crimes such as murder or rape. It became law on July 5, 1957, but only after a fierce debate. It was an issue that continued to crop up from then until the end of the century. Sparky asserted that the death penalty was morally wrong: "It's not the prerogative of a man to take another man's life." The evidence showed that the death penalty did not deter violent crime, Sparky argued, citing the frequency of murder in states with capital punishment compared with those that had abolished it. His main opponent was Republican Senator Wilfred Tsukiyama, who sought to block passage with a filibuster, but failed. Several police chiefs opposed Sparky's bill, which provided for life imprisonment without parole. Sparky's stand would be used against him in subsequent election campaigns.

By the time the 1958 political campaign rolled around, the rule of the oligarchy in the plantation days was faltering and democracy was in full flower in Hawai'i. The Democrats had come to so dominate the state's politics that the Republicans had a hard time finding good candidates to run. Within the Democratic Party, however, factionalism ran rampant. The Democrats were split by personal loyalties and antipathies, by arguments over whether to be pro-union or independent, and by political issues. Some Democrats wanted to continue fighting the old questions of discrimination while others wanted to concentrate on new issues, such as land reform. Perhaps most vicious were the racial and ethnic politics that divided party and state. While Hawai'i had its own flavor in such divisions, they were like those on the mainland where party machines often revolved around Irish, Italian, Polish, Jewish, African-American and Hispanic communities.

Despite those internal fissures, the Democrats carried the day in the election and Sparky again won handily. The Territorial Legislature, anticipating statehood, had been enlarged to 51 seats in the House and 25 in the Senate. Democrats won 33 House and 16 Senate seats and therefore had control of the Legislature. Sparky stood aside from the wrenching disputes inside the party; political accounts of the period hardly mention his name. As a consequence, he was chosen to be majority leader in the 1959 session to replace Inouye, who had moved on to the Territorial Senate. Having not taken sides within the party, Sparky was seen as a leader who might pull the factions together.

In the 1959 session, not much was accomplished because almost every eye in Hawai'i, especially in the Legislature, was focused on the final push for statehood. From the time Sparky had gone to Washington with the statehood delegation in 1954, polls on the mainland showed that 78 percent of Americans favored statehood for Hawai'i. The Hawaii Statehood Commission in Honolulu had in its files copies of 2,000 editorials from newspapers all over the country supporting statehood against 50 opposing.

President Eisenhower was in favor and lobbyists on Capitol Hill reported that a majority of both Houses would approve. Yet the old arguments against statehood persisted among a handful of Congressmen — Hawai'i was not contiguous with the mainland states; Hawai'i would have undue influence in national affairs with its two Senators and one Representative; Hawai'i's population was a polyglot mixture of whites, Asians and Polynesians whose culture was different from that on the mainland; Hawai'i was under the thumb of the communists.

"The deadlock was broken at last in 1958," Daws wrote in *Shoal of Time*. "Jack Burns interpreted the mysterious signals passing back and forth on Capitol Hill to mean that if Alaska was allowed into the union first and separately, then Congress would be unable to justify keeping Hawai'i out any longer." (Alaska was separated from the 48 contiguous states by Canada, thus weakening the argument that Hawai'i should not be a state because it was separated from the mainland by the Pacific Ocean.) That summer, Alaska was voted in as the 49th state. Finally, on March 11, 1959, the Senate passed a similar bill for Hawai'i and the next day, the House voted likewise. Admission to the Union for the 50th state was a reality. Joy and relief erupted in Honolulu.

That set off a political scramble. Up for grabs were the governor's chair, the lieutenant governor's position, two seats in the U.S. Senate and one in the House of Representatives, plus a new Legislature in Honolulu and a referendum to ratify statehood. In this ruckus, Sparky put his election foot wrong the only time in his career. At first, he thought he would run for the State Senate but said "so many people have been urging me to run for the U.S. House or for lieutenant governor that I'm thinking about it."

In April, he announced he would seek the Democratic nomination for lieutenant governor in a four-way primary against Mitsuyuki Kido, who was close to John Burns, Richard Kageyama and Frank Serrao. In his campaign, Sparky asserted, "In my three terms as Representative, I have always striven to give a fair hearing to anyone or any group, whether recognized as a pressure group or not, in order to arrive at decisions on legislation benefiting the people of Hawai'i." On communism, he stated, "I believe that the practices and ideology of communism are totally foreign to the principles of democracy" and concluded that there was little more to be said on that issue.

For Burns, home from his delegate's post in Washington to seek the Democratic gubernatorial nomination, a critical issue was his running mate. In public, he said he was neutral. Privately, so the rumors said, he preferred Kido, who had been part of his circle in capturing the Democratic Party and winning control of the Legislature. Kido had served in the Territorial House from 1946 to 1952, then in the Senate from 1956 to 1959, and was an honorary member of the 442nd Veterans Club, the base of political power for the inner circle. Kido outspent Sparky, with advertisements appearing in the newspapers, especially as the race drew to a close. Burns showed up at a Matsunaga rally in early June but talked about his own campaign without endorsing Sparky.

At the same time, the voters were influenced by a tragedy. A 12-year-old girl named Joanne Yamaguchi was abducted and, several days later, found dead after she had been raped and strangled. A former convict with a long record, John Edward Carvalho, was arrested and confessed to the crime. When federal authorities decided that the accused should be tried in state rather than federal court, it became apparent that he would escape the death penalty because capital punishment had been abolished in Hawai'i by the law Sparky had pushed through only two years earlier. A public outcry erupted that included some finger-pointing at Sparky. Moreover, in the legislative session during the winter, Sparky had defended the law against critics. "I believe those advocating restoration of capital punishment are acting in the face of statistics which prove capital punishment in no way deters crimes punishable by death," Sparky said.

Asked to comment after the murder of Joanne Yamaguchi, Sparky issued a statement: "My deepest sympathy is extended to Mr. and Mrs. Yamaguchi. As a father of five children, including three daughters, I can fully appreciate the sorrow which must be theirs. However, any discussion on the merits of capital punishment at this time, while the family is still grieving, would be inappropriate and in poor taste."

When the votes were counted on June 27, Sparky had lost to Kido by the narrowest margin in any major race, 23,000 to 27,160. He congratulated Kido and promised to support the Democratic slate in the July election. Ever the political analyst, Sparky told the press, "I attribute my defeat to four things:

1. The solid block of ILWU votes which Senator Kido obtained.
2. A skillfully conducted campaign by supporters of Senator Kido that he was the favorite candidate of Delegate Burns.
3. A vicious whispering campaign in the last few days before the election that I was the one responsible for the repeal of the capital punishment law. I think I lost a minimum of 3,000 votes by this campaign.
4. The fact that Frank Serrao and I shared the same type of independent votes."

Sparky also said, "I have been deluged with calls from hysterical women since the Joanne Yamaguchi murder. I can't convince them that capital punishment is never a deterrent to murder." He was upbeat about the future: "I will run again for office; I am not a bit discouraged. The test of a man is not that he shall rise but that he shall fall and rise again."

In the other votes that day, statehood was approved overwhelmingly. Of 174,335 registered voters, 132,773 turned out to vote yes while only 7,971 voted no. The naysayers included 200 native Hawaiians who lived on the tiny, privately owned island of Ni'ihau, off the coast of Kaua'i. Burns easily won the Democratic nomination for governor, and William Quinn, the incumbent as the last appointed governor of Hawai'i, was unopposed for the Republican nomination. The Republican nomination for lieutenant governor went to James Kealoha.

For one seat in the U.S. Senate, Frank Fasi, who was to run repeatedly for one office after another, eked out a win for the Democratic nomination while Hiram Fong, the successful Chinese-American lawyer and entrepreneur, won the Republican nomination unopposed. For the other Senate seat, a former Democratic governor, Oren Long, took the Democratic nomination and Wilfred Tsukiyama, the minority leader of the State Senate, was unopposed for the Republican nomination. In the House, Inouye, war hero of the 442nd RCT and member of John Burns's inner circle, beat out Patsy Mink and Elizabeth Young for the Democrats; Charles Silva was given the nod by the Republicans.

In the general election in July 1959, Governor Quinn shocked everyone, including most Republicans, by defeating John Burns, the delegate to Congress who had been instrumental in bringing statehood to Hawai'i. Democrats blamed their own factional infighting. Quinn said in an interview, "They didn't work as hard as they should have against me. They were complacent and assumed that Jack Burns

Top: The Matsunaga family ca. 1935 (left to right) Satoru Ikeda, Yutaka Ikeda, Mitsuko (Ikeda) Ueno, Chiyono Matsunaga, Kingoro Matsunaga, Dorothy Matsunaga, Andrew Matsunaga and Sparky Matsunaga. Above: Sparky's childhood home in Hanapēpē, Kaua'i, stands abandoned and overgrown shortly before it was razed in the 1970s.

Top: Kingoro, Chiyono and Sparky on Kaua'i in 1959. Above: Seated fourth from left, Sparky poses at a speech contest ca. 1935, with other participants chosen from Japanese language schools throughout the Territory. The panels at rear list each contestant's topic, name and school; Sparky's reads: "Fifty Years of Japanese Immigration to Hawai'i — Matsunaga Masayuki, Hanapēpē."

Charles Fern (left), editor and publisher of *The Garden Island*, presents 19-year-old Sparky, winner of the newspaper's subscription contest, with a check for $1,000.

Top: Sparky (third from left) joined the varsity debate team in his junior year at the University of Hawai'i. Above: At Schofield Barracks on O'ahu, Sparky (front center) was promoted to first lieutenant in June 1942, just before the 100th Infantry Battalion shipped out to Camp McCoy, Wisconsin.

The men of the 100th Infantry Battalion underwent intensive training at Camp Shelby, Mississippi, in preparation for combat duty in Europe.

The 100th Infantry Battalion saw action in some of the bloodiest fighting in northern Italy, including the capture of German soldiers at Oriano (above).

In June 1944, seven months after Sparky was wounded on Hill 600 and hospitalized in Naples, Lt. Gen. Mark Clark awards the 100th Infantry Battalion a Presidential Unit Citation for outstanding performance of duty.

Mother's Day Greetings

Last night again I dreamed of you
As oft I nightly oft I do. I'd seen
I dreamed of scenes as child, I dreamed
of castle-heights & world scenes
As youth, the future schemed.
What blessed sleep to man doth bring
A joyful picture worse to sting
Awakening youth from dreamful glee
In growing light the truth to see.

'Twas not for man to kill a man;
'Twas meant for man to love a man.
Yet who am I but mortals tool
No better than a monarch's fool
To play a part on earth assigned
No choice, no will, afraid, resigned.

Nocturnal sleep as gift to man,
One joyful pictures Lifts all ban,
The worse to sting awakening youth
As reveal the light of
growing light needs the truth

USO

THE YOUNG MEN'S CHRISTIAN ASSOCIATIONS • THE NATIONAL CATHOLIC COMMUNITY SERVICE
THE SALVATION ARMY • THE YOUNG WOMEN'S CHRISTIAN ASSOCIATIONS
THE JEWISH WELFARE BOARD • THE NATIONAL TRAVELERS AID ASSOCIATION

Newly elected U.S. Representative Matsunaga poses for a publicity photo in Washington, D.C. (top) and with fellow dignitaries during President John F. Kennedy's visit to Honolulu in June 1963 (left to right: Sparky, Governor John A. Burns, Senator Daniel K. Inouye, President Kennedy and Senator Hiram L. Fong). Opposite: In Naples in the spring of 1944, Sparky drafted a Mother's Day poem on USO stationery.

In Honolulu in 1964, Sparky meets with business leaders (left to right: Boyd MacNaughton, James Stopford and Sanford Platt) and leads a Friends of Sparky parade during the Hawai'i Democratic State Convention at McKinley High School.

The Matsunaga family poses before the Capitol dome in October 1967. Front, left to right: Diane, Helene, Sparky and Keene. Rear, left to right: Karen, Merle and Matt.

Sparky visits a World War II memorial on Wake Island in November 1962. During his career, his Congressional duties took him as far afield as India (opposite top, second from left, front row, 1965) and Alaska (opposite bottom, second from left, 1964) where his delegation viewed a demonstration of U.S. Army combat readiness in cold weather.

In Congressional circles, Sparky was famous for his hospitality toward visitors from home. In 1970 his guests included Honolulu Mayor Frank F. Fasi and his wife, Joyce, (opposite) and Hawai'i Department of Agriculture Chairman Kenneth Otagaki — a fellow 100th Infantry Battalion veteran — and his wife, Janet.

In August 1967, Sparky was crowned "Alii" (chief) of a 4-H Club exhibition held in the University of Hawai'i's Orvis Auditorium.

was in." Thomas Gill, then a rising star in the Democratic Party, agreed: "Too many people around Burns had fat heads from getting statehood and they made stupid mistakes."

In other elections, Republican Hiram Fong beat Frank Fasi for the six-year term in the Senate, Democrat Oren Long won a shortened three-year term over Wilfred Tsukiyama and Democrat Daniel Inouye doubled the vote over Charles Silva. Finally, on August 21, President Eisenhower signed the declaration admitting "the state of Hawai'i into the Union on an equal footing with other states."

After his defeat in the primary, Sparky went back to practicing law and started to rebuild his political base, giving speeches before whatever audience would have him. He told the annual convention of the Hawaii Federation of Women's Clubs in the spring of 1960 that, in the wake of heinous crimes, there is always a clamor to revive the death penalty but he argued that capital punishment was not a satisfactory solution. The contention that the death penalty deterred murders and rapists, he said with an oblique reference to the Joanne Yamaguchi calamity, "will not hold water."

A newspaper reported that "hardly a Japanese wake or funeral goes by without a Matsunaga appearance." He studied the life of Jose Rizal, the Philippine national leader, and became a member of the Friends of Jose Rizal Society, which won him support among Honolulu's growing Filipino community. The YMCA in Kaimukī got his attention as did the Waikiki Lions Club and the University of Hawaii Preschool Parent Teachers Association. He was a member of the Pacific War Memorial Commission, took part in the work of the Committee on Ethics of the Hawaii Bar Association and was appointed by the State Supreme Court to a committee on rules of procedure.

Sparky was particularly active in the Naturalization Encouragement Association of Honolulu, which had been formed in 1952 to urge aliens to take out American citizenship. This was the start of his interest in issues affecting immigrants, perhaps not surprising for a child of immigrant parents. Since a rudimentary ability to read the English language was a requirement for citizenship, and with about 15 percent of the resident aliens illiterate, the association sought to improve adult education. Altogether, the association was reasonably successful, getting about 1,500 people a year to raise their right hands and swear allegiance to the Constitution of the United States. Among them, to Sparky's great pleasure in 1962, was his father, Kingoro.

Meantime, the Democratic Party was pulling itself together. Robert Oshiro, who was to become a power behind the throne in Hawai'i's politics over the next four decades, chaired a fact-finding committee that sought to determine why Burns, the favorite, had lost to Quinn for governor. "It became very clear," Oshiro said in an interview, "that we can't be infighting all the time." He said that "by consensus, we tried to bring about the concept of a balanced ticket," meaning a racially and ethnically balanced ticket. It was to be critical to the success of the Democrats in Hawai'i from then on. Oshiro indicated that the party's visions of its future at the time did not include Sparky Matsunaga.

Sparky's way in politics seemed to be blocked. As he surveyed the scene in the early days of statehood, he could see that John Burns would run for governor again in 1962. Sparky had already lost a bid to be lieutenant governor, so that was not appealing. He could have run for the State Senate but that would have meant going back to more of the same. Sparky thus shifted his focus from local politics to the national level. There, an opening appeared when Oren Long declared he would not stand for reelection to the Senate when his truncated term was over in 1962. The Burns machine quickly chose Representative Daniel Inouye to run for Long's seat. In turn, that opened up a seat in the House. In addition, the results of the national census of 1960 decreed that Hawai'i would add a second House seat, both to be filled at large from the entire state. Later, Hawai'i would be broken into electoral districts like states everywhere else in the nation.

When Sparky announced in March 1962 that he would run for the U.S. House of Representatives in the November election, the Burns machine was annoyed. They had hand-picked a "unity" slate to avoid primary fights and one that was racially and ethnically balanced. For the two House seats, the party favored Thomas Gill, a *haole*, and Herbert Lee, a Chinese-American. The Japanese-American was Inouye, running for the vacated Senate seat. The gubernatorial candidate was to be Burns, of course, and William Richardson, who was part-Hawaiian despite his haole name, was to run for lieutenant governor.

Oshiro said he went to see Sparky in his law office to ask him to reconsider his bid to run for the House because he was upsetting the racial balance that had been so carefully worked out for the Democratic ticket. Sparky bluntly refused. "Sparky told me," Oshiro said, "'When I look at myself and I look at my age, I feel it's time for me to move into Congress.'" Inside, Sparky was furious. He said later that if he had been asked to step aside because he was not qualified, he might have listened. But to be asked to step aside because of his race was intolerable: "When they used my race as the only reason for withdrawal, I rebelled. I refused to withdraw." Oshiro said he left the meeting with Sparky certain that he would run and would probably win. "He was mission driven," Oshiro said. "He pursued his own ideas and he pursued them relentlessly."

In the primary campaign, Sparky, who was running against Gill and three other Democrats, pounded away at the racial issue, contending that "any slate on a strictly racial basis is strictly un-American." In the primary and in the general election campaign, he called for federal aid to education, proposed medical care for the aged and sought the support of organized labor. In a theme he was to propound for the rest of his career, Sparky advocated a halt in testing nuclear arms. At that time, the Russians had acquired atomic weapons and an arms race between Washington and Moscow was picking up speed. "We're at a critical period where, unless we sit at the conference table and prevent the pushing of the button, we may find our world in utter ruin," he contended. "I feel every candidate for Congress ought to be so concerned with world peace that he would openly discuss his position. All this talk about bridging East and West will come to naught without a solution to world peace."

On that platform, Sparky topped the list of six Democratic candidates in the October primary with 48,762 votes, edging out the candidate backed by the Burns group, Thomas Gill, who got 48,093 votes. In the three-way race on the Republican side, Albert Evensen and Richard Sutton won. John Burns and William Richardson won the nominations for governor and lieutenant governor while William Quinn and Calvin MacGregor become the Republican nominees. Inouye won the Democratic nomination for the Senate by trouncing Frank Troy, 80,707 to 5,476.

During the ensuing campaign, the Cuban missile crisis erupted when the U.S. discovered that the Soviet Union had deployed missiles, presumably with nuclear warheads, in Cuba, only 90 miles from Florida. Sparky came out clearly in support of President John F. Kennedy's response despite his misgivings about the use of military force as an instrument of national policy: "President Kennedy's request for immediate withdrawal of offensive weapons from Cuba appears to be a reasonable one. If the Soviet Union has peaceful designs, it should have no reluctance to comply with this request. A refusal can only mean an offensive intent, and the people of the United States and of other nations in the Western Hemisphere must accordingly unite in support of the unmistakable position our President has taken."

Shortly after, Sparky added, "With our general election only a little more than a week in the future, this grave new crisis has paled all other issues into relative insignificance. But we must maintain our perspective. We must continue to think and plan for our future. The coming election is vital, perhaps more so now than ever before. America needs men of goodwill who will exercise calm judgments in their deliberations in Congress, men who will not fear to continue to negotiate for peace, for civilization itself is at stake."

In the November election, Gill and Sparky came in only 50 votes apart, winning the two seats by counts of 123,649 and 123,599, respectively. The press in Hawai'i noted the contrasts between the two: Matsunaga being polite, conscious of protocol and a believer in gradual change; Gill seen as blunt, confrontational and often labeled a radical.

Sparky saw the differences more in style than in political philosophy. "Tom is abrupt and not as patient with views he considers shortsighted," he said. Gill said that Sparky played things safe. "That," said Gill, who was in Congress for only one term, "is why he was there for so long."

Having been elected to Congress, Sparky did make one change. Before the election, he sported natty bow ties. After he won and prepared to go to Washington, he switched to somber four-in-hands. ❖

Freshman Term
1963–1964

Sparky sat quietly toward the rear of the House of Representatives watching the elaborate, sometimes flowery rituals and the occasional lighthearted banter as the 88th Congress opened on January 9, 1963. His was the only Asian face in a sea of white faces that was almost all male. There were a half-dozen African-Americans and Hispanic-Americans sprinkled through the crowd.

Nonetheless, he had been uniformly well-received in the Capitol, Sparky wrote friends back home, even by some colleagues from the Deep South, where racial segregation still prevailed. In the first order of business, John McCormack, the Democrat from Massachusetts who was to have a marked influence on Sparky's career in the House, was elected Speaker over Charles Halleck, a Republican from Indiana. As that had been determined in party caucuses the day before, the formal vote was strictly along party lines.

Halleck joked, "The result of this election comes as no surprise to me. I was told I was ahead in the early returns. Mr. Speaker, I am getting a little tired of losing these elections to you Democrats, but I have not given up."

McCormack responded in kind, acknowledging that "in the early returns I was behind." He noted, however, that "the Democratic stronghold came in and I was elected." Turning to Halleck, he said, "Charlie, with all my respect for you and my friendship for you, I hope your ambitions will be long delayed."

McCormack became serious and launched into a peroration about the place of the House in American democracy. Sparky listened attentively. "This is the greatest legislative body in the world. I am proud of the record of this body, and particularly in the field of national defense and a firm foreign policy," McCormack said. "We have a strong Congress, which is of paramount importance because of the threat imposed on free peoples and free nations by international communism, an evil sinister movement determined upon world domination."

He paid tribute to President Kennedy as "a man of great ability, a man of keen and penetrating mind, a man who evaluates soundly and a man of unlimited courage" in meeting the challenges of the Cold War, especially the Cuban missile crisis only a few months before. "With such a leader and with a strong Congress acting in cooperation, I have no doubt as to the result; the cause of freedom and liberty will prevail."

The Speaker was sworn in, then asked Sparky and the other members to rise as he administered the oath of office collectively.

Hardly had the Representatives resumed their seats and disposed quickly of six procedural matters when bipartisan amity evaporated and a quarrel erupted, the outcome of which was to govern much of Sparky's tenure in the House. Carl Albert of Oklahoma, the Democratic majority leader, proposed that the powerful Rules Committee, which was the Speaker's right arm in controlling the flow of legislation, be enlarged to 15 members from 12. He proposed adding two Democrats and one Republican to give the committee ten Democrats and five Republicans compared with eight Democrats and four Republicans. That change had been adopted temporarily in the previous Congress to break the hold that a coalition of three conservative Democrats and four Republicans held on the committee. Now the Democrats wanted to make the shift permanent.

Albert argued that "every committee of the House has an odd number of members except the Committee on Rules where a tie vote thwarts the entire legislative process." Halleck, the Republican leader, shot back that President Kennedy was behind the proposed change because he feared the committee could block legislation he wanted. "The President's statement," Halleck contended, "is something of an affront, not only to the Republican members of the Rules Committee, on which I served at one time, but to all members of the Rules Committee — and I am not so sure the affront does not apply to the whole Congress." Halleck continued, "It is unwise, it is unnecessary, it is inadvisable and I think it highly improper that we adopt it at this time." Both sides charged the other with trying to "pack" the committee.

Representative Melvin Laird, a Republican from Wisconsin, suggested what he called a "fair play" amendment that would allow the expansion of the committee but would fix membership at nine from the majority and six from the minority. The debate raged on for more than the allotted hour until the previous question was moved and Sparky cast his first ballot as a member of Congress, voting with the Democrats along party lines, 235–196, to enlarge the Rules Committee. He did not know it then but that change made it possible, four years hence, for him to join the influential committee at a relatively early stage of his career in the House.

Even before he had been sworn in, Sparky was elected president of the incoming class of 67 new Congressmen, 36 Democrats and 31 Republicans, which, more than anything else, underscored his acceptance in Washington. Here he was the only Asian-American in the House, from a small, faraway, oceanic state that had been part of the Union for less than four years, and he was chosen by his classmates to be their leader. During the round of briefings and orientation sessions, the newcomers got to know each other and when it came time to choose a class president, it went to Sparky more by consensus than formal vote. Helene joked, "Maybe nobody else wanted it." The post was largely ceremonial and social but nonetheless it got Sparky off to a good start.

As befitting a freshman Congressman, Sparky kept quiet for the first few weeks and, indeed, took a low posture during most of his first term. Even so, he began laying down a pattern of work habits that carried through his House years and into the Senate. First priority went to constituent services, taking care of things, large and small, that the voters back home wanted, whether it was a tour of the Capitol, straightening out a visa problem or interceding with Selective Service. Next came legislation on the floor of the House; Sparky believed that the duty of a legislator was to legislate. Many of the bills he introduced were those, such as tax laws, that affected the daily lives of Americans, whether on the mainland or back home in Hawai'i. He sought to open up immigration, to restrict migrant workers because they took jobs from Americans, to cut taxes, to defend foreign aid and to promote veterans' benefits.

Sparky, a quick study, began learning the intricacies of the House's parliamentary procedures and soon started to thrive on the give-and-take on the floor where he established himself as an orator in a fraternity that loves words. He also quickly learned that committee work could be dreary and, despite its importance, he never really took to that aspect of the House's work. He attended to it because he had to. Most of all, whether in legislation, floor debate, in committee or outside of Congress, Sparky fought for civil rights and against discrimination at every turn.

Altogether, he made the transition from local politics to national and international issues with relative ease. At the end of that first year, Sparky told *The Honolulu Advertiser*, "My first year in Congress has been the greatest year in my whole life. It is fascinating and rewarding to be part of the national and international scene. The pulse of the world is felt in Washington."

Shortly after being sworn in, Sparky was assigned to the Committee on Agriculture, a good post for a Congressman from a state in which sugar was vital to the economy and the sugar industry was powerful. He displayed little enthusiasm for the assignment, however, perhaps reflecting his years of poverty on the plantation on Kaua'i, and within a few months sought a new assignment on the more influential Committee on Banking and Currency.

When word of that got back to Hawai'i, the sugar industry swiftly pressed Sparky to desist. Donald Maclean, the president of the California and Hawai'i Sugar Refining Corporation, wrote to Sparky asking him to stay on the agriculture committee as sugar legislation was certain to come up the following year. "The pressures from growing areas competitive to Hawai'i will be great," Maclean said, "and it seems to me there will be an exceptional opportunity to be helpful to Hawai'i if you are at that time a member of the House Agriculture Committee." Other sugar executives, labor leaders and lobbyists weighed in with the same message. Sparky, well aware of sugar's political clout at home, quickly relented.

Although he minded his manners and the House's protocol, Sparky displayed his quixotic side early on. Among the first bills he tossed into the House hopper was one calling for a constitutional amendment that would provide for four-year instead of two-year terms for Representatives. What possessed an obscure freshman from a brand-new state to make such a brash proposal has been left unrecorded. The bill sank out of sight. At the same time, he began lobbying for his favorite project, which was to have Congress name a poet laureate of the United States. That campaign was not to come to fruition for more than 20 years, after Sparky had reached the Senate.

Sparky picked March 18, 1963, the fourth anniversary of President Eisenhower's signing of the bill admitting Hawai'i to the Union, to make his maiden address to the House. The topic, timing and delivery of the first speech of a new Congressman is traditionally chosen with care as this first impression influences the member's subsequent standing. Sparky focused on his home state: "History will record that Hawai'i became part of the United States in a unique way. It was not by war or military occupation or by economic conquest or colonial exploitation. Hawai'i became identified with the United States by an assimilation of the political and social ideals of America....Is it not a fact worth meditating on, that the tie which binds the people of Hawai'i to the United States is not that of race or history, nor that of force or economic exploitation, but that of ideals freely accepted?"

Calling Hawai'i the "westernmost outpost" of President John Kennedy's "New Frontier," Sparky asserted, "Hawai'i is the showcase of American democracy for all the world to see. There, out in the middle of the Pacific Ocean, peoples of diverse cultures have proven beyond a doubt that they can live together and work together in harmony and in concert toward their own social, political, economic and cultural betterment. They have proven by actual experiment that the ideals of Americanism can and will work."

As Sparky finished, Majority Leader Albert rose to congratulate him for "his very eloquent oration" and said, "The gentleman has not overdrawn the qualities of the great state he represents." One after another, Democrats and Republicans stood to echo Albert's remarks. Representative Barratt O'Hara, a Democrat from Illinois, said Sparky's fame as an orator had preceded his swearing in "and on a most historic occasion, he has lived up to his reputation."

When Representative Durward Hall, a Republican from Missouri, noted the contributions of former Governor William Quinn, a Republican, to statehood, Sparky gently reminded him that Quinn was no longer governor: "We are enlightened now and have a Democratic governor." Several members, such as Representative Don Edwards, a Democrat from California, noted the value of Hawai'i as a bulwark against communism: "Hawai'i serves not only as a model for her sister states but also mirrors for all the peoples of Asia crushed under the tyranny of communism the possibility of popular self-government based on interpersonal respect without regard to race and creed."

Thomas Gill, the other representative from Hawai'i, underscored a fact of political life in multiracial Hawai'i: "I can state without danger of contradiction that had Congressman Matsunaga been dependent wholly upon the vote of citizens of Oriental extraction, he would not be here today. I can also say with a great deal of certainty that had I been mainly dependent on the votes of those of Caucasian ancestry, I would not be here today, either." Even though the political language of the House is often flowery, through not so ornate as that in the Senate, the praise of Sparky's speech was remarkable.

In June, Sparky was invited to join President Kennedy's entourage aboard Air Force One to fly to Hawai'i where the President was to address the U.S. Conference of Mayors on civil rights. Sparky was as excited as a kid at Christmas. "It was a wonderful way to go home — in the company of the President," he wrote a friend. He had a chance to talk with President Kennedy on the long flight and coached him on how to begin a speech in Hawai'i with the greeting "aloha," in which the second syllable is drawn out. Even with his Boston accent, President Kennedy was able to master it. It was during the arrival ceremony at the Honolulu airport that the President addressed the governor, the mayor and Senators Inouye and Fong formally, but Sparky by his first name. Sparky beamed.

In his arrival remarks, the President said he had come to talk about "how the American people can live more happily and more securely together." He paid tribute to Hawai'i: "There is no place where it is more appropriately said and understood than in this part of the United States, than on this island. Reaching into the Pacific, yet part of the United States, this island represents all that we are and all that we hope to be." In his formal speech the next day, Kennedy further referred to the burning national issue of desegregation: "The mayor of every metropolitan city, in every section of America, must be aware of the difficult challenges he now faces and will face in the coming months. I am asking you, in short, to be alert, not alarmed."

After returning to Washington, Sparky wrote to Donald Brown, a political supporter in Honolulu: "The President was so pleased with the wonderful reception he received in Hawai'i that he had no objections to signing a few autographs. The enclosed is for your daughter, Melinda." Never one to miss a political opening, Sparky asked Brown, "Will you attempt to obtain copies of the TV films taken by any of the studios covering the arrival of President Kennedy which you believe could be used in my next campaign? Also still shots from news photographers which might be usable." Noting that he had slept only four hours in three days because of the hectic schedule during the President's visit, Sparky closed: "For all the sleep I lost over the weekend, I can't write another sentence."

As the President predicted, the challenges were but a few days in coming. Right after he returned to Washington with Sparky in tow, the President federalized Alabama's National Guard to force the University of Alabama to admit two black students. On June 12, a leader of the National Association for the Advancement of Colored People (NAACP), Medgar Evers, was murdered in his home in Jackson, Mississippi. A week later, President Kennedy asked Congress to pass a far-reaching Civil Rights Bill, which set off a fierce debate in the House.

Sparky threw himself into this struggle. Testifying before the Labor Subcommittee on Education, he pleaded for an end to discrimination in schools: "No American child should be subjected to the indignity of being denied admission into a school because and only because he happened to be born of colored parents." In response to a skeptical letter from the Reverend Jesse Nicholas in Wahiawā, Sparky said, "It should be taken for granted in this land of the free that a man should not be subjected to the indignity of having to go from restaurant to restaurant to find a place where he may be served when hungry, nor have to go from hotel to hotel or motel to motel to find a bed where he may sleep when traveling. Some of our citizens from Hawai'i have recently been subjected to such indignities in areas very close to Washington on the basis of their sun-tanned skins....I have personally never been subjected to this type of indignity but I can assure you that I will exert every effort to spare another human being from such indignity."

A focal point that summer was the March on Washington for Jobs and Freedom on August 28 led by the Reverend Martin Luther King, Jr. and other African-American leaders. About 200,000 people, including large numbers of whites, turned out for the march and to hear King deliver his ringing cry for equality: "I have a dream....I have a dream that my four little children will one day live in a nation where they will not be judged by the color of their skin but by the content of their character."

Curiously, for one so committed to equality and civil rights, Sparky spoke out against the march, saying it was not wise because it might degenerate into violence, and he did not turn out for the event. Nor did many other members of Congress. Tom Gill, the other representative from Hawai'i, was there and was critical of Sparky for not going. "Sparky was cautious," Gill recalled years later. "He didn't get too far out on a limb, where it was dangerous."

After it was over, Sparky wrote to a voter back home: "The affair was incredibly well-planned and conducted. There were 6,000 city police, national park police and military police handling the crowd, and the troublemakers were sealed off from the crowd before they could do anything. There were no spectators as such. It was a sober, well-dressed crowd, and most of them gave the appearance of just having come out of church wearing their Sunday clothes."

A couple of days later, Sparky addressed a gathering of the Japanese-American Citizens League (JACL) in Cleveland (JACL had taken part in the march). "I must confess," Sparky said, "that I was against the march due to a genuine apprehension that there would be violence and bloodshed, and as a consequence the civil rights movement would be set back by many, many years." Then he said something rarely heard from politicians: "Thank God that I was wrong."

Even so, Sparky argued, "Demonstrations, however peaceful, are not going to solve our civil rights problems. The Negro-American knows this best, for even after the Big March he has returned home to find the walls of discrimination unleveled, to his segregated school and restricted housing, to 'white only' signs at public accommodations, to a jobless future and daily humiliations." He said Negroes needed allies and applauded JACL for supporting the civil rights movement.

When David Trask, a prominent Democratic state legislator, wrote to say he did not understand Sparky's position, Sparky sent him a copy of the Cleveland speech along with a letter: "It would have been much easier and politically more expedient for me to say I approved of the march...Because of my genuine belief that the civil rights cause would be hurt if any violence and bloodshed resulted, I said I was not in agreement with advocates of the march…I am sure you know me as one who speaks his thoughts outright despite the political consequences. This may be one of my weaknesses as a political office seeker, but I have found it a source of personal strength and satisfaction."

As debate over President Kennedy's Civil Rights Bill heated up, Sparky received mail from all sides. In a long letter to Stephen Murin of the United Public Workers in Honolulu, Sparky analyzed two schools of thought: Those who said "all or nothing" and those who argued "take what you can get now and come back to fight again another year." He said he was inclined to all-or-nothing, although that might not be the wisest course. "Republicans plus Dixiecrats equal a majority in both houses of Congress," Sparky wrote. "Some of us had hoped that the white churches of the South would become a rallying point in the solution of this moral issue. However, it now appears that the profit motive has gone further in producing changes than has morality."

Recognizing that few African-Americans had the money to make choices, Sparky said, "Our goal will not yet have been achieved until we have improved the economic status of the Negro." When Dr. Rodman Miller of the Waialua Agricultural Company urged Sparky to vote against the bill, Sparky's reply was terse: "I am sorry but I do not agree with you."

While that debate swirled on, Sparky delivered a carefully prepared, closely reasoned and sometimes spirited defense of the annual foreign aid bill, not a popular cause in the House. Asserting that "a great deal of misinformation has been circulated" about foreign aid, Sparky homed in on its effect on the balance of payments, which is the sum total of funds flowing into and out of the country through trade, investment and other financial transactions. It was headed into deficit at that time.

"This confusion arises out of the mistaken assumption that because foreign aid goes outside of the United States, the entire foreign aid program should be listed on the debit side of the balance-of-payments ledger," Sparky said. "Even the eminent *New York Times* recently erred in making this assumption." The newspaper, he contended, overlooked "the fact that most foreign aid money is spent right here in the United States." More than 80 percent of foreign aid expenditures the year before had been spent in the U.S., Sparky said, representing "nearly $4 billion worth of contracts for the U.S. business community." He cited figures to buttress his point and concluded, "The balance of payments problem must be solved, but the way to solve it is not by cutting our foreign aid program. Foreign aid is a sound investment in our own future security."

Representative Edmond Edmondson, a Democrat from Oklahoma, agreed. "I think the gentleman has certainly demonstrated with some very fine authority …that the problem is not that simple and that whatever defects and whatever the difficulties may be in our foreign aid program, it certainly cannot be demonstrated by any process of true logic that it is at the root of our difficulty with…the balance of payments."

But Representative Ed Foreman, a Republican from Texas, was angry: "I am surprised to hear the plaudits paid our irresponsible and wasteful foreign aid give-away program, most of them socialistic and many of them communist today."

Sparky replied, "Many nations without foreign aid, which we have given, would have turned communist even before now."

Foreman shot back, "Name one."

Sparky: "India, the bulwark of democracy in the East."

Foreman: "In my opinion they are more communist than they are democratic."

Sparky: "Is communism and democracy intermingleable?"

Foreman: "I do not think they are."

Sparky: "Then why does the gentleman say that India is a state of mixed communism and democracy?"

Foreman: "I say they are closer to communism than they are to democracy."

The exchange ended when Sparky, with a touch of sarcasm, said, "I thank the gentleman from Texas." Not content to let it go, he came back the next day with a chart showing the procurement arising from foreign aid funds in each state. Six, including Texas, received over $10 million in orders. Hawai'i got none.

On November 22, 1963, tragedy struck America. President Kennedy was gunned down by an assassin's bullet in Dallas. Like almost every American, Sparky was stunned, more so than anything since the Japanese attack on Pearl Harbor. He was at the Capitol when he got the news. Congress quickly adjourned and Sparky went to his home in Bethesda, a suburb in Maryland. His son, Matt, was having a party to celebrate his fifth birthday when Sparky walked in and broke down weeping as he told Helene and his family what had happened. Matt said it was one of the few times he had ever seen his father cry. No one, even the children, felt like keeping the party going so they were helped into their sweaters or coats and trundled off home. Sparky and Helene went to a private viewing of Kennedy's body in the White House and then to pay their respects when Kennedy lay in state in the Capitol but did not go to the funeral in St. Matthew's Cathedral nor on the long walk to Arlington Cemetery. Helene said Sparky stayed home to watch the proceedings on TV and to grieve.

Four days after the assassination, Congress was back in session and a day in December was set aside for eulogies for the late President. Sparky didn't wait and was recognized for one minute to speak about the President he deeply admired. His words seemed like a cry from the heart: "What manner of being was this who could be so filled with hatred so as to take the life of a man whose whole heart and mind were dedicated to world peace and goodwill toward mankind? Was this a product of our vaunted society? Where had we failed? And why? Why? Indeed, the greatest tragedy in our nation's modern history has given us cause for some real soul searching."

In early December, on the day for eulogies, Sparky added, "He was mankind's man, a champion of the poor and lowly and of the rich and exalted, and though he walked with kings he never lost the common touch."

As the nation mourned the dead President and watched President Lyndon Baines Johnson form his administration, Congress resumed debate over foreign aid and civil rights. Sparky continued to plead for both. In World War II, he asserted, "We learned and came to accept the fact that we are, indeed, involved in the affairs of mankind. In dealing with foreign aid legislation in recent years, however, there has begun to be a faltering in that acceptance of responsibility. One can detect a wavering in the resolution that has marked our conduct of foreign affairs during the past two decades."

In an appeal that would be heard into the next century, Sparky asked, "Will this nation, its people and we their elected representatives continue to face up to the challenge that confronts us in the world?…Or will we seek to turn away and to retreat into a new isolationism?" Sparky concluded, "Neither politically nor morally can we allow reluctance to overcome us. We must not falter in this great work." The bill was passed early in 1964.

On the sweeping Civil Rights Bill of 1964 that would guarantee the right to vote, forbid discrimination in public accommodation and assure equality in education, Sparky sought to be a voice of reason and conciliation amid an often bitter debate in the House. Just after two Congressmen had come close to calling each other liars, Sparky entered the fray: "It is understandable that those among us whose ancestors owned slaves would today oppose passage of the Civil Rights Bill. We who support the pending legislation understand this, and we want our good friends from the South to know that we do understand. We realize what an emotional and tumultuous problem is here involved.

"But we want our southern friends to understand," Sparky continued, "that by constitutional amendment, our supreme law of the land freed the Negro from servitude 100 years ago and what we are attempting to do here is merely to give meaning to that greatest of human documents." Driving home his point, Sparky said, "American society can be true to itself, therefore, only as rights are accorded to every person because he is a person....Discrimination based on race, color, religion and national origin directly contradicts such an idea of rights. It tends to destroy the integrity of the American way of life." He concluded, "I therefore ask those who oppose this measure to join us in passing it because it is the right thing to do."

Whether Sparky changed any minds in the debate that continued for five more months is impossible to know but the bill was passed in July and signed by President Johnson. On the day of passage, Sparky cautioned both whites and blacks against using the new law to provoke civil disorder: "The white American must realize that the Negro-American is going to fight for his rights, frequently in blind anger and bitterness, and must be treated with greater understanding. The Negro-American, on the other hand, must exercise the patience of Job and seek to remedy wrongs only through the peaceful means provided by the new law."

On Washington's birthday in 1964, Sparky was exhilarated to have been asked to read George Washington's Farewell Address to the House, a tradition rarely performed by so junior a member. It appears to have been this address that brought Sparky to the attention of the Speaker, John McCormack. "Mr. Speaker," Sparky began, "it is with a deep sense of humility that I now attempt to lend voice to the immortal words of George Washington as spoken in his Farewell Address to the people of the United States." This was the wonderfully literate speech that Washington delivered on September 17, 1796, in which he warned, "Why, by interweaving our destiny with that of any part of Europe, entangle our peace and prosperity in the toils of European ambition, rivalship, interest, humor or caprice?" American engagement abroad, the first President cautioned, should be limited "to temporary alliances for extraordinary emergencies."

Sparky, who had practiced the speech diligently, warmed to his subject and was rewarded with high praise. After he closed, the Majority Leader, Carl Albert, said he had heard the Farewell Address read 18 times, but "I have never heard it read better than it was read today. Our colleague from Hawai'i has really done a masterful job."

The Speaker himself chimed in, "In my 35 years as a member of the House, I have never heard Washington's Farewell Address delivered in a better or more effective manner." Leo O'Brien of New York: "Our colleague from Hawai'i made those immortal words leap into new life....Of all the occasions upon which I have been proud of being the floor manager for the bill which brought Hawai'i into the sisterhood of states, I was never more proud than today."

With that, Sparky came under the wing of Speaker McCormack. They were an odd couple — the tall, commanding Irish "pol" from Boston and the short, affable Japanese newcomer from Hawai'i. Underneath, the similarities were evident. Both were from immigrant families, McCormack's having come across the Atlantic, Sparky's across the Pacific. They had grown up in large, impoverished but tightly knit families, and struggled for education and early jobs. Both were lawyers for whom law was a stepping-stone, not an end in itself. They shared a love of the English language, fine oratory and politics. McCormack needed the minority support that Sparky symbolized (even if Sparky didn't think of himself as being in a minority), and Sparky responded by becoming intensely loyal to McCormack.

Sparky's rhetoric scored again the following month, when he spoke to the Inter-American Defense College in Washington on "This I Believe," an exposition of his concept of democracy. "I was taught that as an American, regardless of race, color or creed, I could aspire to the highest office in this land. This I believed as a child, and of its truth I am convinced as a man," he told his audience of North American and Latin American officers and civilians. Sparky recited the trying experiences of Japanese-Americans in World War II and asserted that, despite their adversities, they did not turn against America because "they had faith in the American dream, in this thing we call American democracy." Sparky reviewed the ills of America, including the strife over civil rights, but asserted that the failures were not in the system but in citizens who had failed to live up to the ideals of the nation. "As the son of an immigrant plantation worker who has realized his American dream, I ask you to take this message back to your people — that American democracy is an idea dedicated to the freedom and dignity of the individual man, regardless of his race, color or creed."

In his remarks on the floor of the House, Sparky was eclectic. He applauded the Peace Corps as "the greatest success story in man's quest for peace through human understanding in modern times." With an eye on the votes of Filipino-Americans in the forthcoming election in November, he inserted into the Congressional Record tributes to Emilio Aguinaldo, the Philippine freedom fighter; Jose Rizal, the nationalist; and General Douglas MacArthur, the liberator of the Philippines in World War II. With another eye on the voters, he defended the naval station at Pearl Harbor from those who would move some of its operations to their own states, stalled action on a bill that would permit free import of instant coffee in competition with Hawai'i's Kona coffee and helped to persuade the Agricultural

Committee to report out a bill extending the Sugar Act that favored the industry in Hawai'i. He supported appropriations for the new East-West Center, a research and educational institute at the University of Hawai'i. He also did something rare for a member of Congress, which was to insert in the Congressional Record a word of thanks to the Library of Congress's Legislative Reference Service, which did research for Congressional speeches and bills.

In his personal life, Sparky's father, Kingoro, whom he deeply loved and respected, died in April 1964. Sparky flew home immediately for the funeral and a year later arranged for a Buddhist memorial service for Kingoro in a small chapel in the Capitol, believed to be the first and perhaps only Buddhist service ever held there.

Throughout his first term, and indeed for the rest of his Congressional career, staying in touch with the voters back home was at the top of Sparky's list of priorities. It was a bit difficult, given the distance between Hawai'i and Washington. Unlike his colleagues from the East, South and Midwest, Sparky couldn't go home every weekend. In Washington, he averaged about 30 visitors a week, not counting those in large groups. "I talk with them all," Sparky told *The Honolulu Advertiser*, "show them the Capitol, and we usually have our pictures taken." His colleague, Tom Gill, was more like most Congressmen in seeing only selected visitors and not showing them around. "I was not a tour guide," Gill said.

Here started the custom for which Sparky was to become famous — taking constituents to lunch in the House and later the Senate dining rooms, paid for out of campaign funds. It began with an elderly couple from Maui who visited the Capitol in 1964. A neighbor who knew Sparky had called to ask him to give them a few minutes of his time; they had never before left Hawai'i. He treated them to lunch, took them on a brief tour of the Capitol, and, when shaking hands to say goodbye, the man said, "Sparky, you know I work for Maui Pineapple 40 years. And 40 years I pay Uncle Sam taxes and he no give me back nothing. But I no grumble. Uncle Sam today pay me all back." From then on, Sparky consistently ran up the biggest tabs in the House and Senate dining rooms as few other members did anything like that.

Sparky's correspondence set him apart from many of his colleagues. Like other Congressmen, he received about 100 letters a day. At first, unlike many Congressmen who sent perfunctory form letters in reply, Sparky answered them personally even if it meant staying in the office until 2:00 or 3:00 in the morning. "One thing I've learned," he said, "is that if you skip the mail one day, you have 200 the next day and if you skip for two days, you have 300 to read and sign." As the volume of his mail grew and he became more senior, Sparky's office maintained a thick file of paragraphs that had been carefully drafted and from which key statements could be drawn for the staff to prepare hundreds of letters to respond to queries that were similar. The range of issues was staggering and the correspondence reflected the constant pressures on members of Congress. Even so, Sparky replied personally to as many of the incoming letters as he could.

This correspondence not only built his reputation among his constituents but, more important, caused him to define his political thinking on national and international issues. From those letters emerges a literature on Sparky's reasoning that showed him to be sometimes pragmatic, other times idealistic, occasionally visionary but rarely profound. In this collection, Sparky laid down a base line from which his thinking could be measured as he matured politically. It is a body of thought that showed Sparky's versatility, many of his positions being well thought out and articulated but without much of a center line or unifying principle running through them. Sparky was seen as a liberal but was hardly doctrinaire. He often moved to the middle of the road and even tilted to the conservative side of the spectrum occasionally.

In response to a query from a political newsletter, Sparky ticked off positions on ten issues. He strongly supported a Civil Rights Bill that he said would "do much to end the problem of police brutality." He favored providing information on birth control to those requesting it. He believed that economic and technical assistance should be emphasized over military assistance. He favored trade with communist nations so long as it did not help their military forces. He urged reform of the tax system to plug loopholes for the oil industry. He proposed a commission to determine whether the military draft should be continued, and was among the very earliest of the nation's political leaders to do so. Sparky opposed admitting Communist China to the United Nations. He supported the Alliance for Progress, President Kennedy's plan to aid Latin America.

The issue of federal aid to private schools illuminated the pragmatism of Sparky's thinking. On one hand, he favored such aid to Catholic and other private schools: "It does not seem fair to exclude religious primary schools from federal aid when those who maintain them also pay taxes to maintain our public schools." On the other hand, Sparky saw prayer in public schools as a different issue and drew the line against mandatory or open prayer: "No one should be allowed to foist his religious practices on another."

That became a touchy issue in May 1964, when several Congressmen proposed constitutional amendments prescribing that schools conduct prayer sessions. Sparky said he was flooded with hundreds of letters and cards, the majority supporting the amendment. In what was then a rare form letter, for which Sparky apologized to his constituents, he asserted, "The amendments proposed seem to me to evoke more problems than they would solve. They are all clothed in the evil garment of vagueness." Further, he argued, "the less government has to do with prescribing religious exercises, the better off we will all be, especially those of us who consider ourselves religious people." Sparky cautioned, "Religion does not need the 'crutch' of government support — a crutch that might be used as a club instead to enforce religious conformity among our people. Religion should be born in the home and nurtured in church." He appealed to the voters: "I hope the view which I have herein expressed will cause you to reappraise your position on this delicate issue."

In other letters, Sparky said it was important "that the United States obtain a test ban agreement with the other atomic powers." To a constituent who wanted the U.S. to get out of the United Nations, Sparky said, "We can't just crawl into a box and say, 'Foreigners are no damn good.'" He argued with a voter: "I see nothing wrong with urging the Canadians to participate in the defense of this hemisphere against the danger of nuclear attack by Russia." He explained to another that he had voted for an amendment that would have folded the controversial House UnAmerican Activities Committee (HUAC) into the Judiciary Committee, but lost. Then he voted to retain the committee: "You've either got the votes or you haven't, and I was not prepared to vote for complete abolishment of the HUAC." A constituent wanting a federal tax reduction found sympathy, but Sparky cautioned that decreases would require unacceptable cuts in spending, including cutbacks in Hawai'i: "Everything from the gross income of labor in Hawai'i to our highway building program would suffer."

Sparky's thoughts on civil rights came through in a letter to G.E. Bushnell, a business executive in Honolulu who had written to ask Sparky to vote against the Civil Rights bill of 1964. Sparky replied, "I wish to point out that there are now distinguished federal judges, members of Congress, college professors, scientists and businessmen of Negro ancestry who are far superior in every way to many of those who discriminate against them." Sparky argued that the most that any law could do would be to "make it possible for him to be judged as an individual, not as a member of a race."

A troubling issue then, as now, was the fate of native Hawaiians who were at the bottom of the economic ladder. Perhaps the biggest stumbling block to resolving their problems was the fierce struggles for power within the Hawaiian community, which comprised about 20 percent of Hawai'i's population. Rev. Abraham Akaka, a prominent Hawaiian leader, wrote to Sparky wanting to know where he stood. Sparky replied, "A fair opportunity must be afforded the homesteader to build a decent home for himself and his family and to develop his land to a point of profitable returns." He said a program must be set up to provide "the necessary revolving funds for long-term, low-interest loans to the homesteader." He proposed federal and state funds be appropriated for vocational training, adult education and scholarships. Sparky cautioned, however, that "such legislation would not have much chance in Congress without the unanimous or near-unanimous agreement of the Hawaiian people themselves."

Some of Sparky's letters were directed at high policy. He wrote to George Ball, the Under Secretary of State, to oppose an excise tax on the purchase of foreign securities. He thanked Kenneth Belieu, an Assistant Secretary of the Navy: "It was with great satisfaction that I received your report about homeporting the initial contingent of Pacific Fleet Polaris submarines at Pearl Harbor." Other letters involved not-so-high policy but were important to Hawai'i. Sparky asked Alan Boyd, the chairman of the Civil Aeronautics Board, to approve the rates of two charter airlines that flew papayas to the U.S. mainland. He wrote to Ben Dorfman, the chairman of the U.S. Tariff Commission, "to protest the proposed lowering of the tariff rate on Philippine pineapple juice." Sparky supported a trade union in Honolulu that wanted to block the import of prefabricated sash, doors and cabinets from the Philippines — and this from a member of the Rizal Society who sought votes from Filipino-Americans.

There was also low policy. Sparky wrote about a proposed small boat harbor in a letter to Henry Haanapu of the Democratic precinct at Kalaupapa, the isolated settlement on Moloka'i that is a sanctuary for patients afflicted with leprosy: "If anyone tells you he can pass an appropriation bill before we get an appropriation for the engineering plans, don't believe him. It's *hoo-mali-mali*." (*Ho'omalimali,* the Hawaiian word for "flattery" or "cajolery," might be interpreted in this instance as "an inept bribery attempt" or "polishing the apple.")

Trying to resolve individual problems soaked up much time. Ann Michiko Hanamura, a naturalized citizen, ran into trouble because she had returned to Japan, her place of birth, to care for her invalid grandmother. The Passport Office at the State Department warned her that, under the law then, she could lose her American citizenship if she went to Japan too often. The day Sparky received her letter, he called the State Department and found the bureaucrats there unrelenting on her case. He wrote Mrs. Hanamura and urged her to write to the Passport Office to explain her situation in detail. She did and received a legalistic, bureaucratic reply from Edward Hickey, the deputy director, warning her that "expatriation would result" if she went back to Japan.

Sparky introduced a bill that would remove most of the differences in legal treatment of native-born and naturalized citizens. Meantime, the Supreme Court decided on May 18, 1964 that the law distinguishing between native-born and naturalized citizens was unconstitutional. In Sparky's absence due to illness, E.E. Wiles, his legislative assistant, wrote to Mrs. Hanamura: "You may now return to Japan without fear of losing your citizenship." She replied with a letter of gratitude to Sparky.

In the spring of 1963, Sparky received a flood of letters from right-wing people, some in Hawai'i but more from California, Texas and Louisiana. "There is a recurring theme of hatred running through these letters," he said on the floor of the House. "The President; Departments of Agriculture, States and Treasury; Jews; the colored; foreigners in general; labor unions and the United Nations seem to be the favorite objects of attack." He answered some of the letters. John W. Mahony, of the American Legion in Hawai'i, complained that Sparky had smeared military officers in his comments about right-wingers. Sparky agreed that "the great majority of retired generals and admirals are fine people." But he went on to say, "Uncomfortably large numbers of them have become active members in such organizations as the John Birch Society." A few letters went unanswered and into a file labeled "Crackpot."

Once in awhile, Sparky expressed frustration. He told Allan Saunders, a civil rights activist in Honolulu, that a bill had been passed to extend the Sedition Act of 1917, which sought to restrict freedom of speech, "with Tom Gill and I being two of only 40 voices crying out in the wilderness on this one." He said that while many Congressmen claim that right-wingers do not influence them, "I cannot help noticing a certain skittishness when the chips are down."

He wrote to David Benz, president of a printing company, asking for more time to pay a campaign bill because he had been forced to dip into his own pocket to cover campaign expenses. "I am finding it extremely difficult to make ends meet," Sparky wrote. "My monthly commitments right now exceed my income to a point where I have been forced to give up certain real estate investments which call for monthly payments." He said, "I have never felt this pinched in all my married life, and the thought of another campaign next year, before I've even paid for the last, is enough to give me nightmares."

Occasionally, Sparky verged on the testy. Sara Murdock of Honolulu suggested that Sparky reread the Constitution. He replied, "I frequently referred to the Constitution in the course of my law practice, I studied Constitutional law at Harvard Law School and I refer back to the Constitution from time to time in connection with my duties as a Congressman." With uncharacteristic partisanship, he wrote to William Tilley in Montana: "Congress was getting on pretty well at the beginning of the session, Bill, but lately the hog-thieving Republicans have been lining up too many of the so-called Dixiecrats to vote along with them."

When Vince De Fazio of Pearl City wrote a critical letter, Sparky snapped back, "I cannot see any excuse for writing a letter like that….Honest criticism from constituents who make an attempt to inform themselves is acceptable. However, I do not appreciate this kind of know-nothing letter." In replying to a postcard from Tom Shields of Kailua, Sparky was abrupt: "I cannot at this point agree with you. Thank you for writing."

Sparky could be sarcastic. After Marie Lum of Honolulu had commented on several issues, he replied, "Some of the businessmen in Honolulu who vote for resolutions in various organizations for 'government economy' are the very persons who write me requesting federal funds for projects which will benefit their businesses." He defended the National Council of Churches: "It is unreasonable to believe that the nation is in the hands of one big communist organization." On other issues, Sparky said, "I don't know what kind of 'information' you are receiving but I think you would be well-advised to ask how and where such information originated." To Robert York of Honolulu, however, he lamented, "The influence of a freshman Congressman upon decisions outside of the legislative branch of government is not too great." Sparky wrote to Ralph Johnson, president of the Hawaiian Electric Company, to agree that a tax cut would stimulate both the national and Hawaiian economies but warned that cutting what he called "overkill" in the defense budget would produce large-scale reductions in spending.

A voter who complained that Sparky had exhibited an "I know what is best for you" attitude, got this reply: "If you read some of my daily mail, I believe that you too would agree that some of our citizens need assistance in straightening out their thinking." He had to write several times to senior officials of government agencies to remind them that Hawai'i was not a foreign country but one of the 50 states in which English was the mother tongue.

Sometimes Sparky's dry wit surfaced. He told Carmella Wilson of California, "I have not changed Washington in my first four months in office." K.W. Grimley, the executive secretary of the Alabama Tuberculosis Association, wrote that a physical examination done while Sparky visited a demonstration showed that his lungs were clear. Sparky replied, "It was certainly a welcome relief to know that my lungs are normal. As you know, that part of our anatomy is most vital to the profession in which I am engaged." And he wrote the Honolulu chapter of the Society for the Preservation and Encouragement of Barber Shop Quartet Singing that he would be glad to support a proclamation designating a National Harmony Week: "I am glad that there is at least one non-controversial issue pending action."

Sparky often asked voters for their views. He sent copies of six bills intended to restrict medical experiments on animals to Dr. J.M. Strode in Honolulu, asking him to "let me know which provisions, if any, you consider to be unreasonable restrictions upon the use of animals in experiments." Without waiting to be questioned, Sparky asked his constituent Fred Taniguchi of Kaua'i, "I would very much like to have your views about the licensing of another radio station on Kauai."

Like all politicians, Sparky sought favors. He asked Ronald Lambert, the principal of the University Elementary School, to admit the son and daughter of friends, Mr. and Mrs. Shizuo Oka. Hoover Tateishi, Sparky's administrative assistant, wrote to Albert Teruya of Times Super Market asking for a shipment of Kona coffee for a congressional coffee hour. Another time, Sparky recommended to Acting Governor William Richardson the appointment of Eugene Duvauchelle of Moloka'i to the post of executive director of the Department of Hawaiian Home Lands.

In letters to leaders of the Democratic Party in Hawai'i, Sparky was cordial even though Governor Burns and his supporters had opposed him. But he could not resist needling Robert Oshiro, the Democratic Party chairman who had written him to see what issues he would like inserted into the 1964 state platform (it was Oshiro who had asked Sparky to step aside in 1962 in favor of a racially balanced ticket). "Actually, Bob, the only thing we in Washington really have to have to get re-elected is a united Democratic Party at election time," Sparky said with tongue in cheek. "The 1962 campaign showed what can be done with unity."

Like some politicians, Sparky wrote to people in Hawai'i about personal matters. He sent condolences to Andrew Kamauoha for "the untimely death of your beloved mother, Mrs. Ella Kamauoha." He congratulated Kuraichi Hirokawa "for leading your Hanapepe ball team to the AJA state championship." He sent congratulations to Esmeraldo Arruiza on becoming an American citizen: "I am sure you realize that you are now a full-fledged member of the greatest nation on the face of this earth." He wrote to Gladys Brandt to applaud her appointment as principal of the Kamehameha School for Girls, adding, "I wonder if you remember me as your yard boy while you lived at Port Allen?"

After Mrs. Stanley Makekau complained that she had never received a letter from a Congressman, Sparky wrote to explain that Hawai'i did not have full representation in Congress until it became a state in 1959. He closed: "Permit me, as your representative to Congress, to add my congratulations upon the birth of your third child." He told his friend and supporter, Tony Kinoshita, "I feel indeed fortunate in having a 'brother' like you, always pitching in for me. Frankly, I'd be lost without you and your calabashes and friends." A calabash in Hawai'i is an extended family, although not related by blood.

Donna Tamanaha, a ninth-grade student on Moloka'i, wrote to ask for Sparky's help on a civics assignment. "Since I am an Oriental, I wondered how the Southern senators and representatives accepted you?" Edward Wiles, Sparky's legislative assistant, replied to meet the student's deadline: "Congressman Matsunaga has found that the Southern Senators and Representatives accept him fully, as has Senator Dan Inouye. In fact, Spark has remarked that he is the beneficiary of 'discrimination in reverse.' That is, the Southerners actually go out of their way to do favors and kindnesses for him. If anything, it is a help to be an Oriental in Congress. Even the fact that they have trouble pronouncing 'Matsunaga' is a benefit. From the President and the Speaker of the House on down, they call him 'Sparky.' He is one of the best-known Representatives in Congress."

A poignant letter came from Tamie Kawano Miyamoto in Hilo, the younger sister of Yasuo Kawano, the soldier who had been killed in action at the same time Sparky had been wounded in Italy. On a trip home to Hawai'i, Sparky had gone to the Big Island, as the island of Hawai'i is known in the state of Hawai'i, and while there, had slipped off to lay flowers on Kawano's grave. Mrs. Miyamoto wrote to thank Sparky: "Your thoughtfulness will never be forgotten." Sparky replied, "Your brother was so loyal and true to me as my messenger and friend that I shall forever cherish his memory.... Yasuo died a noble death, fighting for the highest of ideals."

All those letters paid off. At the end of the Congressional session, Sparky went home to campaign for reelection. Tom Gill dropped out of the House to challenge Hiram Fong for his seat in the Senate, and lost. Patsy Takemoto Mink was selected by the Burns group to run for Gill's seat. The election, which was still for two seats at large, saw Sparky win with 140,224 votes, Mink get 106,909 and the two Republicans trail way back. ❖

Vietnam and Rules
1965–1968

Having easily won reelection in 1964 and 1966, Sparky settled into his second and third terms in the House, from January 1965 to January 1969, amid the most turbulent years in America since the end of World War II. America's plunge into the quagmire of Vietnam was at its deepest; no issue had so divided America since the Civil War. Anti-war demonstrations rocked the land, universities closed, the military draft was corrupted. The civil rights movement surged with the march of African-Americans from Selma to Montgomery, Alabama. An attempt by North Korean commandos to murder President Park Chung Hee of South Korea and the North Korean seizure of the U.S. intelligence ship *Pueblo* in neutral waters brought the U.S. perilously close to a second war in Asia.

The Cold War between the Soviet Union and the United States became colder. African-American leaders Malcolm X and Martin Luther King, Jr. were assassinated and race riots erupted in more than 100 cities from Washington to San Francisco and from Los Angeles to Newark, leaving behind wastelands of burned homes and stores. Senator Robert Kennedy, seeking the Democratic presidential nomination, was assassinated. After the Tet offensive in Vietnam in early 1968, President Johnson all but abdicated the presidency in March when he said he would not stand for reelection that fall.

Inundated with all this, Sparky was ambivalent about America's involvement in Vietnam, as were unknown numbers of other Americans. Those who supported the war and those who opposed it were well-known as they spoke out. A third, silent group, perhaps a majority, thought the war was not worth the sacrifice but did not relish undercutting the soldiers fighting in the field. Like Sparky, they seemed to shift their positions as the war wore on. At first, Sparky opposed the administration's policy, then shifted to support the war, evidently more out of loyalty to President Johnson than out of conviction. Sparky's stance was, at best, lukewarm.

In contrast, Sparky was pleased about his appointment to the powerful Rules Committee under the guidance of the Speaker, John McCormack, and there made his mark as a skilled parliamentarian as well as on the floor of the House. The Rules Committee is a cabinet to assist the Speaker and other leaders of the unruly 435-member House in getting things done in a legislature then controlled by substantial Democratic majorities. The 15 members of the Rules Committee are among the most influential in the House and are considered to be part of the leadership.

In legislation, Sparky was enthusiastic about the Great Society, President Johnson's program designed to eliminate poverty. He was energetic in supporting a drive for greater civil rights and fought racism and discrimination whenever it came up. He asked Congress to repeal a "coolie" trade law that was obsolete but insulting, scolded members of Congress for careless use of pejorative expressions and got into a tiff with Vice President Spiro Agnew after Agnew uttered the word "Jap" in public.

Sparky continued to pursue causes that some of his colleagues thought fanciful. He tried to get Congress to adopt a perpetual calendar, to establish a poet laureate of the United States and to have the last surviving American square-rigged sailing ship, *Kaiulani,* returned to the U.S. Built in 1899 in Bath, Maine, *Kaiulani* had plied the sugar trade between Hawai'i and the West Coast until 1910. Subsequently, she was an Alaska fishing vessel, was used in a movie entitled *Souls at Sea,* carried lumber from Washington state to South Africa during World War II, then sailed to Tasmania after which she was ignominiously towed to Sydney and laid up as a coal hulk. *Kaiulani* was rescued by a Filipino businessman to carry lumber. Finally, President Diosdado Macapagal of the Philippines returned the vessel to the U.S., where Lyndon Johnson turned her over to the National Maritime Historical Society.

On one occasion, Sparky stuck his tongue in his cheek to claim that Japanese explorers, not the Viking Leif Ericson nor the Italian explorer sailing under a Spanish flag, Christopher Columbus, had discovered America. He offered legislation that would authorize a "Discover America First Day" as a national holiday. "The Italians would celebrate Columbus, the Scandinavians would celebrate Ericson, and I would celebrate the Japanese," he said. A historian wrote to say that his claim was not too far-fetched — that the first people to find North America were probably Asians who crossed the Bering Strait from Siberia to Alaska, and then migrated east of the Rocky Mountain to become the Indians of the Great Plains and Mexico.

As he gained seniority, Sparky moved into an office suite in the Cannon House Office Building numbered 442, which recalled, of course, the 442nd RCT. As he gained even more seniority, Sparky declined to move to newer and more desirable quarters because that return address on his mail to Hawai'i was too good to lose — even though he had not served in the 442nd RCT, it having arrived in Italy after he had been wounded.

When the 89th Congress convened in January 1965, the U.S. had been engaged in Vietnam for more than ten years, since the summer of 1954, longer than most Americans realize today. The numbers had grown from a handful of 350 American military people in 1955 to 23,300 in 1965; several Americans had been killed in action. At first, the American mission had been to advise the South Vietnamese government and army in its struggle with communist North Vietnam and its guerrilla arm in South Vietnam called the Viet Cong. The fight had not gone well for the South Vietnamese, and Americans had taken on more and more responsibility. Finally, in March 1965, President Johnson ordered the first ground combat troops from the Third Marine Division in Okinawa, Japan, to land in Vietnam. Soon after, they were authorized to begin offensive operations. The 173rd Airborne Brigade arrived from Okinawa in May and a brigade from the First Infantry Division in Ft. Riley, Kansas, landed in July. By the end of the year, 184,300 Americans were in Vietnam and 636 had been killed. That commitment expanded until it peaked in early 1969, when 543,400 American soldiers, marines, sailors and airmen were "in country."

Throughout this period, Sparky vacillated, perhaps because of his own experience in World War II and because he was beginning to form a conviction that negotiation, rather than fighting, was a better way to settle things. He seemed torn between his aversion to the American role in Vietnam and his allegiance to President Johnson, who was driving the nation into an ever-deeper morass. If Sparky, who vigorously objected to policies or decisions being made on the basis of race, had qualms about Americans bombing Asians, he appears not to have made them public, except once, late in the war.

In his first term in Congress, Sparky had backed the American advisory effort in Vietnam. He took part in a Marine Corps forum, asserting that the U.S. role "was not 'intervention' but an attempt to help the government of a newly independent nation to meet some of its most critical problems." He said, "The U.S. has no political ambitions in Southeast Asia." In response to calls for neutralizing South Vietnam, Sparky argued that such proposals ignored the fact "that North Vietnam continues flagrantly to violate" agreements not to interfere with South Vietnam nor to post forces in neighboring Laos. "There is no reason to believe that an agreement on neutralization reached today with North Vietnam would be respected by it any more than the previous Geneva agreements," he said.

In a letter to a constituent, Mrs. Ruth Snyder, in August 1964, Sparky said, "It is my belief that the actions of the United States in Vietnam must be directed toward the containment of the spread of hostilities in Southeast Asia....Having experienced war, I am for that action which will bring peace." He cautioned that a withdrawal of the U.S. from Vietnam could cause a bloodbath there and in Malaysia, Thailand, Burma, even in India.

Another constituent, Mrs. Carolyn Rankin, wrote in February 1965: "I would like to see our government pull out of Vietnam or allow our men to fight this war as they have been trained to do." Sparky replied, "The war in Vietnam is a real frustration." He again warned of aggression throughout Southeast Asia but not escalating the war to the point that Communist China entered it. "Our citizens would not want," he said, "a full-scale conventional war against a nation which can draw its supply of fighting men from a population of nearly 800 million." To a Californian, Jeff Elliott, Sparky wrote two weeks later in a similar vein: "The war in Vietnam is dreary, likely to be long and costly, of uncertain result unless we develop a strong South Vietnamese government capable of leading its own people — but very necessary."

During this time, Sparky began to be skeptical but took part in the debate in the House without openly attacking the President's policy. In an exchange with Representative Benjamin Rosenthal, a Democrat from New York who opposed President Johnson's stance on Vietnam, Sparky said, "I too was somewhat disturbed by the action that the President had taken in Vietnam....The question is: With whom do we negotiate? It takes two to negotiate."

Sparky asked Rosenthal if he thought the administration was making every effort to negotiate. Rosenthal replied that "perhaps those efforts would be more fruitful with a reduction in bombing." Sparky concluded, "I hope that his (Rosenthal's) thoughts will be conveyed to the administration."

Sparky's thinking on Vietnam was reflected in articles, polls and speeches he put into the Congressional Record, which allowed him to express a position without being controversial. When the first combat troops went into Vietnam, Sparky delivered a radio report to Hawai'i in which he said he had spoken with the President and Secretary of State Dean Rusk at a White House dinner. "I am now convinced," he said, "that the President has no intentions of escalating the war but is taking such steps as need to be taken towards bringing peace in Southeast Asia."

On negotiations, he quoted Rusk as saying, "The only response we have had from the Viet Cong has been an absolute denial of any direction or connection with the guerrilla warfare now going on in South Vietnam." Sparky rose on the floor in May to support the domino theory: "Whether we like it or not, we have made a commitment in Vietnam....For — let us make no mistake about it — if South Vietnam falls, the great arc of free-world defense between Korea and Pakistan will be in grave danger." Sparky argued, "The outcome in Vietnam is still uncertain. But our foreign aid program in South Vietnam is still keeping the embers of hope alive." He said it had two objectives: "To strike at the root causes of insurgency; and second, to help keep Vietnam's economy afloat and avoid disastrous inflation."

Sparky suggested that his mixed feelings on Vietnam could be seen in a letter to the editor in *The Honolulu Advertiser* by Charles Osgood of the University of Illinois, who was a visiting professor at the University of Hawai'i. Inserting it into the Congressional Record, Sparky said it was something "every responsible American should read." Osgood contended President Johnson had made clear that "we intend to escalate the conflict as far as necessary to obtain our objectives" even if that meant a "military confrontation with China or ultimately Russia." While the President said he wanted to negotiate a settlement, Osgood questioned, "Is it possible that neither President Johnson nor his intimate advisers have the foggiest idea of what could be gained by negotiation — or perhaps do not expect negotiations to materialize in any case?" Osgood concluded, "I'm afraid the administration has swallowed a baited hook. The bait was the temptation to use our awesome military power as a political tool."

Similarly, Sparky inserted an editorial from the *Honolulu Star-Bulletin* entitled "Morality and Vietnam." It noted, he said, "that hardly anyone in public life has raised the question of whether morality has any bearing on the U.S. position and its attitudes with respect to the war in Vietnam." Sparky applauded but did not offer his assessment of the moral position of the U.S. in Vietnam. He was more forthright in September when he said, "The Viet Cong's goal is the overthrow of the existing government."

Late in the year, Sparky joined a Congressional delegation led by Representative Clement Zablocki, a Democrat from Wisconsin and chairman of the House Foreign Affairs Subcommittee on East Asia, that spent a month in Saigon and other capitals in Southeast Asia. Henry Cabot Lodge, the American ambassador in Vietnam, took one look at Sparky and said, "Spark Matsunaga, aren't you the young man from Harvard Law School who went to Washington to lobby me for Hawaiian statehood?"

Sparky said, "How could you remember such a little incident which happened so many years ago?"

Ambassador Lodge replied, "It isn't too often that a U.S. Senator tears up his own 'Dear Colleague' letter."

The delegation stopped in New Delhi, India, where they ran into a band of Americans protesting the war. Zablocki, who was short-tempered, told them, "You are poor misguided souls." Sparky, in contrast, walked around the periphery of the protesters with one of them, Ann Maceachron of Ithaca, New York, and told her, "I once felt the way I think you now feel. But I've made a study of the situation, and now concur fully with the U.S. position. I think you're misinformed and sadly misguided." Sparky said later, "We must fulfill this commitment so other free nations in the area will have faith in our word. We must prove to the world that we will not tolerate any form of military aggression."

In Pakistan, the delegation was walking down a narrow street when a well-organized demonstration began with cheerleaders directing the crowd in chants of "Americans go home." Sparky, in an interview with *The Honolulu Advertiser*, recounted that he fell behind. "As the other Congressmen went on along, they were jeered and people stuck out their tongues. But as I went by, they cheered and shouted, 'Chinee, Chinee.'" Sparky said that when he got clear of the crowd, he turned and held up his hand. "I'm not Chinese, I'm American," he told the crowd. "I'm an American Congressman, but I'm of Asian descent — just like you." Sparky chuckled, "They didn't believe me. They cheered me again, thinking I was making fun of the Americans who walked ahead."

Sparky returned to Washington to tell United Press International: "More and more, I became convinced that the way to shorten the war was to show a greater determination to assist South Vietnam in ejecting all infiltrators from the north and proving to the North Vietnamese that we will not in any way tolerate military aggression as a means of international relations."

Early in 1966, Sparky vigorously supported economic aid to Vietnam, asserting that "little is known of our fight to provide a permanent line of defense in the struggle for men's minds in Vietnam." He cited the 9,000 school classrooms built in the last five years, 14 million textbooks, teacher training and a television network to reach into the hamlets for adult education. Reflecting his own wartime experience and showing that he could still be moved by tales of heroism in combat, Sparky inserted into the Congressional Record article after article about men at war, often those portraying soldiers from Hawai'i.

A pained letter from a constituent in early 1966 brought home the dilemma of Americans who disagreed with the U.S. role in the war but wanted to act within the law. Jack Gillmar, who was studying for an M.A. at Harvard, wrote: "From my knowledge of history and current events, I have decided that the position of my country in the Vietnam conflict is wrong. I view the hostilities there as basically an internal conflict and one in which we have no legal, national or international right to participate."

Gillmar asserted that he believed in the right of Americans to dissent from government decisions after "thoughtful consideration and clear conscience." On the other hand, he noted that "I am obligated by federal law to serve in the armed services of our country when drafted. You and your colleagues of Congress have put me in a difficult position." He asked if there was not an alternative, such as the Peace Corps or the War on Poverty.

Sparky wrote to Selective Service director Lewis B. Hershey, who replied that whether the Vietnam conflict was proper was outside the jurisdiction of Selective Service. Hershey repeated the standard formula that an American who based his objections on other than religious reasons did not qualify as a conscientious objector. Specifically, he said the Peace Corps and the War on Poverty were not substitutes for military service.

Gillmar said in a telephone interview later that he served in the Peace Corps for three years in Micronesia, during which the draft board did not call him up. When he left the Peace Corps, he was a few months shy of his 26th birthday, the cutoff date when he could be drafted, and was not called during that time. If he had been, he said, "I would definitely have left the country because I was not going to fight in a war I did not believe in."

Sparky's vacillation continued. He wrote to a constituent, Manning Ford, in July 1966, that peace came at "the price of having our friends, our loved ones, martyred on the battlefields of the world. This we must accept until men realize that these disputes can only be settled at the negotiation table. The war in Vietnam is not a popular war, but it is a necessary war."

He joined with 43 other Democrats and two Republicans in Congress a few days later in a statement denouncing South Vietnamese leaders for suggesting that South Vietnam invade North Vietnam. The Congressmen urged the Johnson administration "to redirect its energies more forcefully in pursuit of a peaceful, political settlement of the war." When Sparky announced in August that he would seek reelection, he made no mention of Vietnam. He joined 22 Congressmen to plead with North Vietnam to take part in a peace conference proposed by Thailand; Hanoi had earlier rejected the proposal.

"We strongly urge North Vietnam to reconsider its out-of-hand rejection of this proposal," the plea said. "It is difficult to understand why North Vietnam has failed to welcome such a conference." During the election campaign in October, Sparky attacked his Republican opponent, James Kealoha, for calling President

Johnson's Vietnam policy "one of the greatest blunders in American history." Instead, Sparky praised President Johnson for seeking a negotiated end to the war: "We have made every effort to bring the enemy to the negotiation table, but they have refused."

In the 1966 elections Sparky won handily as did fellow Democrat Patsy Mink, with 140,000 votes each, against two Republicans who got 62,000 to 67,000 votes in balloting for the two seats at large.

After he had been sworn in again, Sparky contended in March 1967 that the Rev. Martin Luther King, Jr., the African-American civil rights leader, was damaging the nation by opposing President Johnson on Vietnam. "Martin Luther King has called this an 'unjust war,'" Sparky said. "I'm all for dissenting views being expressed, but King is performing a disservice and may be helping to lengthen the war." Sparky asserted that the North Vietnamese leader, Ho Chi Minh, "realizes he cannot win militarily. He realizes he cannot win politically. He is now trying a third way….Ho will not come to the conference table as long as he thinks he is winning the war for public opinion."

Yet Sparky defended the right to protest, inserting into the Congressional Record a carefully wrought address on dissent by Judge Masato Doi, who had been decorated for his service in the 442nd RCT. "Expression of dissent," the judge said, "is not to be equated with treason." He had just acquitted a college student of contempt in an anti-war protest. A poster displayed by the student, Noel Kent, "was not intended to represent the American flag but was displayed by him as a symbolic portrayal of his violent disagreement with present American policy in Vietnam." Judge Doi said he personally favored U.S. policy in Vietnam but asserted, "Even if the idea is one which we despise, the answer is that in an atmosphere of freedom, truth will prevail in any contest with error."

When Senator William Fulbright, the chairman of the Senate Foreign Relations Committee, criticized President Johnson's Vietnam policy in a speech in Honolulu, Sparky charged that the Senator had made "no real effort to understand what the President is trying to do." Sparky told a gathering of teachers on the Big Island (Hawai'i), "Every step in the escalation has been a calculated step, calculated to prevent nuclear holocaust and calculated to prevent Russia and China from coming into Vietnam. The President deserves a lot of credit for what he is doing….If we did what the hawks propose, we'd be facing 100,000 Red Chinese soldiers the next day. The thing to remember is that the war could end tomorrow if Ho Chi Minh would come to the negotiating table."

A few days later, in August 1967, Sparky defended forthcoming elections in South Vietnam, saying that the government in Saigon should be credited with seeking to hold fair elections despite the obstacles thrown up by the war. He lamented in an interview with *The Honolulu Advertiser*, "Even when I make a talk on a specific subject not related to Southeast Asia, the matter of Vietnam always comes up in the question-and-answer period. There seems to be a feeling of 'What can we do about it?' 'How long will it last?' But the most frequent question is why big, powerful America doesn't go all out and crush North Vietnam. I tell them that it is not our policy to crush other governments. What we want is to give the South Vietnamese the opportunity to freely choose their leadership. If they choose communism, that's up to them but they cannot have it forced on them."

The casualties that military people from Hawai'i suffered in Vietnam may have affected Sparky's thinking. In May 1967, he put a report into the Congressional Record showing that the combat death ratio of soldiers, sailors, marines and airmen from Hawai'i for the period from January 1961 through February 1977 was by far the highest in the nation. Hawai'i had experienced 9.17 deaths per 100,000 in population, well ahead of West Virginia's 6.82. Part of that might be explained by a comparatively large number of military people stationed in Hawai'i before being sent to Vietnam.

In speeches during the summer and fall of 1967, mostly on trips back home to Hawai'i, Sparky hardly mentioned Vietnam. He talked instead about high school graduates going on with their education, about the challenges to Hawai'i of jet travel, about how young people should accept the responsibilities of good citizenship — without addressing the painful dilemma of military service in Vietnam. He deplored "the military drummer beating everlastingly in the background and the nation in a constant state of tension," and cast doubt on progress in reaching the goals of President Johnson's Great Society. Toward the end of the year, Sparky tried to lift up his audience by noting: "Ours is a nation going through an intensive creative period, a period marked by rapid changes demanding innovative adjustments." It was as if Sparky, like perhaps a majority of Americans, just wanted Vietnam to go away.

The Tet Offensive, named for the Vietnamese lunar New Year holiday, began on January 30, 1968, in an all-out Viet Cong campaign to persuade the South Vietnamese to join them in overthrowing the government in Saigon and driving the Americans into the sea. The Viet Cong nearly succeeded, breaching the walls of the American embassy in Saigon under the eyes of American television cameras before they were repelled. They captured the ancient capital at Hue, where they massacred 2,800 civilians, and mounted attacks against 30 of 44 provincial capitals. During the offensive, the U.S. suffered its worst rate of casualties during the week of February 10-17, when 543 were killed in action and 2,547 were wounded.

Late in February, the Viet Cong were driven out of Hue and the offensive petered out. They had failed to rouse the South Vietnamese but they had broken the back of political support for the war in America. President Johnson, in effect, abdicated on March 31 by stating that he would not be a candidate for reelection that fall. Three days later, the North Vietnamese agreed to begin negotiations.

Sparky was strangely silent during this episode. He had nothing to say on the floor of the House, and made no comments to the press. He seemed as shell-shocked as the rest of the nation. He did take to the floor to urge that the United Nations handle the North Korean seizure of the U.S. intelligence ship *Pueblo,* which the North Koreans had captured on the high seas off North Korea just before the Tet offensive.

During the Democratic presidential nominating convention in Chicago that summer, there was tumult inside the convention hall and on the streets where anti-war protesters and police fought pitched battles. Inside, Sparky said that Democrats "fight each other more than any other political beings" and pleaded for an end to quarreling between hawks and doves. "We are all Democrats concerned with attaining the earliest possible peace in Vietnam. In a real sense, the difference lies in the tactics to be applied in attaining peace in Vietnam — the goal is the same." Negotiations with the North Vietnamese made little progress as President Johnson ordered the bombing of North Vietnam to continue.

Sparky continued to have little to say about Vietnam until asked during his reelection campaign in the fall of 1968. At a meeting with editors of the *Honolulu Star-Bulletin,* Sparky was queried about whether he thought the U.S. should stop the bombing in an effort to entice the North Vietnamese to bargain seriously. "I feel that Vietnam is the prime issue facing the country today," Sparky replied. "Because of it, we have not been able to proceed as rapidly and in as full force as we would like on domestic problems. To effect an early settlement in Vietnam, I feel that we have got to remain flexible, bearing in mind that flexibility arises only out of our known strength, not weakness. Any settlement in South Vietnam is going to be made politically, not militarily. For this reason, when Vice President Humphrey (Hubert H. Humphrey, the Democratic nominee for President in 1968) offered his proposals to go one step beyond where President Johnson had gone, I immediately came out in support of his position on the basis that the risk would be worth taking. If the proposed bombing halt appears likely to lead to serious peace negotiations, we ought to take that risk."

Asked whether that would help Humphrey's chances, Sparky said, "I would say it would have a profound effect on the chances of Mr. Humphrey being elected." Sparky left the issue there until after the election in which Humphrey was defeated and Richard Nixon elected.

In contrast to his uncertainty about Vietnam, Sparky was enthusiastic about joining the Rules Committee. As the 90th Congress was being organized in January 1967, Speaker John McCormack, Majority Leader Carl Albert and majority whip Hale Boggs of Louisiana approached Sparky to ask him to serve on the committee. Sparkly accepted with alacrity. He was relatively junior to be selected, most members having had six to 12 years of service before joining the committee.

Sparky was chosen for several reasons, perhaps chief among them was his friendship with the Speaker. When McCormack was asked whether he had consulted the Rules Committee chairman before appointing Sparky, he replied, "Absolutely not. The Rules Committee is an arm of the leadership and the Speaker must have complete freedom to select those members on whose personal loyalty he can reasonably depend." There was speculation that McCormack had chosen Sparky because all members of the Rules Committee were white and Sparky provided minority representation. McCormack denied this.

By this point, Sparky was seen as a team player who voted with the Democratic Party 80 percent of the time. He held what was known as a "safe seat," having been elected three times by large margins, which meant that he could vote on some issues without worrying too much about what the voters back home might think. The appointment meant giving up his place on other committees because House regulations said members of the Rules Committee could not serve on other committees; that would have given them too much power.

When Sparky left the Agriculture Committee, where he could protect the sugar industry and other agricultural interests in Hawai'i, that caused some consternation back home. Criticism came mostly from vested interests and people who didn't understand how Washington worked or the importance of the Rules Committee.

The Rules Committee sorts through the 15,000 bills introduced in any one Congress, including those coming over from the Senate. Of those, 3,000 would be considered by legislative committees such as Ways and Means, Interior, Agriculture, Commerce, Armed Services or Foreign Affairs. After committee hearings and votes, bills that are reported out go to the Rules Committee, which decides whether a bill will go to the floor and in what order, the length of the debate and whether amendments will be allowed.

The Rules Committee acts as a court of appeals when other committees bottle up bills. Its decision on the conditions under which a bill will reach the floor is called a "rule," and the rule must be approved by a majority of the House. The chairman of the Rules Committee determines which member of the committee will manage the parliamentary process under which the rule will be considered. Rarely, and only after complicated proceedings, does the House overturn a rule proposed by the committee. The Rules Committee screens out bills that a Congressman has introduced to please a constituent or pressure group but which would have made bad law, taking the heat while the pressured Congressman escapes the wrath of his voters. The committee does not have life-and-death control over the legislative process but it can come close, and its members are among the most influential in the House.

When Sparky joined the committee, he was seated next to Representative Thomas P. "Tip" O'Neill, the Democrat from Massachusetts who was later to become Speaker of the House. Sparky said that he and Tip "recognized ourselves in each other: 'work-and-wage Democrats' of immigrant stock who had come up the hard way, gaining our political experience in our respective State and Territorial houses." Sparky went on: "It was from him that I learned 'The Rules of the Road' of poet John Boyle O'Reilly, wisdom-in-rhyme which has served me in good stead." O'Reilly was an Irish revolutionary convicted by the British and sent to a penal colony in Australia. From there he escaped to America where he became editor of a newspaper in Boston. Excerpts from the poem include these words of caution:

"Who heeds not experience, trust him not."
"When honor comes to you, be ready to take it;
　But reach not to seize it before it is near."
"Be silent and safe — silence never betrays you;
　Be true to your word and your work and your friend;
Put least trust in him who is foremost to praise you,
　Nor judge of a road till it draw to the end."
　"Good neighbor and citizen; these for a code,
And this truth in sight, — every man on the planet
　Has just as much right as yourself to the road."

After several years on the committee, Sparky wrote a book about the Rules Committee with the help of a scholar, Dr. Ping Chen of Eastern Illinois University.

It provided a rare glimpse of the inside workings of a committee that operated then in secrecy, holding executive sessions behind closed doors, voting by hand and not recording who voted for what and publishing no minutes. The book, entitled *Rulemakers of the House*, was reasonably candid, with Sparky illuminating his successes and his failures.

In one instance, Sparky found a way around a legislative roadblock by proposing that the committee report out a bill with a Senate amendment to extend a Voting Rights Act to give 18-year-olds the right to vote. Representative Richard Bolling, a Democrat from Missouri, backed Sparky's proposal, arguing, "There is a strong possibility that unless we accept the Senate bill we will never have an opportunity to take further action on the matter. I urge that we support Matsunaga's resolution since a conference would not work." Sparky's proposal was voted out of the committee and adopted by the House.

When Sparky wanted to be the floor manager of a bill to extend the Sugar Act, however, he was preempted by a more senior member, Representative B.F. Sisk of California, whose constituents were equally interested in sugar. Another time, Sparky stubbed his toe with the committee chairman, Representative William Colmer of Mississippi, a crusty Southerner who was protective of his prerogatives. Sparky had asked a staff aide to put a bill on the committee agenda without first clearing it with the chairman. In an executive session, Colmer berated Sparky for what the chairman saw as an infringement on his authority and refused to schedule Sparky's bill, in effect killing it. Sparky did not make that mistake again.

A dilemma confronted Sparky when a bill to extend the military draft came before the Rules Committee. He was adamantly opposed to the bill and let it be known that he would oppose reporting it out. On the other hand, the Democratic leaders thought it necessary to keep the draft going so long as the U.S. was engaged in Vietnam. Carl Albert, by this time the Speaker, beckoned Sparky to his desk on the floor one day to ask, "Sparky, you're okay on the rule for the draft conference report, aren't you?" When Sparky said he intended to vote against it, Albert suggested a way out: Vote for the rule on the bill in the committee, then vote against it on the floor. Sparky, out of loyalty to his party's leadership, did so.

As a floor manager, Sparky was in his element. An early test came not long after he had been appointed to the Rules Committee, when he was named to manage the rule on a bill that would continue civilian government over the Trust Territory of the Pacific Islands. It was a relatively uncontroversial bill that would provide modest increases in spending on the Caroline, Marshall and Mariana Islands (except Guam, a U.S. territory) that the U.S. administered under a trusteeship set by the United Nations. Sparky explained the bill and the rule, which was followed by brief debate and the adoption of the rule.

In October 1967, Sparky ran into a little more trouble in managing the rule on a bill that would prohibit the obstruction of criminal investigations; a legislature full of lawyers might have been expected to approve it easily. Sparky opened, "My colleagues will be amazed to learn, as I was, I'm sure, that under the present law there is no protection for potential witnesses prior to the institution of proceedings."

Representative Basil Whitner, a Democrat from North Carolina, rose to object to a word in the proposed bill. Representative Emanuel Celler, a Democrat from New York and chairman of the Judiciary Committee, readily agreed to an amendment but declined to accept that of Representative William Hungate, a Democrat from Missouri. And so it bounced from Congressman to Congressman, and Sparky's head moved back and forth as if he were watching a tennis match.

Finally, Representative Wayne Hays, a Democrat from Ohio who was considered a curmudgeon, said, "I had understood that this was a little, non-controversial bill. It does not seem to be so little and so non-controversial." He added, "I do not want any part of this bill. If you are going to bring it up tonight, I just want you to know that I am going to insist on a quorum being here while we discuss this little, non-controversial and unimportant piece of legislation." Sparky noted, apparently with relief, that there were no further requests to speak and asked for a vote. The resolution passed.

In October 1968, Sparky got into a quarrel with Representative H.R. Gross, the Republican from Iowa whom former Speaker Thomas Foley called "the conscience of the House." Gross arrived in his office every day early in the morning, read every bill coming up and spent much of the day on the floor; a biography said he answered 95 percent of the roll calls. He introduced little legislation himself but closely questioned advocates of bills, especially on cost.

In this case, Sparky sought a rule for a two-hour debate on the National Foundation on the Arts and the Humanities Act, a cause dear to his heart. In opening the debate on the floor, Sparky quickly summarized the bill, which would give the foundation $55 million in 1969 and $80 million in 1970. Sparky had barely finished when Gross was on his feet, drilling Sparky on the numbers.

Gross said, "All I was trying to do was to find out how, in all conscience, the Rules Committee would bring out a rule on this bill if the amount involved exceeds the President's budget figure. The President (Johnson) is apparently calling for austerity. If the President means what he says and says what he means, how did this bill get a rule?"

Sparky tried to pass off the criticism lightly: "The Rules Committee, of course, considers things which are of the spirit as well as of money. This is a good bill and I am sure that if the gentleman from Iowa supports the bill, he will some-day while on his rocking chair, in speaking to his grandchildren, say with pride 'I supported that bill.'"

Gross snapped, "That is what the gentleman from Hawai'i thinks, and only what he thinks. If I ever get to a rocking chair, I will not be talking about this kind of expenditure in a day and age when the government and the taxpayers are sur-feited with debt." Gross continued, "Where does the gentleman propose to get the money for this purpose?"

Sparky asserted the taxpayers "would be more than willing to pay for a program as noble as this which will continue the great cultural aspects of our civilization."

Gross: "I wonder how high a price you are putting on spirit these days. I do not know what kind of spirit or spirits you are talking about."

Sparky: "As the gentleman knows, if we look back into the history of mankind, we will find that those characteristics of civilization which have lived on to this day are those which deal with the spirit, the arts and the humanities."

Gross was unrelenting and Sparky sought to toss the ball to others. Gross interrupted sarcastically, "I thought the gentleman was an expert on this subject. He apparently voted for it in the Rules Committee or he would not be handling the rule."

Representative John Anderson, the Republican from Illinois who was a member of the Rules Committee and later a third-party candidate for President, questioned the wisdom of appropriating funds for the arts when the war in Vietnam was soaking up billions of dollars. "Until that war has been finished, it ought to be the main business of this country, of this government and its people."

Gross was pleased and turned to renew his debate with Sparky: "Since the gentleman from Hawai'i apparently voted to give a rule to this monstrosity, and is something of an expert on it, I wonder if he could tell me whether a $2-million allocation has been made for scholarships to research."

Sparky, evidently exasperated, said, "I will have the gentleman know that the gentleman from Florida (Claude Pepper) was supposed to handle this rule, and he is really expert in this area, but I was called upon at the last minute to present the rule in the absence of the gentleman from Florida. I am not making excuses but I am just telling the facts." With relief, he yielded to Representative Frank Thompson, a Democrat from New Jersey , who said, "I am fascinated by the Doc Gross show." After batting down several of Gross's erroneous assumptions, Thompson said, "I am willing to answer the gentleman from Iowa with respect to any number of obviously frivolous and fictitious grants which he named. I do not mind playing games with him. I think he has a great sense of humor."

Thompson defended the bill at some length but Sparky got control of the debate again to remind the House, "We are now considering the rule, not the merits of the bill. We on the Rules Committee have in the past been chastised for not giving the House the opportunity." Representative Frank Annunzio, a Democrat from Illinois, interrupted to ask when was the last time the House failed to adopt a rule. Sparky, apparently weary of the wrangling, said, "When the rule on the rat control bill was first considered." He did not elaborate. Representative Ogden Reid, a Republican from New York, interjected, "A majority of the Republicans on the committee voted for this bill coming to the floor." Sparky thanked him, moved the previous question and got the resolution passed.

Although Sparky got bumped around occasionally, within a couple of years he had mastered the intricacies of parliamentary procedure, quietly making a reputation for fair play, being accessible to members of both parties and for economy in his arguments. The Democrats controlled the House during Sparky's tenure there, which, of course, contributed to his standing. Sparky had become so influential by 1972 that Majority Leader Hale Boggs told a researcher from the activist Ralph Nader's office, "It's getting to the point where you have to see Sparky Matsunaga to get a bill passed around here."

When Sparky returned to Hawai'i in October 1968 to campaign for reelection, his Republican opponent, Mayor Neal Blaisdell of Honolulu, accused him of being "irresponsible" for giving up a seat on the Agriculture Committee to join the Rules Committee. He asserted that Sparky "prefers self-prestige to performance." The mayor, who was evidently not well-informed about the workings of Washington, appeared not to understand that members of the Rules Committee had a throttle on legislation, including bills on agriculture, and could either kill them or see that they got to the floor.

Blaisdell contended that Sparky would lose his place on the Rules Committee if Richard Nixon was elected. Noting that the majority party had ten seats on the committee, Blaisdell declared, "He is the ninth-ranking Democrat and would be the first to go in a Republican administration." Blaisdell apparently did not understand that the U.S. does not have a parliamentary government and that control of House committees changed only when a different party gained control of the chamber, not when the White House changed hands.

Sparky defended himself in an interview with the *Honolulu Star-Bulletin*: "Perhaps I can best state it by quoting Speaker of the House McCormack who said that 'membership on the Rules Committee is equivalent to membership on all standing committees.' He went on: "Having a seat on the Rules Committee is like having 19 additional Congressmen from the district the member serves.' The Rules Committee is the top committee of all committees." Sparky noted that "the Civil Rights Act of 1968 came out of this committee by an 8-7 vote. So did the Higher Education Act, the Vocational Education Act, the Federal Pay Raise Act, the Gun Control Act and others. You can see the importance of my one vote: Hawai'i's vote."

In the election a few weeks later, the voters chose Sparky over Blaisdell by more than twice as many votes, 161,950 to 78,730, sending Sparky back to Washington for a fourth term.

Throughout these middle years in his tenure in the House, Sparky was vigilant for any trace of racism or discrimination. He introduced a bill in 1966 to repeal the "coolie" trade laws that had been on the books since 1862 and 1875 to prevent Chinese and Japanese laborers from being imported as indentured servants. "However commendable they may have been at one time," Sparky told the House, "these laws are obsolete." He argued that the word "coolie" carries "an unfortunate connotation" in Asia, and people in Hawai'i, with its large population of Asian descent, were more sensitive than other Americans to the image generated by these laws. ("Coolie" is derived from the Chinese *ku-li*, meaning hard labor.) Eliminating the laws, Sparky asserted, "would remove a possible source of misunderstanding and promote better relations between the United States and Asian countries."

There was no debate and the bill was passed immediately by voice vote. The Senate, however, did not act on the law and Sparky was back the next year with the same bill and the same words. The bill was passed again without debate but it took Sparky several years before he could get the repeal through the Senate and to the President for signature.

Things were not nearly so bland when amendments of a voting rights bill were being debated. Democratic Representative Basil Whitener, a Southerner from North Carolina who opposed the bill, stated: "So if you have a Chinaman running for Congress out in California and some Japanese *nisei* stands up in a crowd and yells, 'I do not like Chinese and I do not think he has any business in Congress,' and then throws an egg at the Chinaman and a piece of eggshell scratches the eyelid, we are going to put the Japanese in the penitentiary for ten years or take $10,000 from him or both. That is how absurd this bill is." Whitener went on in that vein. (Sparky said he heard Whitener use the word "Jap," although the Congressional record shows "Japanese." "Chinaman" to a Chinese-American has the same pejorative connotation as "Jap" to a Japanese-American.)

When Sparky was recognized, he was seething. "I take it the gentleman means, by 'Chinaman,' a Chinese-American or American of Chinese descent?"

"I mean a Chinaman" Whitener snapped. "He may be a red Chinese Chinaman. He might be from Red China and might just have gotten off the boat, from a stowaway position, off a slow boat from Red China."

Sparky asked, "And by 'Jap,' the gentleman means American of Japanese descent?"

Whitener, apparently realizing he was being led into a trap, shifted his ground. "Of course, this is all irrelevant. Perhaps my knowledge of the English language is not as good as it should be. I believe my knowledge of what this bill will do is fairly accurate. Suppose we strike out any reference to *nisei* and Chinese and let it be Greeks and Arabs, or Greeks and Turks."

"In this day of international tension," said Sparky coolly, "perhaps the suggestion to strike out all derogatory references to any racial group would be acceptable to this august body." In the end, the House rejected the amendment that Whitener supported.

About the same time, Sparky received a telegram from Gladys Mizuno, a voter in Hawai'i who was in New York, protesting dialogue in a TV serial about Batman and Robin that referred to "shifty-eyed Japs in America." She asked, "Was the AJA World War II sacrifice so meaningless that we remain silent?"

Sparky shot off a letter to Thomas Moore, president of ABC-TV, noting the objectionable terms and asked that they be not be repeated. He sent a copy to Ms. Mizuno, who hastened to tell Sparky that the film she had seen was a World War II revival, not a current serial. Sparky immediately corrected the record with Moore, who thanked Sparky for setting things straight and noted that "our programming department puts forth a great deal of effort to ensure that our shows are entertaining without being offensive."

Similarly, Frank Hayashi of Bellrose, New York, sent Sparky a copy of a letter he had written to the *Long Island Press* objecting to the word "Jap" in headlines, such as "Japs as Dodgers to bring Koufax" and "Jap girls announce ball games." Hayashi pointed out how derogatory the term was to Japanese-Americans and asked the paper to refrain from using them. Sparky was campaigning in Hawai'i but a staff aide wrote Hayashi to ask him to write Sparky again if the *Long Island Press* persisted in using the offending term.

During the 1968 election race, Spiro Agnew, the Republican vice presidential candidate, walked into the back of the campaign plane to talk with the press and noted that Gene Oishi of the *Baltimore Sun*, whom he called a "fat Jap," was asleep.

That got out and, along with Agnew's references to Poles as "Polacks," raised a hullabaloo. Sparky jumped up in the House to ask to speak out of order and said, "Webster defines 'Jap' as a shortened form of 'Japanese' used in contempt. Mr. Agnew knows, or should have known, this. He should be instructed that one does not make friends by insulting people of other racial backgrounds, particularly through mouthings of racial prejudice." Agnew, who by chance was in Hawai'i a day later, was unrepentant despite the large Japanese-American community in Hawai'i, asserting that Democrats "must really be desperate" to bring this up during a political campaign.

Earlier in the same campaign, Sparky widened his focus on racial issues in a speech to Japanese-Americans in California in which he said that poverty, more than anything else, spawned race riots. He blamed the war in Vietnam for soaking up funds that should have gone into President Johnson's War on Poverty: "It is clear that the War on Poverty could have been fought with greater success if we had been able to give it our undivided national attention and our undiluted national resources."

Referring to the World War II experience of Japanese-Americans being thrown into concentration camps, Sparky said, "Many of you present here tonight are acquainted with the horror of racial hatred." He went on to say, "Japanese-Americans have overcome the forces of prejudice as have others before them, and they have joined the mainstream of American democracy. There is no reason to believe that the Negro-Americans will not in time overcome their difficulties, too."

In legislation, among Sparky's favorite proposals was to have the United States establish the position of poet laureate similar to that in Britain. He brought this up as an amendment to the National Foundation on the Arts and the Humanities Act in February 1968, and delivered carefully crafted remarks to support his case. "It is the encouragement of man's creative imagination for an even more intense practice of the lovelier energies with which we are here concerned," he said. "We have established in the sciences that the possibilities for invention are limited only by the degree to which we are willing to encourage further investigation. It is within our power to unleash the same unlimited potential for creativity in the arts.

"The arts and the humanities," Sparky continued, "have made great contributions to our understanding of the first two-thirds of the 20th Century. The rise of science and the pestilence of war, however, have dominated the temper of our times. If man is to transcend his own inventions in the age of the computer, in the age of potential annihilation, we must give equal consideration to the regenerative forces of the arts and humanities. We cannot continue to rationalize the economic plight of the American humanist." He concluded, "Who can deny that out of this humble body may some day arise a mind pregnant with celestial inspiration, whose greatness may be heightened by his aspirations to become Poet Laureate of the United States."

Sparky evidently held the chamber in thrall but Frank Thompson, the Democrat from New Jersey, rose to say and, as much as he regretted opposing Sparky's proposal, the amendment was not germane to the bill itself and should not be allowed. He was upheld by the chair. The poet laureate issue was thus put off for another day.

Sparky's forward-looking views were perhaps best seen in his advocacy for gun control, an argument that has continued into the 21st Century. In July 1968, he urged passage of a firearms control bill, asserting, "The evidence makes it over-whelmingly clear that there is an urgent need for stronger gun control legislation." Among the statistics he cited: "Privately-owned firearms have caused more American deaths since the turn of the century than all the wars in which the nation has been engaged. Some 630,000 Americans have been killed in war since 1776 as compared to 800,000 persons who have been killed by privately-owned firearms since 1900." He concluded, "We have seen the growing use of firearms in violent crimes in this nation. To allow this trend to go unchecked is to render a great dis-service to the American people. It is now time to lay aside specious objections and see what strong gun control laws can do to reduce America's horrendous crime rate."

In contrast to Sparky's vision on gun control, he was at his whimsical best when he introduced legislation in September 1967 that would have mandated what was known as a "perpetual calendar." Devised by Dr. Willard Edwards of Honolulu, it would place the same date on the same day every year. Each quarter would have two 30-day months and one 31-day month. That would leave one extra day, New Year's Day, that would not be in any month but would be set apart from the others and called January 0 in computers.

He told the House, "Lest it be considered a crackpot of an idea, I have given the proposed calendar and its creator my very serious study." He contended, "The perpetual calendar is a scientific plan to correct the two costly faults of our present calendar, unequal divisions and lack of fixity. Its approval by this body will hasten the date of its adoption. Its civil use will actually save hundreds of thousands of hours and dollars now lost annually through needless accounting and calculation caused by existing calendar irregularities."

Workers paid by the hour, for instance, earn less in February but have the same monthly bills. For accounting and comparative purposes, Sparky said, "There is actually no such thing as a comparable period in our present calendar system."

He contended, "The perpetual calendar will permit everyone to celebrate his birthday, wedding anniversary and all holidays on the same day of the week every year. This will make it easy to remember anniversaries."

The Congressional Record does not show how many people were on the floor when Sparky spoke but it does show that no one objected. Indeed, no member of Congress had anything to say, pro or con, to the proposal and it was chalked up to another of Sparky Matsunaga's quixotic ideas. The bill was referred to the Committee on Foreign Affairs, for reasons lost to history, and so far as could be determined, was never heard of again.

One day while listening to a debate drone on in the House, Sparky put his head back to daydream and found himself counting the stars surrounding the Great Seal of the United States on the ceiling. To his horror, he found only 48 instead of 50 and asked Speaker McCormack to have that corrected. Later, a highlight of a tour of the Capitol was the guide's account of how Sparky's stars got put up: "Within the center of the ceiling is the great American eagle and encircling it are 50 stars for the 50 states. Originally, there were only 48 stars when the freshman Representative from Hawai'i, Spark Matsunaga, took the oath of office. He was the first Representative to count the stars and noted only 48. He then asked the Speaker of the House, John McCormack, when would the two stars for Alaska and Hawai'i be added. The Speaker retorted if the Representative from Hawai'i could find another member of the House who would count the stars while sitting in the Chamber, he would add the other two stars. Representative Matsunaga asked two friends, Bob Leggett and John Hanna, both Representatives at that time, if they would count the stars and verify the amount to the Speaker. They counted 48 and presented their findings to the Speaker. With that, the Speaker told Spark that he would have the stars added as soon as the House adjourned. On that note, Representative Matsunaga requested that Hawai'i's be added at the head of the eagle instead of the tail."

Sparky teased his colleagues from Alaska to make sure they understood that the extra star at the eagle's head was that of Hawai'i. ❖

Divided Government
1969–1976

When the 91st Congress convened in January 1969, Sparky returned to Washington as an experienced, respected and popular legislator in a Democratic Party that continued to control the House and the Senate. His political life, however, underwent wrenching changes. The election of Richard Nixon, a Republican, as President and of Spiro Agnew, a former governor of Maryland, as Vice President, gave the U.S. a government divided between the Republican White House and the Democratic Congress. Divided government has almost always been difficult and was all the more so then because the tumult over Vietnam roared on with full force. For Sparky, not since his days in the Legislature of Hawai'i, when Republicans Samuel Wilder King and William Quinn had been appointed to the governor's chair, had he served in a divided government.

Sparky didn't much care for President Nixon or Vice President Agnew either ideologically or personally, although former Representative Don Fuqua, Sparky's friend from Florida, said, "He tried not to let it show in public." During these years, Agnew would be forced from office in disgrace and Nixon would resign to escape impeachment. Representative Gerald R. Ford, the Republican from Michigan and Minority Leader of the House, whom Sparky liked and respected despite their political differences, succeeded to the vice presidency and, in 1974, to the presidency.

In those years, peace talks with North Vietnam dragged on, anti-war demonstrations grew, four students at Kent State University in Ohio were killed by National Guardsmen and the nation was shocked when the My Lai massacre in Vietnam was revealed. Publication of the Pentagon Papers, a secret history of the war, stimulated more anti-war sentiment but the B-52 bombing of North Vietnam in late 1972 brought the North Vietnamese back to the negotiating table where an agreement was reached in early 1973. American troops were out of Vietnam by the end of March although the last Americans did not leave until April 1975, when they barely escaped before the onrushing North Vietnamese forces entered Saigon.

This was the era of Watergate, when Republican undercover operatives were caught breaking into Democratic Party offices in the Watergate complex. President Nixon was reelected in a landslide in 1972 but the White House's role in Watergate overshadowed his accomplishments in foreign policy. His opening to China in 1972 and his visit to Moscow, the first by an American President, later that same year to forge a strategic arms agreement with the Soviet Union were notable.

Change in Sparky's political life came not only from divided government but the retirement of his mentor, Speaker John McCormack, who was succeeded by Representative Carl Albert of Oklahoma. Sparky was a friend of Albert's but not so close as McCormack. Even so, in early 1973 Albert made him a deputy whip, whose task was to help rally Democratic members to the leadership's banner. That, along with his place on the Rules Committee and later on the Democratic Policy Steering Committee, which sought to bring cohesion to the Democratic legislative program, cemented Sparky's place in the House leadership.

Nixon's presidency, moreover, freed Sparky from his loyalties to President Johnson over Vietnam. Sparky soon turned against the U.S. military engagement there, denounced Nixon harshly and, for the first time, raised the cry of racism in U.S. policy. Sparky vigorously supported a drive to curb the President's ability to get the nation into war without Congressional approval, and was an outspoken leader in the campaign to eliminate the military draft and to form a volunteer armed force. He backed voting rights for 18-year-olds, he said, "because they have earned the right to vote by bearing the responsibilities of citizenship," a reference to military service. In foreign policy, Sparky spoke for an independent Taiwan, the island off the coast of China claimed by Beijing, at the same time President Nixon was seeking an opening to China that would include an ambiguous stand on Taiwan.

On civil rights, Sparky led the struggle to repeal a law known as the McCarran Act that permitted the government to detain American citizens without trial on suspicion of disloyalty. He took up the cause of a Japanese-American woman known as "Tokyo Rose" who had been unjustly accused of treason and helped to get her a pardon from President Ford. He resumed his effort to have the "coolie" trade laws repealed. And when a lawyer for White House officials in the Watergate hearings referred to Senator Daniel Inouye as a "little Jap," Sparky hit the ceiling.

In legislation, Sparky supported most tax reforms. He advocated laws to help preserve newspapers and helped to push through laws that required elected officials to disclose their financial standings. He supported a Constitutional amendment that would have provided for direct election of the President instead of through the electoral college, an issue that came up again when President George

W. Bush was elected in 2000 with a minority in the popular vote but a majority in electoral votes.

Sparky argued for increases in social security benefits and was successful in pushing through environmental legislation that placed controls on dumping waste in the ocean. He lost a debate over whether the nation should adopt the metric system. Sparky proposed that the government establish a Department of Peace that would pull together foreign aid and related activities but it sounded like another State Department and got little support. He fought for reform in campaign financing, a battle still going on more than a quarter century later.

For Hawai'i, Sparky fought a losing battle to retain price supports for sugar, a dying industry because the cost of union labor made Hawaiian sugar less competitive. He campaigned for funds for the memorial to those who died aboard the battleship *U.S.S. Arizona* on December 7, 1941. He was not successful in getting an amendment intended to protect jobs at the Pearl Harbor shipyard but managed to have Hawai'i exempted from daylight saving time because "Hawai'i is further south and closer to the Equator than any other state in the Union" with less variation in the length of days.

Sparky occasionally took stands that seemed out of character. Although he considered himself a man of science and technology, he opposed the supersonic transport (SST) aircraft because its noise concerned people in Hawai'i. "This is a kind of pollution nobody needs or wants," Sparky said. Despite his stand for civil liberties and against political oppression, he praised President Park Chung Hee of South Korea when he was inaugurated in Seoul in 1971 after having been elected by questionable means and having demonstrated many attributes of the dictator he would become.

On the lighter side, Sparky had a running rhetorical battle with Representative H.R. Gross, the dour Republican from Iowa. Sparky, who loved the give-and-take of civil disputation, more than once rose to Gross's bait. One day in the spring of 1970, Sparky brought to the floor a bill intended to encourage tourism in national parks, just the sort of expenditure the parsimonious Gross disliked. Gross opposed the bill as unnecessary and took a swipe at members of Congress "junketing out to Hawai'i."

Calmly, Sparky replied, "If the gentleman had gone on any one of the trips, I believed he would have returned a more knowledgeable and happier man and able to make greater contributions to the nation through better legislation."

Later, Gross wanted to know if Hawai'i received a form of foreign aid known as counterpart funds. Sparky replied, "No. I will have the gentleman know, although the gentleman may not have voted for the bill, that Hawai'i was admitted as a state of the Union in 1959."

As Sparky brought up a bill to extend an international coffee agreement that benefited Hawai'i, the only state in the U.S. that grows coffee, Gross growled that it would raise coffee prices for consumers. Sparky said, "The last time the gentleman from Iowa raised a question about a product of Hawai'i, he confessed he had never tasted Hawai'i's delectable papaya. I hope the gentleman is not saying he has not enjoyed our Kona coffee."

Gross was no slouch himself when it came to debating points. He once introduced a resolution that he managed to have titled H.R. 144, a play on his name. Another time, Sparky brought up a bill for the Rules Committee with a provision that Gross approved. The Iowan, who intensely disliked the Rules Committee, exclaimed, "This is the fourth rule presented in about 20 minutes that is wide open: No waivers or points of order. The legislation which it makes in order is subject to amendment. Mr. Speaker, this massive atonement of the Rules Committee for its errors of omission and commission in the past is almost unbearable."

One day in 1969, Sparky asked a favor of his friend, Speaker McCormack. A new statue of Father Damien of Moloka'i had caused curiosity among visitors to the Capitol. Police officers told Sparky that people had questions about the boxy frame and deformed face of the Belgian priest. So Sparky called Governor Burns to ask for an explanatory plaque to be affixed to the base. When it arrived, Sparky learned that it was against the rules to have such signs in the Hall of Statues so he went to Speaker McCormack to ask for an exemption. The Speaker said he couldn't break the rules even for a friend.

Sparky said, "I put on my saddest countenance — my most hangdog expression — and slunk slowly toward the door." Then he heard the Speaker say, "If you put it up when I'm not looking, I may not order it to be taken down." Sparky had the sign quietly put up, then invited the Speaker to a ceremony marking the occasion — and to make sure no one took it down.

On the overriding issue of President Nixon's role in Watergate, Sparky said in the spring of 1973 he did not think the President would be impeached. By fall, he had swung around to say impeachment was inevitable and that 98 percent of the mail from his constituents favored dismissing the President. "Right now, I can't see how Congress is going to escape that course unless the sentiment of the people takes a different course," he told an audience in Honolulu. To another group, he said, "Don't be surprised if the President, within the next few weeks or months, resigns from office." At the end of 1973, Sparky opined, "If the investigation now in progress warrants it, we must proceed with the impeachment of the President to restore faith in the American system."

Meantime, Vice President Agnew resigned after being investigated for bribery, extortion, tax fraud and conspiracy. Agnew pleaded no contest to tax evasion and on October 10, 1973, just before he was fined $10,000 and sentenced to three years on probation, he resigned. Sparky was surprised, saying he thought Agnew "would fight to the bitter end." He added that he would have no problem voting for a Republican replacement: "It would be unthinkable that the President would name anyone other than a Republican."

After Nixon nominated Ford to be Vice President, Sparky said, "I have not agreed with Jerry Ford on many issues in the 11 years I have served in the House, but his conduct has been such as to elicit my respect for the man despite his understandably misguided position on the issues. He has been highly partisan at times but so have we all on occasion. Besides, under our two-party system, as minority leader he has had to play his assigned role as the villain. And those of us with theatrical experience know that the villain's role is the most difficult to play." In a serious vein, Sparky applauded Ford's integrity, saying, "I have learned one unimpeachable thing about him: Jerry Ford always keeps his word."

In the winter and spring of 1974, Nixon's position was steadily eroded when several key aides were indicted for covering up the Watergate break-in and Nixon himself was named an "unindicted co-conspirator." Nixon sought to suppress tape recordings of conversations in the Oval Office but the Supreme Court ruled against his claim of executive privilege. About the same time, the House Judiciary Committee voted to impeach Nixon for obstructing justice, abusing presidential power and refusing to obey House subpoenas. After that, it seemed clear that Nixon would be impeached by the House and convicted in the Senate. On August 8, he resigned and left office the next day. Vice President Ford was sworn in as President.

Like others in Congress, Sparky pledged to support President Ford but that did not last long. When the new President unexpectedly pardoned Nixon in September, Sparky was displeased but not so openly as many other Democratic leaders. "I'm afraid this will cause millions of Americans," he said, "to lose faith in the initial strong favorable disposition which they had toward our new President."

By 1969, a majority of Americans had either given up on the Vietnam War or were actively opposed to it and demanded a withdrawal of U.S. forces. In his campaign for the presidency, Nixon had claimed to have a plan, which events showed he didn't, to end the war with honor. Instead, the armed forces were condemned to fight for four more years with little public support. At the end of 1968, some 30,600 Americans had been killed in action. By the end of 1973, after American forces had gone home, that number had risen to 46,163. Another 12,000 had died of illness, accidents or other non-combat causes.

Sparky began to turn against the war when he campaigned for Vice President Hubert Humphrey in his 1968 presidential campaign against Nixon. After Nixon won the election, Sparky became outspoken in opposition. Invited to address the Veterans of Foreign Wars in Honolulu in June 1969, Sparky set off on a new tack before an audience generally supportive of U.S. military operations. "More than any other thing," Sparky said, "the war in Vietnam has produced deep divisions among the American people...Americans are becoming more and more disturbed over mounting casualty reports and the seeming endlessness of our involvement...I share these misgivings."

Sparky said he opposed both further escalation and a withdrawal of U.S. forces. Rather, he argued for a political settlement with a coalition government that included the communists. He called on Nixon to persuade the South Vietnamese to accept such a settlement.

In his criticism, Sparky was careful to draw a line between his distaste for Nixon's policies and his admiration for soldiers in the field. "It is tragic," he told the House in December, "that in the emotional debate over our future course in Vietnam, the heroic efforts and sacrifices of American servicemen may have been overlooked." Nor did he refrain from criticizing North Vietnam: "I would like to add my voice to the rising tide of outraged world opinion against the government of North Vietnam as the result of its inhumane treatment of American prisoners of war."

As Nixon began pulling U.S. forces out of Vietnam in the summer of 1969, Sparky stayed away from the large anti-war demonstrations in October and November and let them carry the message. By year's end, U.S. forces were down to 475,200 from the peak of 535,000. When Nixon ordered an incursion into Cambodia in April of 1970, Sparky joined Senator Inouye in criticism. "Communist violations of Cambodia neutrality will not justify any similar action on our part," he said. "I believe the President is making a mistake seeking a military solution rather than a political settlement."

Early in 1971, Sparky intensified his dissent. "The war must end," he said in the House. "Congress must move to reassert its constitutional responsibilities to 'raise and support armies' and to 'declare' war." He called for the withdrawal of all American troops by December 24, 1971, which he said "could present the people of this nation with the most cherished Christmas gift since the end of the Korean conflict." He hammered at the North Vietnamese for their brutal treatment of American POWs and asserted in March that "our prisoners of war have become pawns in a chess game of war and politics." He said, "Let us propose to the Hanoi government that we will withdraw all American troops from South Vietnam by a certain date if it will release all American POWs by that same date."

Two months later, Sparky joined Representative Bill Chappell, a Democrat from Florida, to challenge Nixon's constitutional authority to wage war without the express authority of Congress. This was the sort of fundamental argument that Sparky relished. "If we have learned but one lesson from the tragedy in Vietnam," he chimed in, "I believe it is that we need definite, unmistakable procedures to prevent future undeclared wars. 'No more Vietnams' should be our objective."

In the fall, Sparky applauded a motion by Senator Mike Mansfield, the Democratic Majority Leader from Montana, who wanted all U.S. forces withdrawn in six months so long as the POWs were released at the same time. "We have diverted $130 billion from urgent domestic needs," Sparky complained, "to conduct a war everyone wants terminated." Those pressures caused Nixon to reduce U.S. troop strength in Vietnam to 156,800 by year's end.

Meantime, in Paris, Nixon's negotiators broke off peace talks with North Vietnam in March 1972, asserting the U.S. would not negotiate until the North Vietnamese indicated they were serious. The President ordered the Air Force to resume bombing North Vietnam in mid-April, which triggered off new anti-war demonstrations across the U.S. Sparky, among others, denounced the President: "Since President Nixon's professed march toward total military disengagement from Vietnam seems to falter...the Congress must now take the initiative to end the war." In Paris, Hanoi's negotiators returned to the table for two weeks, then halted the talks again.

In response, Nixon intensified the bombing and ordered the port of Haiphong to be mined. Sparky inserted into the Congressional Record a brief protest that reflected his rising desperation. The President, he said, "has completely usurped the constitutional power of the Congress to declare war. An even greater tragedy is that the Congress has supinely acquiesced and even supported the President." The only way to end the war, Sparky asserted, "is to cut off all funds." A proposal to adopt a War Powers Act gained momentum; it would curb presidential authority to get the U.S. into a war like that in Vietnam. Sparky noted that "as sudden and unexpected as the attack on Pearl Harbor was, we went to war only after its declaration by Congress." The resolution passed the House by an enormous margin, 345 to 13, but died in the Senate. It was not for another year that both houses of Congress passed the bill and then only over President Nixon's veto.

A few days later, as a mark of his anguish, Sparky brought race into the debate. "Is the war in Vietnam a racist war?" Sparky asked in the House. "Years from now, when the tumult and shouting surrounding Vietnam have subsided, history may record that the United States — a predominantly white nation commanding the greatest resources and the most advanced military technology ever known — systematically destroyed an Asian agricultural nation the size of North Dakota merely because its people wore yellow skins. Would we pursue this policy of massive bombing and total destruction if the foe were a small, white Western nation?" Sparky let the question hang in the air.

In contrast, he had little to say when the Paris Peace Accords were signed in early 1973, the last of the U.S. forces were withdrawn and 590 American POWs were released by North Vietnam. When President Nixon sent bombers over Cambodia in May in retaliation for North Vietnamese violations of the peace agreement, Sparky joined other Congressmen in stirring up a storm. As before, Sparky focused on the constitutional issue: "The President today has engaged this nation in warfare in Southeast Asia without any declaration of war by the Congress... If the President, as Commander in Chief of our armed forces, wishes to engage this nation in warfare, let him come to the Congress and ask for a declaration of war."

This led to a raging debate over the President's constitutional authority to wage war. Since the beginning of the Republic, Congress has from time to time challenged the President's power to engage the nation in war. The struggle was particularly intense in the early 1970s when emotions over Vietnam were rubbed raw. Out of this came the proposed War Powers Act, which was intended to require the President to obtain the consent of Congress before committing U.S. armed forces to hostilities. Sparky was in the thick of the fight as an advocate for the act.

Debate rumbled on until July 1973, when Representative Clement Zablocki, chairman of the Foreign Affairs Subcommittee on East Asian Affairs, brought the War Powers Resolution to the floor. It would require the President to consult with Congress before sending the armed forces into battle. Sparky supported the bill with enthusiasm, concluding, "The time for Congress to take this action and to reassert its constitutional role is long overdue." The bill passed, 244-170, and was approved by the Senate with amendments two days later.

After a Senate-House conference ironed out differences, it came back to the House where Sparky spoke just before the vote in October, a tactic he evidently believed could change some minds even at the last minute. Noting "the cloud of a possible veto," he urged Republicans to vote for the bill. The House approved it, 238 to 123. Sure enough, President Nixon vetoed the bill. In the ensuing debate about whether to override the veto, Sparky argued, "Mr. Speaker, when we raised our hands here in this chamber on the opening day of this session, we swore, each and every one of us, that we would uphold the Constitution of the United States. Here is the opportunity to prove that we meant what we said." Both the House and the Senate voted to override the veto.

Just as the War Powers Act was a product of the war in Vietnam, so was the struggle to end military conscription and to recruit a volunteer force. The draft, which had been in place since before World War II except for a brief lapse, had become corrupted. Almost 16 million exemptions out of 26.8 million eligible young men were gained by claiming personal hardship, marriage and fatherhood; the ministry or teaching; or conscientious objection. Physical, mental and psychiatric defects were feigned, medical records were falsified and not a few sons of the rich bought their way out of service by staying in school. They stood in stark contrast to the 10.8 million men, of whom 7.5 million were volunteers, and 261,000 women who served in the armed forces during the Vietnam era. An unknown portion of the men were induced to volunteer by the threat of the draft.

When that corruption was added to the widening dissent against the war itself, Americans across the political spectrum urged an end to the draft. In 1970, President Nixon appointed a commission chaired by former Secretary of Defense Thomas Gates that concluded: "We unanimously believe that the nation's interests will be better served by an all-volunteer force, supported by an effective standby draft, than by a mixed force of volunteers and conscripts."

Even before the Gates Commission reported, Sparky joined 30 Congressmen on March 16, 1970 to introduce a resolution calling for an all-volunteer force. Sparky often spoke outside Congress to urge repeal of the draft. Early in 1971, he and Representative William Steiger, a Republican from Wisconsin, joined forces with 80 others to introduce a bill, about which Sparky said, "The bipartisan group of sponsors of the measure represent a wide range of ideological differences and an equally wide range of individual motivations." Some saw the draft, he said, as "an unwarranted infringement of the basic liberty of our citizens." Others said it was a way for the President to ignore congressional intentions. His bill was intended, Sparky said, "to make the military service attractive to the point that young men will volunteer in sufficient numbers to meet our national defense needs."

After several liberals objected to the volunteer force because they feared that the burden of military service would fall on African-Americans, the drive to end the draft got vital help from Rev. Ralph Abernathy, an African-American who was president of the Southern Christian Leadership Conference. He testified before the

Senate Armed Services Committee that fear of a volunteer army being drawn mainly from the ranks of the poor and black "is not only unappreciated, it is downright repugnant from the point of view of the black soldier who is ordered to die for a 'freedom' that he has never known." Abernathy concluded that continuing the draft would be imposing another "form of involuntary servitude" on black Americans.

Debate began in Congress on March 30, 1971, after the Armed Services Committee voted to extend the draft for two years while raising pay and moving toward a volunteer force. Representative Bella Abzug, a fiery liberal Democrat from New York, sought to amend the bill to end the draft on January 1, 1972, while Representative Michael Harrington, a liberal Democrat from Massachusetts, wanted it to end on June 30, 1971. Representative Charles Whalen, a Republican from Ohio, proposed extending the draft for only one year. Representative Samuel Stratton, a conservative Democrat from upstate New York and a member of the Armed Services Committee, argued for the extension, asserting, "We ought to have some time in which to see whether this volunteer proposal, and doing it by the increases in pay, will actually work."

Throughout the three-day debate, Sparky supported one amendment after another to limit conscription but went down in defeat each time. Finally, noting that pay increases had been included in the bill, Sparky said, "We hope that by such a salary increase, we will be able to induce more young men to volunteer for service so that we will have a *de facto* volunteer army." In the end, Congress, fearful of ending the draft suddenly, voted on April 1 to keep it alive until 1973. The vote was 293–99, with Sparky voting against the bill in a final, if futile, effort to end the draft.

Nearly two years later, on January 23, 1973, the same day the Paris Peace Accords were signed, Secretary of Defense Melvin Laird announced that no more young men would be drafted. That did not end the controversy as President Nixon sought to keep the Selective Service System alive. Sparky led another charge, telling a church group in late February, "The end of induction is only a step toward our goal...there is an opportunity today to end Selective Service and the continuing threat it poses to a free society." Sparky introduced a bill to eliminate Selective Service but it died in the Armed Services Committee where there was overwhelming support for the draft.

In the end, the Selective Service System survived as a government agency but the President was stripped of authority to order young men to register for the draft or to be inducted. While Sparky and his allies had failed to repeal the draft law, their opposition had, in effect, pressed the Nixon administration to turn to a volunteer force. The administration might have dropped the draft eventually but protests from large numbers of Congressmen forced that decision to be made sooner than later.

In September 1971, there took place in the House one of those rousing struggles that are the mark of a robust American democracy. Sparky brought up a bill that would repeal Title II of the Internal Security Act of 1950, sometimes called the McCarran Act after its sponsor, Senator Pat McCarran, a Republican from Nevada. The law had been passed over President Truman's veto during the anti-communist hysteria led by Senator Joseph McCarthy, Republican of Wisconsin. The clause that Sparky wanted repealed provided that the government could, in an emergency, detain without due process any citizen or alien suspected of treason. While this law had not been in effect when Japanese-Americans were incarcerated after the outbreak of World War II, it made legal what had been done illegally eight years before.

It had taken Sparky two years to get his bill to the floor, having first introduced it in June 1969 with Representative Chet Holifield, a Democrat from California, as co-sponsor. Sparky told the House then that the McCarran Act "violates the constitutional guarantees and judicial traditions that are basic to our American way of life." The government had built six detention camps, two in Arizona and one each in Pennsylvania, Florida, Oklahoma and California. Sparky noted that in 1967, as dissidence over Vietnam spread, "wild rumors spread through the black ghettos, across the college and university campuses and among war protesters."

Holifield added, "As long as Title II is on the books, it could be used, and some American citizens would probably be arrested and detained before its constitutionality could be ruled on by the courts." Holifield had seen Japanese-Americans arrested in California during the war just because they were of Japanese descent. "I am proud to say that I spoke out against the so-called 'protective custody' at the time, though I was in a small minority who dared to do so."

Sparky and Holifield picked up 125 co-sponsors and numerous endorsements from civic organizations but the bill was referred to the House Committee on Internal Security and died there when Congress ended in early 1971. That committee, led by Richard Ichord, a conservative Democrat from Missouri, had little sympathy for civil rights over internal security.

Undeterred, Sparky and Holifield reintroduced the bill in 1971. At the same time, Ichord presented a bill that would have modified the McCarran Act, but only slightly. Both bills were referred to the Rules Committee on which Sparky sat.

Sparky argued for a rule under which his bill would be considered first and the Ichord bill as an amendment or substitute. The committee agreed. In the floor debate, Representative Joe Evins, a Democrat from Tennessee and floor manager of Sparky's bill, came right to the point: "Is there a place for concentration camps in America?" The answer, he said, "obviously is no." His opponent, speaking for the Internal Security Committee, was Representative Allen Smith, a Republican from California, who noted that Title II had never been used, thus "now we are talking about something, which in my opinion, is much ado about nothing."

With those statements setting the tone, the argument went back and forth for two days. Sparky's bill was backed by Representatives John Anderson, the Republican from Illinois who ran for President as an independent in 1976; Robert Kastenmeier, a Democrat from Wisconsin who had chaired the Judiciary Subcommittee in hearings about the issue; Abner Mikva, a Democrat from Illinois who later became a respected federal judge; and Emanuel Celler, a Democrat from New York and the venerable chairman of the Judiciary Committee. Celler asserted, "The very idea of a detention camp connotes Hitler and Mussolini," the Nazi German and Fascist Italian dictators of World War II.

When an exchange with Ichord became testy, Celler lightened the mood by thanking Sparky for reminding him of a stand against Title II he had taken in 1950. "There are three qualms of life," Celler said. "First is the lapse of memory, and now I cannot remember the other two." The House broke out in laughter and applause. Then Celler became serious: "Although the detention act has never been used, it provokes fear and distrust, violates the civil rights of citizens and serves no useful government purpose. It belies our much vaunted freedom. It is as loathsome as a hangman's rope to a convict."

Representative Wendell Wyatt, a Republican from Oregon, presented a poignant argument: "I served as a special agent in the FBI during the latter part of 1941 and the first half of 1942 (in Seattle)....I personally observed the almost indiscriminate rounding up of alien Japanese and U.S. citizens of Japanese ancestry....I observed many, many injustices, not only with respect to persons but also property rights. I witnessed forced sales of personal property, and many tearful good-byes. We know now but did not realize then, that we acted out of hysteria, and needlessly." Wyatt concluded, "We have adequate laws without Title II to protect the internal security of the United States." Representative John Conyers, a Democrat from Michigan and an African-American, asserted, "The mere fact that we could debate this provision justifies the fear on the part of many of my constituents that black people could be victims of the same oppression as that of the Japanese-Americans."

When debate resumed the next day, Ichord carried the spear for the amendment drawn up in his committee. He was supported by representatives such as John Ashbrook, a Republican from Ohio, who asserted that Ichord's bill "directs itself to...the situation where we have disloyal Americans, where we have saboteurs, where we have insurrectionists, where we have those who are bent on changing our government by war, by invasion, by subversion." John Flynt, a Democrat from Georgia, contended that if the nation's survival depended on rounding up citizens as had happened to Japanese-Americans, "I would do it again without hesitation."

In summing up, Ichord said, "I ask the members of the House today to legislate not on the basis of unfounded fears but on the basis of fact and logic....At this time, I rise in the security interest of the country." He said the contest was between those who favored Sparky's bill, "which would prohibit the apprehension of saboteurs and espionage agents," and those who favored his bill, "which would permit the apprehension of saboteurs and espionage agents."

Just before the first vote, Speaker Carl Albert rose to support Sparky: "This is an attempt to erase from the statutes of the United States a law which has been...the last vestige of any authority to incarcerate people because they are related to people who are at war with us." Representative Gerald Ford of Michigan, then the Republican floor leader, said he would support Sparky's bill and called for a vote. "The well is dry," he said. "No further debate will sway the conviction of any member." Ichord's bill was voted down, 124–272.

Then came the vote on Sparky's bill, which was passed 356–49, an overwhelming victory. Savoring his success the next day, Sparky lauded his colleagues for their "exercise of good judgment" and thanked his supporters and the Democratic leaders. Turning to the Republicans, he said, "My idealistic image of the Congress was made to appear brighter by the bipartisan support I received." He concluded, "Together we have proven to the world that we Americans mean what we say when we say there is no place for concentration camps in America."

Nor, in Sparky's view, was there any place for the "coolie" trade laws. Sparky had several times introduced a bill to repeal them but they had got lost in the legislative shuffle or never made it through the Senate. This time, Sparky again asked the House to adopt the repeal because Senator Fong had succeeded in getting an identical bill through the Senate. The House approved it without objection and the repeal became law on October 20, 1974.

As a member of the Rules Committee, Sparky helped to revise two critical elements of the immigration laws in 1973. The first, Sparky told the House, "would make it illegal to knowingly employ aliens" who had not been lawfully admitted or who had violated their visa status by taking unauthorized jobs. Sparky argued that the bill sought to protect Americans "who suffer from job competition posed by these illegally employed aliens." It passed the House, 297–73.

Later that year, Sparky introduced a bill that would allow families to bring their relatives living in Canada, Mexico and elsewhere in the Western hemisphere to the U.S. As Sparky noted, an overhaul of the immigration laws in 1965 had made it possible for immigrants from Asia to settle in the U.S. as easily as those from Europe. The proposed law, which passed 336–30, extended that privilege to the Western hemisphere.

In the summer of 1973, during a break in the Watergate hearings, an attorney for two senior aides to President Nixon lit a fuse under Sparky by calling Senator Inouye a "little Jap." A reporter had asked the attorney, John J. Wilson, whether he had been bothered by questions from Senator Lowell Weicker, a Democrat from Connecticut. "Oh, I don't mind Senator Weicker," Wilson said. "What I mind is that little Jap," referring to Senator Inouye, another member of the committee. Wilson didn't realize he was speaking into an open microphone; his slur was heard and reported in the press. The next day, Sparky rose in high dander to lash Wilson not only for his pejorative reference to Senator Inouye but for defending his remark by saying, "I wouldn't mind being call a 'little American.'"

"Mr. Wilson should indeed be called a little American, if not un-American, for, blinded by racial prejudice, he could not recognize that Senator Inouye is all-American," Sparky said. He recited Senator Inouye's war record, noting that "in defense of America and its citizens, including Mr. Wilson, Senator Inouye literally gave up his right arm." Sparky invited Wilson to visit Hawai'i, whose population was then 27 percent Americans of Japanese ancestry: "He may then be able to recognize an American when he meets one."

Sparky was testy another time when the chairman of the Rules Committee, Representative Ray Madden, an aging Democrat from Indiana, needled Sparky several times for coming late to meetings. Finally, Sparky remonstrated with Madden: "Why are you always picking on me, Mr. Chairman? Is it because I look like a foreigner?" According to Sparky, there was no further ribbing from Madden.

Sparky helped to right an injustice to a Japanese-American woman who had been accused of treason for broadcasting to American G.I.s as one of several "Tokyo Roses" during World War II. It took political courage to take up the issue as it could have left Sparky open to accusations of being soft on alleged traitors because they were Japanese-Americans.

Iva Toguri, who was born in Hawai'i on July 4, 1916, went to Japan in July 1941, to care for a sick aunt and was trapped in Japan when the war broke out. With her native English, she worked for a news agency, then for the Danish embassy and finally for Radio Tokyo where she played music, read the news and chatted amiable nonsense. After the war, she returned to the U.S. but was arrested, tried and convicted on the testimony of fellow workers, some of them Japanese-Americans who sought to save their own skins. She was sentenced to ten years in prison, fined $10,000 and lost her American citizenship. Toguri was released for good behavior after serving six years and two months, and went to rejoin her family in Chicago.

There the story stood until early 1976, when press accounts reported that Toguri had been wrongfully accused. That caught Sparky's attention and he put them into the Congressional Record with a plea that Toguri's citizenship be restored. "I have joined in the effort on behalf of Iva because she seeks no retrial of her case even though it now appears that she was made a scapegoat," Sparky said. "She only wants a presidential pardon and in no way claims that she was made a scapegoat." In asking colleagues to join him, Sparky said restoring Toguri's citizenship would show the government's "kindness and tolerance toward those whom it once prosecuted." He wrote to President Ford and persuaded the President to sign a pardon, which he did on January 19, 1977, his next-to-last day in office.

Occasionally, Sparky ventured into foreign policy, notably with a speech about Taiwan that advocated a policy opposite to that of President Nixon. From 1949, when Mao Zedong's communists had come to power in China, through the Korean and into the Vietnam wars, relations between the U.S. and China were often bitter and always without diplomatic relations. A critical issue was the fate of the island of Taiwan, off the coast of China, which the Chinese claimed as a province. The Nationalist Chinese regime, known as the Kuomintang, fled to Taiwan after being defeated by the communists, claimed that it was the rightful government of China and vowed to return to the mainland. Washington had diplomatic relations with the Nationalists, who also represented China in the United Nations.

President Nixon, in an effort to play a China card against the Soviet Union in the Cold War, sought to repair relations with China by visiting Beijing to meet with Mao. The issue of Taiwan was high on the agenda. In July 1971, five days before Nixon announced that he would travel to China the following winter, Sparky made the case for a Taiwan independent of China, but which no longer claimed to rule the mainland. In a speech in Honolulu, he said, "There is a deep-seated longing for political freedom and possibly independence among the 12 million

Taiwanese. A plebiscite, supervised by the United Nations, offers the most democratic and feasible method of ascertaining the real wishes of Taiwan's 'silenced majority.'"

Sparky agreed with a Taiwanese scholar, Chen Lung-chi, that "Taiwan is Taiwan and China is China." He opposed suggestions that Taiwan be placed under Chinese political control and the Nationalist seat in the U.N. be given to the communists. "There could not possibly be a more inhumane proposal in the cold and calculating game of international power politics," he said. "The advocates of such a proposal, in my opinion, show a callous lack of concern for the wishes of 12 million Taiwanese who yearn for self-determination, the very principle upon which this nation was founded."

Because Sparky's speech was delivered in Hawai'i, 5,000 miles from Washington, Nixon appears not to have noticed it. Both the Taiwanese and the Chinese noticed it, however. Soochow University in Taiwan awarded Sparky an honorary Doctor of Laws degree even though the government of Generalissimo Chiang Kai-shek did not like his advocacy of an independent Taiwan. When Sparky went to Hong Kong the next day, Chinese authorities declined to give him a visa. Sparky told a newspaper the Chinese said they couldn't spare anyone to show him around because of a Communist Party conference. When Sparky asked whether the refusal had anything to do with his visit to Taiwan, he quoted a Chinese official as saying, "Why should we object to your visiting Taiwan when it is already a part of China?"

Sparky, who had long been keen on arms control, became an activist during this period. He opposed deployment of an anti-ballistic missile (ABM) system in 1969, asserting that it was too costly, that it would need expensive upgrades and that it was a "Maginot Line" that could be overwhelmed by a superior force. He questioned whether the U.S. needed a deterrent in chemical warfare and complained that the Pentagon had not kept Congress adequately informed on chemical and biological weapons.

It was Sparky's opposition to the Nixon administration's plan for the largest-ever underground nuclear test in Alaska that got him moving on arms control. The test, code-named Cannikin, was to take place in November 1971 under the island of Amchitka in the Aleutian chain at a cost of $19.7 million. The test was to ascertain whether a warhead 250 times more powerful than the atomic bomb dropped on Hiroshima in 1945 would work on an ABM missile. "This explosion is not essential to our national defense," Sparky argued in July. "Furthermore it is likely to jeopardize progress at the SALT — Strategic Arms Limitation Talks —and it could well prove to be an ecological disaster."

After losing a fight to have funds deleted from an appropriations bill, Sparky wrote to President Nixon with a plea not to go through with the test. "I strongly urge that the test be canceled on grounds that it will needlessly endanger lives and property, and may jeopardize the SALT talks," he wrote. "A major earthquake, triggered by the huge underground blast or its aftershocks, could send a series of 'tsunamis' (seismic tidal waves) sweeping across the Pacific Ocean, bringing death and destruction within a matter of hours to the West Coast of the United States, Hawaii, Japan, Taiwan, the Philippines, the Trust Territory and other Pacific Islands." The day before the test, Sparky sent another message to President Nixon, telling the House, "Never have I felt so frustrated in any effort to accomplish some good as I feel today." In his letter, Sparky urged that the test be canceled even at this eleventh hour.

Some of Sparky's vocal opposition may have been to cover his *ōkole* (Hawaiian for that part of the anatomy on which one sits) with his constituents. Part of it appears to have been based on information from anti-nuclear and environmental activists. Part of it was his dislike of almost anything President Nixon did. Whatever the motivation, none of his dire warnings came to pass. The seismic shock of the underground detonation registered 7.0 on the Richter scale, which classified it as a major earthquake. A crater a mile wide and 60 feet deep was caused by the collapse of the cavity in which the explosion took place and there were rockfalls on the coast of the island. Environmentalists have alleged that radiation leaked. But there were no tremors or tidal waves in the Pacific region and the SALT talks with the Russians went forward.

To underscore his admiration for America's warriors and to bring federal construction money to Hawai'i Sparky proposed on December 7, 1971 that the House provide shore facilities for the memorial dedicated to the 1,177 sailors and marines whose remains were entombed in the sunken battleship *Arizona*. Ten years earlier, Congress had authorized construction of a memorial above the battleship that lay on the bottom of Pearl Harbor.

"The Arizona Memorial," Sparky said, "has since become a truly national memorial, visited annually by citizens from every state in the Union." They were ferried out by motorboat but, Sparky argued, "existing shore facilities are painfully inadequate." He asked that a shelter be built so that visitors would not be forced to wait for the shuttles under the sun or in the rain, for a theater to show films of the attack, a museum and the usual creature comforts. In a tactic that became his trademark, Sparky rounded up 100 co-sponsors — one by one — including the Congressional delegation from Arizona and the chairman of the House Veterans

Affairs Committee. When the bill got to the floor in August 1972, there was no opposition and it was passed on a voice vote. The Senate, however, failed to act and so Sparky reintroduced the bill in April 1973, with 120 co-sponsors from 37 states. It, too, would await another day.

In political campaigns, Sparky had little trouble in the 1970 election in defeating Republican Richard Cockey, a retired naval officer and President Nixon's classmate at Duke Law School. In a revision of electoral districts, Congress had divided Hawai'i into two districts instead of the at-large arrangement since statehood. Sparky's district was urban Honolulu while that of Patsy Takemoto Mink, who ran unopposed, was rural O'ahu and the neighbor islands.

The next time out, however, Sparky ran into the fight of his life when he was challenged in 1972 by an aggressive Republican State Senator, Fred W. Rohlfing. From the start, Sparky acknowledged the strength of his opponent, saying, "I plan to run as though I were the underdog." Both campaigns were well financed, Sparky reporting a war chest of nearly $100,000 and Rohlfing $85,500. Race undoubtedly played a part in the campaign, the western portion of Sparky's district being heavily Asian-American, which favored him, while the eastern part was heavily haole, which favored Rohlfing.

Rohlfing was no racist, by any means, denouncing right-wingers as "an intolerant, loud and abusive element" as he sought to revive Republican hopes by building a multiracial party. In some ways, Rohlfing was a Republican Matsunaga — independent, outspoken on certain issues and a reformer. During a debate, they clashed over Sparky's ability to win favors for Hawai'i in Washington, and Rohlfing accused Sparky of losing touch with Hawai'i. Sparky defended his place on the Rules Committee: "For Hawai'i to have one of its only two members sitting on that committee is fortunate, indeed."

Sparky got help from his son, Keene, then an officer in student government at the University of Hawai'i, who arranged a forum at which Sparky could address university students. The outcome of the election was the closest in Sparky's career; he won the vote count, 73,800 to 61,100. In the next campaign, in 1974, against a political unknown, Republican William B. Paul, Sparky had an easier time and won, 71,550 to 49,000.

In the background was Sparky's yearning for a seat in the Senate. He had considered running against Senator Hiram Fong in 1970 but thought the better of it as Fong, even though a Republican in an increasingly Democratic state, was well entrenched. Moreover, Keene said mutual friends promised Sparky that if he did not challenge Fong in 1970, Fong would retire in 1976 and leave the way clear for Sparky.

By 1974, Sparky was talking openly about running for the Senate. Even though he was in the Democratic leadership of the House, Sparky's family and friends said that being elected to the Senate — and being addressed as "Senator" — had been his boyhood dream. Perhaps more important was the influence derived from being one in a chamber of only 100 members as opposed to the 435 in the House. A Senator from a small state, such as Hawai'i, could have as much power as a Senator from a big state, such as California, since each state had two votes in the Senate.

After Senator Fong let it be known that he would not stand for reelection in 1976, Sparky lost no time in making his move. He picked Club 100, home of the 100th Infantry Battalion Veterans, to announce that he would run for the Senate. On a cool day in January 1976, he said in the assembly hall of the modest, one-story building that the club "is not only an indelible link with the past but is also a basis of hope for the future." Facing a battery of microphones and television cameras and surrounded by family and supporters, Sparky said the club symbolized "the values that our country is seeking, almost desperately, to rekindle today in this 200th anniversary of its birth." As if he could see to the end of the century, Sparky said, "There is abroad in the land today a spirit of cynicism and indifference that threatens the very roots of our democracy."

First Sparky had to run against Representative Patsy Mink in the Democratic primary. It was no secret that Sparky and Patsy did not much care for one another. Indeed, Senator Inouye predicted "a bloody campaign." Sparky disagreed: "I do not intend to spill anyone's blood, including mine." He went on to say, however, "It's going to be a hard-nosed, no-nonsense campaign. The American people have lost confidence in no-compromise, ultra-liberal zealots," a less-than-subtle reference to Mink, "and die-hard conservatives," which referred to anyone the Republicans nominated. That was to be former Governor William Quinn, who had been out of politics since he was defeated for reelection in 1962 and, pressed by GOP leaders, had reluctantly agreed to run against Sparky.

During the primary campaign, Sparky asserted that he should be elected because he had the ability "to get along with one's fellow legislators, to pull together, to make them aware and sympathetic to your viewpoint." That, he argued, "is what good representation in Washington is all about." Asked whether he was pointing a finger at Mink, who had a reputation for a sharp tongue and a feisty attitude, Sparky shied away from a direct attack. "My record will show," he asserted, "that I have been effective because of my ability to bring people together."

In one instance, Sparky clashed openly with Mink, accusing her of having reneged on an agreement under which she would not run for the Senate if Sparky helped her to get on the House Appropriations Committee, a coveted assignment because the committee controls spending bills. "For some reason," Sparky said while campaigning at the University of Hawai'i, "that agreement was unilaterally canceled by her." Mink vehemently denied the charge: "Absolutely no such commitment was ever made." Nothing was ever proven one way or the other.

On the issues, Sparky and Mink had voting records that were alike, with one exception. Sparky had supported the U.S. role in the Vietnam War until President Johnson bowed out, then shifted to oppose the war. Mink opposed the war from the beginning, and often in vociferous terms. Hawai'i's unions mostly opposed the war, and a unified political action committee led by Tony Rutledge, the prominent labor leader, supported Mink. Sparky, however, raised and spent almost twice as much money on his campaign — $225,000 to $118,000 for Mink.

In the end, Sparky won the primary in September, 75,889 votes to Mink's 58,547, carrying every island except Mink's home island of Maui. Mink left Honolulu for Washington shortly after the primary and sat out the campaign without offering to support Sparky.

The Republicans gave Sparky little time to rest. The primary was on a Saturday, the results were known on Sunday and on Monday, the Republican nominee, William Quinn, attacked Sparky's integrity for having the editor of *Hawaii Business* magazine on his payroll as a part-time campaign writer. The GOP candidate asserted that Sparky's allegation during the primary that he and Mink had agreed that Mink would not enter the primary was "a flagrant disregard of proper procedures for the conduct of congressional affairs."

Quinn hammered away at what he called Sparky's "improprieties" and accused Sparky of having failed to get a sugar bill extended by the Senate. Quinn was nominally supported by Senator Fong and got outside help from Senator Ted Stevens, a Republican from Alaska, and Senator Howard Baker, a Republican from Tennessee. Even so, Quinn's campaign was lackluster and he acknowledged in an interview: "I never really put out any heat against him."

For his part, Sparky emphasized his 14 years of experience in the House and contended that he could have an immediate effect in the Senate. "It's not as if I were starting out cold," he said. He argued that it was almost certain that the Democrats would win the White House and control the Senate and that he, therefore, would have more influence than a Republican. Although union leaders endorsed Quinn, Sparky took aim at the rank and file by contending that the top priority of his campaign was to get the faltering American economy moving again so as to provide more jobs. On the idealistic side, he argued again for a Department of Peace and for a peace academy: "I look forward to the time when our nation will be the first in the world to establish peace academies, which unlike the military academies, will teach the tools of peace rather than militarism."

A scandal in Washington, in which members of Congress received campaign donations from a Korean named Park Tong-Sung, threatened Sparky briefly. Known in the U.S. as Tong Sung Park, he was an agent of influence for the Korean Central Intelligence Agency seeking to sway U.S. policies affecting Korea. Sparky acknowledged that he had received a $1,000 campaign contribution from Park, which was legal at that time and had been properly reported, but asserted that there were no strings attached. Sparky and his press spokesman, Ed Howard, pointed out that Sparky had written to President Park Chung Hee (no relation to Park Tong-Sung) of South Korea protesting his repression of political opponents.

When the ballots were counted in November, Sparky had won, 162,300 to 122,700, taking 56 percent of the votes. He appeared dazed by his victory. "I am so overwhelmed," Sparky told a thousand supporters at his campaign headquarters in downtown Honolulu. Being elected a United States Senator, he said, "is a dream I have had since I was a junior at Kauai High School," where his civics teacher, Robert Clopton, had first raised the possibility. Elected to the Senate that same day was S.I. Hayakawa of California , who defeated the Democratic incumbent, Senator John V. Tunney.

Thus, there would be three Japanese-Americans in the Senate as Matsunaga and Hayakawa would join Senator Inouye there. Hayakawa got a jump on Sparky because Senator Tunney resigned effective January 1, 1977 to allow the governor of California, Edmund Brown, to appoint Hayakawa to finish out Tunney's term and gain seniority over the Senators who took their seats three days later. Senator Fong, Governor Ariyoshi and Sparky didn't get organized to do the same thing. ❖

United States Senator
1977–1982

S hortly after two o'clock on the afternoon of Tuesday, January 4, 1977, Spark Masayuki Matsunaga, son of a dirt-poor immigrant plantation worker from the remote village of Hanapēpē, Kauaʻi, was sworn in as a United States Senator. Along with him were 33 other Senators-elect who presented themselves at the desk in the well of the Senate chamber to be sworn in alphabetically in groups of four. With Sparky were Richard G. Lugar of Indiana, John Melcher of Montana and Howard M. Metzenbaum of Ohio. Each was escorted by the senior Senator from his home state; Senator Inouye accompanied Sparky. After the oath of office had been administered and each had signed the book of oaths, they were greeted, the Congressional Record says, with "applause, Senators rising."

This was another time of singular change in American politics. Many old faces had been pushed out of office by voters unhappy with setbacks abroad and scandals at home. President Gerald Ford was defeated in the election of 1976 by former Governor Jimmy Carter of Georgia, a Democrat who ran against the old political order. In the 1974 Congressional elections, 85 new Representatives had been elected to the House. In 1976, another 64 new faces were elected, meaning that 35 percent of the House had changed since Watergate. The era of divided government ended with Democrats once again in control of the White House and both the Senate and the House.

That lasted only four years as the Republican, Ronald Reagan, assumed the presidency in January 1981. In the Senate, where change comes more slowly because only one-third of the members stand for election every two years, 29 of 100 members, including Sparky, had come to office in the last two elections. The Senate's committee system was reorganized to trim the power of chairmen and to give every Senator a worthwhile assignment. Closed-door markup sessions, where committee votes were taken on proposed legislation, were opened to the press and public. More staff assistance was provided. Votes needed to end a filibuster were reduced to three-fifths from two-thirds. Television coverage of Senate proceedings was initiated.

Even before he reached the Senate, Sparky had thrown in his lot with Senator Robert Byrd, the Democrat from West Virginia who sought to be elected Majority Leader. Senator Mike Mansfield, the Democrat from Montana, had held the position for 16 years before retiring to become ambassador to Japan. Byrd was competing with Senators Hubert Humphrey of Minnesota, Edmund Muskie of Maine and Ernest "Fritz" Hollings of South Carolina. Muskie and Hollings withdrew before the race heated up but the battle was joined by Humphrey, the popular former Vice President, and Byrd. Byrd wrote that Humphrey "conducted a vigorous and spirited campaign but, well in advance, I had stacked up more than enough commitments to win."

Sparky explained why he supported Byrd, a commitment that was sought while Sparky was still in the House. "Shortly after I announced my candidacy for the Senate in 1976, he (Byrd) called on me and told me then of his intention to run for the Senate Democratic leadership post in the 95th Congress and asked for my support," Sparky told the Senate in 1988. "I expressed my surprise that he should pay me such a premature call as I had not even been nominated, let alone elected to the Senate. He assured me that he had every confidence in my election and spoke as if it was a foregone conclusion.

"In questioning him on his positions in regard to the leadership post he was seeking, I soon learned that we were not only compatible in our political outlook but we both shared a keen interest in the history and parliamentary mechanics of both Houses of Congress. I also learned that we had a lot in common. Both of us came from blue collar, rural backgrounds, struggled for an education, were attorneys and entered politics as members of our state legislatures before coming to Washington, initially as Members of the House. I gave him my commitment of support during that 1976 visit and have supported him ever since, and never have I had cause to regret it."

Byrd obtained another commitment from Senator Inouye, who told Sparky that Byrd was likely to become Majority Leader, which he did in early 1977. Byrd rewarded Sparky by appointing him chief deputy whip, the third-ranking position in party leadership. Asked why he had favored Sparky so early, Byrd gave two reasons: "He was an experienced legislator and he was always loyal to me."

Byrd had been the Democratic whip before becoming Majority Leader and had made that post essential to the workings of the Senate. In addition, Senate staff aides pointed out, Sparky held a safe seat and had come to the Senate with a big electoral win and thus could take positions that might be unpopular in Hawai'i. Further, he came from far away and would not travel home so often; having him in Washington meant he was available to work.

The chief deputy whip and the regional whips gathered intelligence and provided the Majority Leader with a confidential tally on issues before the Senate. The whips then sought to persuade undecided Senators on which way to vote. "The whips are primarily responsible for keeping the members of their parties in attendance during the consideration of controversial issues," Byrd wrote in a history of the Senate. "They operate on the cardinal principle of the need to have the right senator at the right place at the right time."

Byrd insisted that the Democrats always have someone on the floor capable of looking after the party's parliamentary interests or, to put it baldly, to make sure no one pulled a tricky maneuver. The Majority Leader, said a staff aide, "liked to be on the floor himself so he did not turn to the whip for help but turned to Sparky."

Senator Alan Cranston, a Democrat from California, was the whip but left much of the work to Sparky. Cranston, more a show horse than a workhorse, spent his time raising campaign funds, promoting nuclear arms control and pushing issues with high political visibility. By default, Sparky became the Majority Leader's faithful lieutenant as he brought to bear his experience in the House, his mastery of political maneuver and parliamentary procedure, and his willingness to operate behind the scenes. Even though Sparky took his cue from Byrd, the Majority Leader denied in an interview that he had been Sparky's mentor in the fashion of Speaker John McCormack in the House. The initiative then had come from McCormack, who had picked Sparky. The initiative in the Senate came from Sparky, who had attached himself to Byrd.

Another priority for Sparky was to establish working relations with Senator Inouye, the senior Senator and acknowledged leader of the four-member Hawai'i delegation in Washington. Sparky and Danny, as they were often referred to in Hawai'i, were quite different in background and personality. Sparky came from remote Kaua'i; Danny from the main island of O'ahu. Longtime residents of Hawai'i say Kaua'i people have a sense of separation from the rest of Hawai'i while those from O'ahu are in the mainstream. Sparky's family was mired in poverty; Danny's had risen to the middle class as his father was an office worker in Theo. H. Davies, Ltd., one of the Big Five firms that dominated the economy of the Islands. Sparky was in the Army before Pearl Harbor; Danny was a high-school boy when World War II broke out. Sparky was commissioned through ROTC and went to war with the 100th Infantry Battalion; Danny enlisted in 1943 at the age of 18, was assigned to the 442nd Regimental Combat Team and rose to be a sergeant before earning a battlefield commission in France. Both were wounded, Danny much more severely in losing his right arm.

Both were lawyers, Sparky graduating from Harvard and Danny from George Washington University in Washington, D.C. Both worked as assistant district attorneys and went into politics at the same time but with a great difference: Sparky was an outsider and a loner while Danny was at the center of the inner circle around John Burns, who had mobilized the veterans of the 442nd RCT into a political force. Sparky made his way in politics despite the Democratic machine; Danny because of it. Sparky, a gregarious, outgoing man, won elections and got things done through his personal popularity. Danny, a more reserved man, consistently displayed a taste for and a mastery of political power.

Institutional imperatives made working together chancy, as with every other pair of Senators. The Senate is the only place in American politics where two people share the same constituency. There is one governor of a state, one mayor of a city and one Representative in Congress for each electoral district. In the Senate, two Senators vie for the same votes and support — and money, even if in different years. It can be even more competitive when the two Senators are of the same party, as in the case of Sparky and Danny.

Asked whether this was true of him and Sparky, Senator Inouye replied, "Absolutely." He said they managed the rivalry by having Sparky assigned to different committees and looking after different issues important to Hawai'i. Senator Inouye said the rivalry was often more fierce between staffs who sought to protect their boss's turf than it was between the Senators themselves. He occasionally had to rein in his staff and suggested to Sparky that he do the same.

Ross K. Baker, a political scientist at Rutgers University, has written in *Friend and Foe in the U.S. Senate* that Senators from the same state and party are vulnerable to six perils:

- Conflicts over spokesmanship, in which each Senator struggled to speak for the state or the party to which both Senators belong.
- Competition for contributors, campaign workers and interest groups.
- Political balance, in which voters could become uneasy by having two Senators of similar political traits and might prefer to have a conservative balanced by a liberal.
- Factionalism, such as big city versus rural splits.
- Competitive staffs. "So zealously are these maneuvers carried out that the two principals must play the role of peacemakers," Baker wrote.

- Disputes over patronage and credit as each sought to show that he or she could deliver favors and funds for the state.

Sparky and Danny avoided much of this competition because Sparky deferred to Danny as the senior Senator. In turn, Danny used his seniority to help Sparky get good committee assignments. "Altogether," said a Senate staff aide who knew them both, "they worked with each other reasonably well, but they were not so close that they'd go out and have a beer together after work."

Sparky slipped easily into the rituals of the Senate, which differed from those in the House but were within the realm of the parliamentary procedure he relished. He learned, for instance, that a Senator was always addressed in the third person on the floor. Senator Byrd was the distinguished Majority Leader or the distinguished Senator from West Virginia. Where members of the House were permitted five minutes to speak during debate, a Senator could hold forth so long as his voice lasted.

Sparky was also a quick study. Only 20 days after being sworn in, he was asked by Senator James Eastland, the Mississippi Democrat who was president pro tempore of the Senate, to act in his stead for a day. While this was a chore often handed to a junior Senator, it was an unusual request of a Senator with such short experience. Some weeks later, Sparky was again called on to take the chair, this time drawing praise from Byrd: "I compliment the distinguished Senator from Hawai'i for presiding over this body with a degree of dedication, efficiency and skill that is so rare as a day in June."

Still later, Senator Hubert Humphrey thanked Sparky for a birthday greeting and added, "I say to the Senator how pleased I am to see him in this body. He makes a fine-looking presiding officer. He has distinction, quality, all of those characteristics that make us proud of him as he presides over this body." Sparky, who could rarely resist a quip, replied, "The chair will state this, that he does not think so. But what is his opinion against the opinion of the senior Senator from Minnesota?"

In the transition from House to Senate, Sparky told *The Honolulu Advertiser* in June: "The principal difference is the personal impact a Senator can have on any legislation before a committee of which he is a member. Very rarely does the Senate turn down a committee member's amendment. In the House, they let you speak and then just vote you down." An editorial in the *Honolulu Star-Bulletin* suggested: "By playing close to the House leadership, he (Sparky) came to hold considerable power in the House. Now he is doing the same thing in the Senate."

Sparky appears to have found working behind the scenes, one-on-one with 99 other Senators, more effective than in the House of 435 members. An episode in 1981 illuminated not only his tactics but his penchant for legislation that affected people's lives even if it did not draw national headlines. He noticed in a tax bill presented by President Reagan that a 15 percent credit for investment in renewable energy projects had been dropped, which Sparky thought would be disastrous for Hawai'i's fledgling renewable energy industry.

"So I went to my Republican and Democrat colleagues in the Finance Committee and explained my concerns," he said. "Then I went to my colleagues on the floor. Before long, I had 59 co-sponsors to an amendment to restore the renewable energy tax credits and a commitment from ten other Senators should it come to a floor vote. Then I went to Senator Robert Dole, the Senate Finance Committee chairman, showed him my list of co-sponsors and supporters of my amendment and suggested that he accept my amendment. He said he couldn't do that because the (Reagan) administration was opposed to it. But he immediately arranged our meeting with Treasury Secretary (Donald) Regan to discuss the matter. Being the Treasury Secretary, Mr. Regan is good at numbers. He saw that I already had 69 votes, which was greater than a two-thirds majority. Being a gentleman as well as a mathematician, he withdrew his objections and my amendment was adopted by a unanimous vote of 97 to 0."

Another carryover was Sparky's habit of receiving visitors from Hawai'i. As many as 200 travelers a week passed through his office in the summer months, with a staff aide doing nothing but looking after voters and Sparky trying to meet every one himself. For most Senators, constituents other than big-campaign contributors were a bother — and even more so for their staffs. Not so for Sparky. He often gave visitors a tour of his office, showing off the golden gavel he was given for presiding over the Senate for 100 hours, and taking them to lunch in the Senate dining room. He often had two or three tables reserved until there were mild complaints that his constituents were taking up too much space. If Sparky couldn't conduct a tour of the Capitol, the staff aide did it with a script written by Sparky. He often snared other Senators to introduce to his constituents, which the Senators sometimes did not appreciate even if they were glad handers.

While Sparky kept a low profile as a freshman Senator, he was by no means reluctant to speak up. "Sparky was an extrovert but not an exhibitionist," said a longtime Senate observer. "He looked like he enjoyed the job where most them of walk around as if they had the weight of the world on their shoulders."

Sparky spent much time tending to his duties as chief deputy whip, operating behind the scenes to keep the Senate moving and speaking up on the Senate floor only when he thought he had something to add. "One of Sparky's strengths," said a Senate staff aide, "was that he did not speak up on every issue. He was a work-horse who could get a lot done by letting someone else take credit for it." Further, he said, "the job of the whips was to enforce consensus. Sparky built relationships because everybody liked him. Many times, they would go along just because Sparky asked them to."

Sparky was assigned to the powerful Finance Committee (which handled revenue and tax bills), to Energy and Natural Resources, and to Veterans Affairs. Later, he was further assigned to the Committee on Labor and Human Resources, which spread his daily work rather thin. On the Finance Committee, the chairman, Senator Russell Long of Louisiana, "became my mentor," Sparky said, "and I could not have had a better one. We share a belief in the use of the tax code as an instrument of social policy as well as of raising revenue for the operation of the government." Sparky did the work of those committees, attending hearings and taking part in deliberations, but he much preferred legislative action and the duties of chief deputy whip.

Sparky was meticulous in mastering the fine points of complicated legislation. In a committee hearing in 1980, he demonstrated detailed knowledge of a bill by closely querying a Treasury official: "Do the proposed regulations affect the ability of a plan using 4/40 or 10 percent vesting to receive a 'favorable determination letter?'" On a tax issue in December 1980, Sparky supported a proposal: "Section 124 of the pending resolution denies use of appropriated funds to disqualify a plan under section 422 (d) (1) (B) of the Internal Revenue Code, provided such plan has a vesting schedule which is equal to or more stringent that the so-called 4/40 plan." On social security, Sparky proposed help for the blind. "Benefits to the blind are eliminated whenever a sightless person begins to earn $468 a month," he told the Senate. "Under my proposal, a person who is blind and has worked six quarters in Social Security-covered employment would be able to qualify for disability benefits."

Throughout his service in the Senate, Sparky defended the volunteer military force that he had helped to establish while in the House. He sought, in vain, to establish a Department of Peace but, successfully, to charter an academy of peace and conflict resolution. He argued for arms control at home and abroad, sometimes with success, sometimes not. The same was true for new forms of energy and for safe disposal of nuclear waste. He was vigilant in looking out for the interests of Hawai'i, fighting a losing battle to save the sugar industry that was no longer competitive. He was equally attentive to issues that concerned Japanese-Americans and other Asian-Americans. Self-determination and statehood for Puerto Rico, if that's what Puerto Ricans wanted, got strong support. He noted it had taken 59 years for

Hawai'i to attain statehood: "I do hope that Puerto Rico will not suffer the same fate." And he continued to pursue his pet projects, such as the direct election of the President, the naming of a poet laureate and getting the proper number of stars affixed to the ceiling of the Senate.

Politically, Sparky enjoyed being in the majority party, especially as he was close to the Majority Leader, Senator Byrd. He does not appear to have been enamored of President Carter, who was not popular on Capitol Hill because he did not cultivate the support of the barons who prized their positions, prestige and prerogatives. As one-time Speaker of the House Tip O'Neill has written: "Jimmy Carter was the smartest public official I've ever known...but when it came to the politics of Washington, D.C., he never really understood how the system worked." Sparky was lukewarm when Carter came up for reelection in 1980.

Sparky commented wryly on being the only member of Congress to accompany President Carter to Tokyo for a summit meeting in June 1979. He said his presence was "window dressing" because the State Department liked to say that the U.S. Senate was "not all white." He sounded miffed in an interview with *The Honolulu Advertiser* because he was not allowed into the high-level meetings themselves.

On the other hand, Sparky's son Keene said his father had taken advantage of the long flight to Tokyo to talk with Carter about religion and politics. Sparky listened to Carter talk about being a born-again Christian and how he hoped to change Washington and the world. Sparky advised the President to make better use of the Democratic leadership in the House and Senate, and emphasized that the U.S. should protect Israel, not only for Biblical reasons but because Israel was the smallest of the underdogs. He thought that Carter's summit meeting with Sadat of Egypt and Begin of Israel at Camp David in 1978 had been among the President's greatest accomplishments. B'nai Brith, the Jewish service organization, later honored Sparky for his support of Israel.

When President Reagan was elected and the Republicans took control of the Senate in 1981, Sparky was in near shock. "I never expected anything like this," he told a reporter. "I knew Carter was in danger of losing to Reagan but I never dreamt the Republicans would gain control of the Senate." He went on: "I've never been in the minority before, even way back when I was in the State and Territorial Legislature. This is a totally new experience for me. I don't know how I'm supposed to behave." The record shows he became sharper and at times more contentious in debate, not only with Republicans but sometimes with members of his own party. Sparky's wife, Helene, however, thought Reagan was charming, and the First Lady, Nancy Reagan, liked Sparky and his ideas for peace, according to Keene Matsunaga.

Sparky kept his sense of humor. When General Alexander Haig's name came up for confirmation as Secretary of State, Sparky voted for him reluctantly, saying he was "apprehensive over what appeared to be an attitude and belief on his part that there are easy solutions — military ones — to what in fact are complicated matters of policy." He quoted President William Howard Taft, a Republican, to give Haig this advice: "War is not the continuation of foreign policy by other means. War signifies the failure of foreign policy."

A short time later, Sparky went to a reception at the White House for a visiting Japanese prime minister. At the appointed hour, the Japanese delegation was ushered in to meet President Reagan and his cabinet. Sparky, despite his protestations, was herded in along with the Japanese. As he went through the receiving line, Secretary Haig welcomed Sparky to Washington and asked if he spoke English. Sparky, with a straight face, replied, "Yes, Mr. Secretary, I do — and I had the honor of voting for your confirmation the other day."

The first big issue for Sparky was the future of the Panama Canal; his role was part of a defining moment for the Senate. The new Majority Leader, Robert Byrd, had set out to recapture the Senate's role in U.S. foreign policy, asserting, "Foreign policy is the joint responsibility of Congress and the President…arbitrary, controversial or secretive unilateral presidential actions do not produce a sound, sustainable foreign policy." Sparky, having sought to make that point on Vietnam, was an enthusiastic supporter.

Since the 50-mile-long canal had been completed in 1914, agitation had boiled up periodically as Panamanians resented U.S. control of the ten-mile-wide Canal Zone that cut through their country. Many of them felt that income from the canal was not shared fairly, even though the U.S. had increased its payments to Panama. After World War II, resentment got stronger and in 1964, anti-American riots led to a suspension of diplomatic relations between the U.S. and Panama. They were patched up when the U.S. agreed to negotiations, which took 12 years to complete. Two treaties were signed by President Carter and the Panamanian leader, General Omar Torrijos Herrera, in September 1977. One provided for Panama to take over the canal and the other said Panama would keep the canal open to ships of all nations.

Byrd, who initially had opposed the treaties, told President Carter he would support them if the right of the U.S. to protect the canal was clarified and if U.S. warships would be given priority transit in an emergency. Carter agreed and Byrd set about laying the groundwork in the Senate. He first invited Sparky and five other Democrats to join him on a trip to Panama. Sparky had already come out for the treaties, saying they would be "a barometer of American intentions in the Western hemisphere."

The others — Paul Sarbanes of Maryland, Donald Riegle of Michigan, Howard Metzenbaum of Ohio, Walter Huddleston of Kentucky and Jim Sasser of Tennessee — were undecided. When the delegation reached Panama in November, Byrd told Panamanian leaders at a dinner: "Any Senator voting for these treaties will pay a high political price. He will gain absolutely nothing personally by doing so. Therefore, you have to be tolerant and patient in bringing people around to understanding these problems and to taking this difficult decision."

During four days in Panama, the delegation met with General Torrijos and traveled around the country. At one point, the general complained in good humor that the flurry of questions made him feel like "a baseball catcher catching pitches from seven different pitchers." The Senators talked with Lieutenant General Dennis McAuliffe, commander of the U.S. Southern Command, who told them there would be more anti-American demonstrations if the U.S. disapproved the treaties. Radical elements might even sabotage the canal, asserting, "If we can't have the canal, you can't either."

The Senate debate on the treaties opened in February 1978, when Byrd sought to insert the provisions on neutrality and emergency use. For more than two months, the Senate deliberated in what Byrd was to call "the longest Senate treaty debate since the Treaty of Versailles in 1919." Senator Frank Church, the Idaho Democrat on the Foreign Relations Committee, was among the leaders advocating passage, with Sparky taking a supporting role. In the forefront of the opposition was Republican Paul Laxalt of Nevada, with support from Jesse Helms Republican of North Carolina and Jake Garn, Republican of Utah.

As often happens in Senate debate, the main points were laid out early and then chewed over to the point of exhaustion. Senator Church argued that the existing arrangement was outdated, that the people of Panama wanted a new treaty, that Panamanian nationalism was rising and that if Washington sought to retain control by force, "the U.S. will stand alone." He asserted the treaties would ensure that the U.S. would continue to have full use of a militarily secure canal.

Senator Laxalt, whose argument had more emotional appeal, complained he had heard "the proponents of this treaty literally apologize to the world for our being in Panama to begin with and literally apologize for what I consider to be a magnificent project and a tremendous contribution to the people of that country. I, for one, am not going to indulge in any breast-beating here because I have nothing to apologize for."

Laxalt contended the canal was "a strategic waterway, absolutely essential to the security of the United States." He asserted Torrijos was close to the Cuban dictator, Fidel Castro, and there would be a danger of communist takeover if the U.S. gave up the canal. Sparky jumped in to say that the delegation to Panama had asked Torrijos whether he would invite either Cuba or Russia to help operate the canal. Torrijos's response, Sparky said, was: "I don't want Panamanian waters infested by communist sharks." Laxalt countered by asserting Torrijos had told him that "Fidel Castro was a friend and trusted adviser." Neither Sparky nor Laxalt persuaded the other.

Several days later, Sparky argued that "it would be disastrous for both Panama and the United States if the Senate did not ratify" the treaties. Most important, he argued, was "that the canal is worthless to us unless it can be kept in operation and we are able to use it." Sparky said he had ridden in a helicopter over the dense jungle on either side of the canal and "came to the conclusion that any determined band of guerrillas could keep the canal completely shut down over extended periods." He asserted, "The new treaties are the best guarantee — in fact the only guarantee — we have to avoid hostilities and to keep the canal open for our unobstructed use."

He contended, "I believe that a negative vote by the U.S. Senate on the pending treaties would be the greatest possible boost for communism in Panama. The enormous frustration that the Panamanians would feel would help the communists convince them that the United States is an imperialist nation bent on exploiting weaker nations." Sparky summed up: "We have fought for other peoples' right to self-determination. Let us not deny the same right to the Panamanians and try to understand that their yearning for self-determination and national dignity cannot too long be contained."

The debate rumbled on intermittently for several more weeks. Occasionally, Sparky, with his impish sense of humor, tried to lighten things up. When Senator Byrd congratulated Sparky for his address, he inadvertently referred to him as the "Senator from Alaska." Sparky interrupted: "Hawai'i. I come from the sunshiny state." Byrd corrected himself, then finished his plaudits.

Sparky sought recognition: "Will the distinguished Majority Leader, the Senator from Virginia, yield?"

Byrd, testily: "West Virginia."

Sparky (tongue in cheek): "Oh, *West* Virginia? Well, now we are even."

The first phase of the deliberations ended on March 16, when the Senate voted 68 to 32 to ratify the Neutrality Treaty, Sparky voting with the majority. Debate resumed for another month, with Sparky rising to assert that Torrijos was not a communist but rather a Panamanian nationalist. When Senator James Allen, a Democrat from Alabama, accused Sparky of being naïve, Sparky kept his cool: "I want to make it clear to the Senator from Alabama that I am as much opposed to dictators as he is. The issue…was whether General Torrijos is a communist." In talking with people who knew Torrijos, Sparky argued, "I personally became convinced that General Torrijos is not a communist." He needled Allen: "I am convinced…that the Senator from Alabama is not a communist. That is only a statement, not praise."

Sparky made similar points in exchanges with Senator Helms and other opponents of the treaties, with no changes of mind evident. The opponents, according to Byrd, proposed a raft of provisions that would have weakened the bills or delayed their passage — 145 amendments, 26 reservations, 18 understandings and three declarations, which amounted to 192 changes. Even so, at 6:00 p.m. on April 18, the second treaty was approved by a vote of 68–32, identical to the earlier vote.

On another vital issue, Sparky was a steadfast advocate of the volunteer military force. He put into the record a report from Rand Corporation, an influential research center in California, and asserted, "Volunteer forces are better military forces in every way. Today's volunteer is both better educated and more able than the draftee of the 1960s…the Volunteer Force is a socially representative mix. Young people from middle and upper income brackets are enlisting in numbers equal to those drafted during the early 1970s." (That last point may have been a bit misleading because middle- and upper-income young men were more adept at getting out of the draft during the Vietnam War than were young men from lower-income families.)

By the fall of 1979, the volunteer force was in bad shape, particularly in regard to the declining quality of recruits. Proponents of military conscription, among them Democratic Senator Sam Nunn of Georgia, a senior member of the Armed Services Committee, contemplated a revival of the draft by proposing that draft registration be resumed. It would require only that young men sign up so that a draft board would know where they were.

Sparky and other critics of conscription, suspecting this was but the opening shot in a campaign to revive the draft itself, were quick to respond. Sparky noted that President Carter "has chosen not to seek any legislative initiative on registration, and he has announced his opposition to the pending legislation." Going back to the draft, he asserted, "would be to disregard the lessons we learned the hard way through the Vietnam War."

Senator Mark Hatfield, Republican of Oregon, and another opponent of the draft, pointed out that Sparky spoke "from the very excellent position of having been a co-author of the voluntary system." When the issue was set aside without passage, Sparky supported a proposal that a commission make a comprehensive study of military personnel needs. It failed to get through, as did a proposal to raise military pay and allowances to attract and retain people in the armed forces.

The issue came up again a few months later, after the Russian invasion of Afghanistan in late December 1979. President Carter, in a reversal, asked in his State of the Union address to Congress in January 1980 that draft registration be reinstated as a signal to the Russians that the U.S. would resist aggression. The House passed legislation to implement the President's request in April but when the bill reached the Senate in June, Sparky and Senator Hatfield led a vigorous resistance.

Advocates of the President's proposal were led by Senator Nunn and Senator Bennett Johnston, a Democrat from Louisiana. Johnston put it bluntly: "This country ought to move to a draft now. The All-Volunteer Force is not working." Subtly, he raised the question of race, since African-Americans comprised a larger portion of the volunteer force than they did in the population at large. "Our armed forces," Johnston said, "ought to represent a cross section of America."

Hatfield said he resented the implication that "an all-black army is going to descend upon us and that somehow an all-black army is a danger for America." He asserted forcefully, and was shown to be right, that the armed forces would be neither all-black nor a danger to the country.

Sparky delivered an impassioned plea against draft registration. He agreed with the President, asserting, "President Carter's concern that the Soviet invasion of Afghanistan poses a very serious threat to our interests and that the United States must react in a firm and decisive manner." He argued, however, that the President's request for draft registration had been received by the American people "with uncertainty, with skepticism, and in some case with protests and demonstrations." Registration would be "a less than meaningful gesture," he argued, and quoted from a Selective Service System report saying registration would be "redundant and unnecessary."

Further, he asserted, "no amount of registration is going to get trained personnel to the war zone in the early stages of a future war. We will have to depend on our reserve forces to replace our early casualties." The problems of the volunteer force, he insisted, were "directly attributable to what has been a steady erosion of pay and benefits."

Finally, Sparky pointed to the Vietnam era: "If we in Congress are really serious about the war powers of the President; if we are really serious about maintaining the coequal relationship with the Chief Executive that we fought so hard during the last decade to attain, then I say to Senators that we must take a long, hard and objective look at just what is at stake in reinstating draft registration." He concluded, "I simply do not believe that America is ready for another era of divisiveness and unrest; the wounds of the Vietnam War have not yet fully healed."

Senator Nunn tried to manipulate the debate but Sparky saw through it, saying, "The Senator has a clever way of twisting things around and, of course, is a very formidable debater." Nunn's argument: "We can pass all the bills we want on pay, we can triple the pay and we will not be able to get an individual ready in a pre-trained manpower pool, and not be able to get a Selective Service System unless we are willing to have some form of registration."

In the end, Nunn's side beat back delaying maneuvers and won by a vote of 58–34. Even so, Sparky had made two points: He had served notice that proponents of the draft would be confronted with effective opposition on reviving conscription. Second, Sparky was right about resistance to draft registration. After it went into effect, so many young men defied the law that, if they had all been arrested, tried and convicted, they would have more than doubled the population of the federal prisons.

The same issue came up in a different guise again in September 1981, after the Reagan administration had taken office. The administration proposed to raise military pay by 14.3 percent across the board, which the House approved. But the Senate Armed Services Committee, a bastion for advocates of conscription, revised that to give large increases for officers and senior non-commissioned officers, arguing this would help to retain them in the service. To pay for that, the committee reduced pay increases for the three lower enlisted grades, saying larger increases were not necessary.

Sparky and Senator Hatfield, once again suspecting the Armed Services Committee of trying to sabotage the volunteer force, proposed an amendment that would shave raises for senior people in favor of greater raises for those at the bottom. The committee's proposal, Sparky argued, "will have a disastrous effect on military recruiting efforts and will, in the long run, undermine the All-Volunteer Force....And as the night follows the day, the committee will come before this body and say the peacetime draft is necessary to maintain our military manpower."

Senator Nunn was joined by Senator James Exon, a Democrat from Nebraska, in defending the committee's bill. "It is a fallacious contention," Exon

In the company of Senator Inouye (partly hidden at right center) and Governor Burns (at right), Sparky shields Lyndon Johnson from the rain during the President's visit to Honolulu in 1968.

Surrounded by members of the Kaneohe Sweethearts, a group of *lauhala*-hatted supporters, Sparky greets a young admirer during the 1968 campaign.

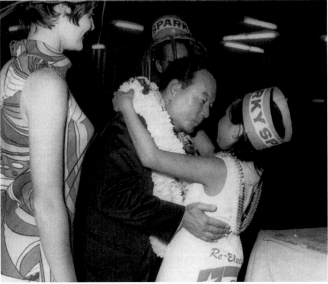

At a *lu'au* (feast) in the summer of 1967, Sparky teaches Vice President Hubert Humphrey the finer points of eating two-finger poi.

Friends and staff play island music in Rep. Matsunaga's office (opposite, top). A behind-the-scenes view of his Senate office reveals comfortable slippers, a Hawaiian Thermometer and a collection of nametags plastered to a desk drawer (opposite, bottom).

Clad in a tapa-print jacket, Sparky works the phones at the Democratic National Convention in 1968 (above). Twenty years later, his supporters take to the streets in his final campaign (left).

In 1973, Joseph Twanmoh, president of Taiwan's Soochow University, awarded Sparky an honorary doctorate in law even though the government of Chiang Kai-shek (with the Senator, above) disliked Sparky's advocacy of an independent Taiwan.

In 1979, Sparky greets Deng Xiaoping, Vice Premier of the People's Republic of China, at the Senate Caucus Room in January (above) and rides with Helene in the Aloha Week Parade through Waikiki in September.

Senator Matsunaga was the only member of Congress to accompany President Jimmy Carter to a summit meeting in Tokyo in June 1979 (at right with Rosalyn Carter aboard Air Force One).

In June 1986, Sparky signs copies of his newly released book, *The Mars Project.* Above: Unveiling of the planned redevelopment of the National Memorial Cemetery of the Pacific at Punchbowl Crater in Honolulu (left to right: National Cemetery System Director John Mahan, Adm. John McCain, Senator Vance Hartke, Veterans Affairs Administrator Richard Roudebush, and Senators Matsunaga and Inouye.)

Sparky greets President Richard Nixon in 1974. Ten years later, President Ronald Reagan welcomes the Matsunagas to a reception (right) in honor of the president of Venezuela. In 1983, Sparky is sworn in (opposite) for his second term in the Senate by Vice President George H.W. Bush, who was also constitutionally the president of the Senate.

Sparky's guided tours of the Capitol usually included a stop at the statue of Father Damien (opposite, top), the Belgian priest who helped care for leprosy patients on Moloka'i in the late 19th Century. In 1980, he dedicates an exhibit on health care at the National Library of Medicine (opposite, bottom), which included historical photos of the Federal Leprosy Investigation Station (above) operated at the Kalaupapa settlement between 1909 and 1913.

Opposite, bottom: Sparky lobbied long and hard for redress for AJAs incarcerated by the U.S. government during World War II. On his left is Senator Robert Packwood, the Republican from Oregon. In August 1988 he works on long-awaited redress legislation (above), a move heralded by editorial cartoonist Corky Trinidad in the *Honolulu Star-Bulletin* (opposite, top).

YOU ARE LEAVING MANZANAR

THE LAST INTERNEE

Helene greets well-wishers on election night in Honolulu in 1976 (top), and the Senators from Hawai'i confer in Washington two months later.

claimed, "for others to say that this was crafted in some way to destroy the All-Volunteer Force." Nunn said targeting pay increases for senior people "makes sense from the point of view of retention; it makes sense from the point of view of the overall viability of continuing the volunteer effort." As the debate continued, Sparky realized he was about to lose and withdrew his amendment with a request that the Senate seek a 9.1 percent pay increase for the lowest grades when House and Senate negotiators met to reconcile differences in their bills.

Sparky got more than he wished as the House insisted on raising pay for the lowest grades by ten percent. He was hard put not to gloat. "The conferees hammered out under difficult circumstances, an excellent compromise between the vastly different House- and Senate-passed pay bills," he said, "which will go far to address the serious manpower problems of the All-Volunteer Force and ensure its continued viability."

It might appear contradictory for Sparky to be a staunch promoter of a strong volunteer force at the same time he was an intense advocate of the peaceful resolution of conflict. In his mind, he saw them not as either/or propositions but rather as and/and. "As long as there are nations that will choose to settle international disputes on the battlefield," he said, "we will need military experts for the nation's security and defense." In the next breath, Sparky argued that just as the United States seeks its best and brightest for the military academies to learn the art of war, so should the nation single out others among the best and brightest to study the art of peace.

From his House days, Sparky brought to the Senate two proposals: Establish a Department of Peace and organize an Academy of Peace and Conflict Resolution. He resumed his quest for a Department of Peace on December 7, 1977, the anniversary of the Japanese bombing of Pearl Harbor, by introducing a bill that would make the U.S. the first nation to establish a cabinet-level department "dedicated solely to the promotion of peace on earth and brotherhood among all men." The Peace Department would pull together the Peace Corps, Arms Control and Disarmament Agency, and the International Development Cooperation Agency. The State Department opposed the concept on grounds that it was not needed and would encroach on its turf. The bill was referred to a committee and sank out of sight.

Even so, Sparky was named chairman of a commission to consider proposals for a National Academy of Peace. The commission comprised nine members, three each appointed by the President, the Speaker of the House and the President Pro Tempore of the Senate. The commission held hearings and deliberated for a year, then recommended to the Senate that a National Academy of Peace be established in Washington "to stimulate broad government, private and voluntary participation in peace endeavors." Sparky told the Senate the academy would cost $31 million to set up and operate for two years, which, he said, "is less than one-tenth of the cost of a single B-1 bomber." The bill to authorize the academy had 52 sponsors and was reported out of committee to the floor in July 1982. There it sat until it was pushed through later.

Not everyone thought it a good idea. A letter to the editor of the *Honolulu Star-Bulletin* called it a "piece of quackery" and a "grand boondoggle" intended to provide Sparky with a job after he retired from politics.

If Sparky was a visionary on the peace academy, he was hardheaded about trying to control violence at home and abroad. With terror having expanded as a worldwide threat, he joined Senator Lloyd Bentsen, the Democrat from Texas, in a proposal that would require the President to suspend arms sales "to those nations which he determines aid and abet international terrorism by granting sanctuary from prosecution to international terrorists." The proposal was agreed to by voice vote. This was two decades before the terrorist assaults of September 11, 2001.

When President Carter proposed in May 1978 that the U.S. sell $4.8 billion worth of jet warplanes to Saudi Arabia, Egypt and Israel in an attempt to increase U.S. influence in the confrontation between Arabs and Israelis, Sparky voted "no." He said it was the "hardest decision" he had yet to make in the Senate because it made him split with Senator Byrd and Senator Inouye, not something he did lightly. Sparky told the *Honolulu Star-Bulletin*: "I would like for my country to get out of the arms race in the Middle East and to concentrate its efforts on the search for a peaceful solution to the political problems in that area."

Sparky lost, in a 54–44 vote, as more Senators agreed with Senator Inouye, who said, "If the Senate had rejected the President's proposal, it would have been unreasonable to have expected the Saudis to sit still and do nothing about it." Sparky said later the President called him at home on a Saturday morning but "I couldn't buy the argument that we were selling the planes to Saudi Arabia for defensive use against the communists."

When President Reagan sought to sell more warplanes to Saudi Arabia in 1981, Sparky was no more amenable. The proposed sale included planes with airborne warning and control systems known as AWACS that guided fleets of fighters into combat. Sparky joined 65 other Senators in writing to President Reagan: "We urge you to reject any such requests from Saudi Arabia." In the Senate, Sparky contended, "The President's proposal, if not disapproved, would clearly jeopardize the security of Israel — our only stable, democratic ally in the Middle East." Under a law on arms sales, the sale required that the Senate disapprove rather than approve it. The resolution rendering that disapproval was set aside by voice vote as Republicans rallied to the President.

On other foreign issues, the attention of the nation was caught in late 1979 by the Carter administration's rediscovery of a Soviet military brigade in Cuba, by the seizure of American diplomats by Iranian radicals in Tehran and by the Soviet Union's invasion of Afghanistan. Consequently, arms control negotiations with Moscow were halted. Sparky had come out early in public for the SALT II treaty that would limit nuclear arms in the U.S. and the Soviet Union but when Senator Byrd and President Carter agreed that Senate should suspend debate over ratifying the treaty, Sparky went along.

Those seeking arms control had better luck with a resolution on nuclear non-proliferation just before President Reagan attended a summit meeting in Ottawa in 1981. The resolution was intended to give the President Congressional backing as evidence that the U.S. was serious about halting the nuclear arms race. Sparky asserted, "So long as we have not resolved the question of nuclear fusion, we should limit the spread of nuclear power, even for peaceful purposes." The resolution was quickly passed 88-0.

In domestic issues, Sparky co-sponsored a handgun control bill in 1979 with Senator Edward Kennedy, the Democrat from Massachusetts whose two brothers, President John Kennedy and Senator Robert Kennedy, had been gunned down by assassins. Noting that "all Senators are fully aware of public opinion on crime nationally," Sparky said Hawai'i had cut its crime rate partly by banning "cheap, non-sporting, concealable handguns, better known as Saturday night specials." A national effort was needed, he said, to buttress state and local efforts. The bill died in the Judiciary Committee as gun enthusiasts lobbied against it. Similar bills in 1981 got no further. A resolution calling for a Senate investigation of Justice Department undercover operations against criminals got through by voice vote with Sparky acting as Minority Leader.

Energy had become a national issue by the time Sparky entered the Senate. A crisis had been triggered by oil-producing nations when they formed a cartel to drive oil prices up in the early 1970s. Near panic followed in the U.S., causing long lines at gasoline stations, an almost frantic search for alternatives to oil and establishment of the Department of Energy in 1977. It was tasked with coordinating the federal government's policy on shrinking resources of oil, natural gas and coal, and with finding ways to reduce U.S. dependence on imported oil. Controversy was abundant and Sparky leapt into it.

As a member of the Finance Committee that had jurisdiction over taxes, tariffs and other federal revenues, Sparky began deliberating President Carter's energy program that called for taxes intended to reduce U.S. energy consumption. After several days of wrangling, Sparky broke a logjam by recounting how Hawai'i had promoted the macadamia nut industry with tax incentives rather than new taxes. Senators from energy-producing states, including Russell Long, the committee's chairman, grabbed the idea and encouraged every Senator to add to the bill as many tax credits as each could think of. It passed, 9-5. Some tax credits were lost on the floor and in conference with the House, but the basics remained.

Sparky got into trouble over that, as critics accused him of accepting campaign contributions from oil interests. The total came to $6,571, by far the smallest amount received by members of the committee and measly compared with the $265,181 received by Senator Bentsen. Sparky brushed the criticism aside, arguing, "There was no way of knowing last October or November during my campaign for the Senate that I would be appointed to the Finance Committee."

He received support from Carl H. Williams, president of the Hawaiian Electric Company, who wrote in the *Honolulu Star-Bulletin* that Sparky's position on the Finance Committee allowed him to prevent Hawai'i from being forced to convert to coal for electrical generation and to retain local regulatory control over public utilities. "Because Senator Matsunaga has the respect of his colleagues," Williams said, "he was able to accomplish those results."

On the floor, Sparky helped to block gasoline rationing. "Gasoline rationing is inherently inequitable and will never be supported by the American people for any length of time," he said. He opposed nuclear breeder reactors that produced more fuel than they consumed because "we have not as yet acquired the technology to do away with the waste matter safely; that plutonium is such that it can be used not only by armies of nations but also by terrorists who may hold not only communities but also nations in blackmail."

When mandatory conservation of energy was proposed, Sparky opposed it, arguing, "Americans have not become and never will become accustomed to a compulsory form of conservation." He was enthusiastic about the Energy Security Act of 1980 that mandated filling a strategic petroleum reserve and making Hawai'i a pioneer in renewable sources of energy. "The probability of a major conflagration in the Persian Gulf in this decade," Sparky said ten years before the Gulf War, "is so high that refusal to build up a strategic petroleum reserve would constitute an inexcusable shortsightedness."

There was hardly an alternative form of energy that Sparky did not advocate, except nuclear power. He got a bill through the Senate that provided for development of coal gasification, but it died in the House. The Senate adopted his proposals for developing geothermal steam, particularly from Hawai'i's active volcanoes, but that, too, failed to get through the House. Sparky was eager to see solar energy developed. He proposed a bill to develop advanced batteries to store electricity but that died in committee. When President Reagan sought to remove price controls from oil in 1981, Sparky argued "decontrol has imposed unwarranted and severe economic hardships on the American consumer," but he was overruled by the Republican majority.

Sparky came back to Hawai'i in June 1981 to promote alternative forms of energy at the dedication of a solar electric power system. "A process leading inevitably to the conversion of millions of residences into miniature solar power plants has begun," he said. "The decentralized solar power system that will reshape the conception and execution of electric power generation throughout the world will date from today's event."

As often happened, Sparky was ahead of his time because solar power has not caught on with the speed that he foresaw. In this case, the home of Henry Wiebke, a retired science teacher on the island of Moloka'i, had been equipped with an array of photovoltaic, or solar, cells mounted on the roof to convert sunlight into electricity. The array was connected to the Molokai Electric Company's grid so that electricity in excess of Wiebke's needs would be sold into the grid.

In another instance, Sparky was at his imaginative best when he proposed tax breaks for owners of vessels who equipped their ships with sails. In seeking to reduce fuel costs for small ships plying among Pacific islands, Sparky's staff came across what was called "sail-assisted technology" that combined motor power and sail power. Computers determined when it would be most economical to switch from motor to sail or vice versa. The motors were not turned off but ran at much-reduced speeds, conserving fuel while the sails propelled the ship. More research turned up oil rigs under tow being helped by big sails. Sparky briefed the Senate Committee on Energy, which led to hearings that he chaired. In the end, his proposed tax break was not adopted but he managed to get an appropriation of $250,000 for a pilot project on the island of Enewetak in the Marshall Islands.

Sparky fared better in protesting a Carter administration plan to store nuclear wastes on Pacific Islands, asserting, "As a Senator whose state lies in the middle of the Pacific Ocean, I was miffed that I had not been informed about the possible storage of nuclear wastes on a U.S. island in the Pacific." The Senate passed a proposal to stop the move but the issue died in the House. Sparky continued the fight and eventually helped to pass legislation that blocked the storage of nuclear wastes in the Pacific.

Sparky was among the Senators who sought to have the Constitution amended so the President and Vice President would be elected by popular vote and not through what he saw as an anachronistic electoral college. "Three times in this country's history," Sparky argued, "in 1824, 1876 and 1888, the presidential candidate who won the popular vote was kept from office because of the strange electoral arithmetic of the electoral college." (This was before the 2000 election in which President George W. Bush was elected with a minority of the popular vote.)

Sparky noted that in the election of 1976, a shift of only 8,354 votes — 4,667 in Ohio and 3,687 in Hawai'i — would have elected Gerald Ford even though he polled 1.7 million votes less than Jimmy Carter. Sparky contended, "We cannot and should not continue to tolerate an electoral system" that posed such a threat to American democracy. In the end, the proposal failed, 51–48, as it had before.

Sparky's interest in the Capitol building began during his early days in Washington. He became an admirer of Constantino Brumidi, the Italian artist who had painted frescoes in the Vatican in Rome and later emigrated to the U.S. where he settled in Washington. Brumidi painted several frescoes in Congressional buildings, perhaps his masterpiece being *The Apotheosis of George Washington*, the circular work that adorns the ceiling of the Rotunda. Other works are in the west, or Brumidi, corridor. The only known quotation left by Brumidi was: "My one ambition and my daily prayer is that I may live long enough to make beautiful the Capitol of the one country on earth in which there is liberty." Both in the House and the Senate, Sparky co-sponsored resolutions that made September 18 Constantino Brumidi Day.

Perhaps that inspired Sparky to his waggish best when he rose in September 1980 to note, as he had in the House, that "up in the ceiling of this chamber are only 48 stars, which means that the stars for Hawai'i and Alaska are missing. And here on the walls of this great Senate chamber there are only 46 stars. So we have not only Hawai'i and Alaska but also Arizona and New Mexico missing. So I plead with the distinguished Majority Leader to exert his influence in bringing the Senate chamber up to date."

Byrd listened, then brushed off the issue dryly: "I thank the distinguished Senator from Hawai'i." Two years later, Sparky submitted a resolution authorizing the Architect of the Capitol to install the stars but that, too, fell on deaf ears.

As ever, Sparky made sure his constituents knew what he was about. That was not easy, given the grueling 12-hour trip from Washington to Honolulu. "Sometimes I come just to make a speech at a major function," Sparky told the weekly newspaper *MidWeek* in 1980. "I arrive about four o'clock in the afternoon, go to dinner, speak that night and leave the next morning."

In 1981 alone, Sparky flew to Hawai'i to promote renewable fuels in January, to present an award to the Waianae Military-Civilian Advisory Committee in April, to lash the Reagan administration for its alleged failures in the savings and loan banking scandal in June, and the next month to report on the status of a tax cut and to celebrate the Fourth of July.

The following month, Sparky was back to attend a Marco Polo award ceremony, to address the Honolulu Exchange Club in Honolulu on the role of the federal government in alternative sources of energy, to tell the Kauai Chamber of Commerce that the Reagan administration should reassess its policy of high interest rates, to applaud the Kalihi Business Association in Honolulu for nurturing small businesses, to inform the Hawaii Estate Planning Council what he had done to get estate tax relief into a bill in Washington and to tell a dinner meeting in Hilo, on the Big Island, what needed to be done to combat inflation — all in a two-week summer holiday.

Before returning to Washington in September, Sparky helped to dedicate the Kupuna project for the elderly on Kaua'i. He was back in Hawai'i twice more that month for a fund-raising dinner and for a press conference with Governor George Ariyoshi to announce an environmental project. In October, Sparky joined a celebration marking the 70th anniversary of the founding of the Republic of China on Taiwan, and, on the same day, told the University of Hawai'i Professional Assembly that a new partnership was needed in higher education.

Sparky did not always get good press at home. Hardly had he taken his seat in the Senate than the *Honolulu Star-Bulletin* criticized him for retaining his brother, Andrew, on his Honolulu office staff despite a federal law that prohibited members of Congress from hiring relatives. Sparky's press secretary pointed out that Andrew had been hired in 1962 and was therefore exempt from a law that had been passed in 1967. The episode quickly blew over.

During the Carter administration, Sparky supported an international agreement intended to protect the U.S. sugar industry, and particularly that in Hawai'i. It passed 80–11, well over the 67 needed to ratify. As time passed, support for the Hawaiian sugar industry, which was becoming less competitive by the year, began to wane. During the Reagan administration, Sparky and other backers of the industry had to pull out all stops to avert efforts to kill price supports, Sparky arguing, "It would simply destroy the sugar industry in the United States, which would mean the loss of 100,000 jobs in America, 30,000 of which would be in Hawai'i."

A bill to establish a national park on the Kalaupapa peninsula on the island of Moloka'i, where those afflicted with leprosy lived, came over from the House. The bill would permit the few remaining residents to live out their lives there, protected from prying visitors. Sparky spoke briefly in support of the bill, then yielded to Senator Byrd, who said, "I hope that I shall be able to get a good night's sleep now that this bill has been called up because Senator Matsunaga has not given me any respite whatsoever for the last ten days, urging me to call up this measure." It was passed by voice vote. ❖

The Creative Impulse
1983-1987

Sparky's second term in the Senate, beginning in January 1983, was surely the most satisfying period of the public service that he began as a lieutenant of infantry on Moloka'i in 1941, just before World War II.

He got off to a grand start when he won reelection by an overwhelming margin in November 1982, with 82 percent of the voters casting their ballots for him — a thundering landslide. Sparky hardly worked up a sweat, scaring off potential challengers in the primary and crushing a Republican unknown, Clarence J. Brown, in the main event. With no real competition in Hawai'i, he ran his campaign more against President Ronald Reagan than against his hapless opponent at home.

Moreover, Sparky ignored a political rule of thumb that says all politics is local. He campaigned on national and international issues and his idealistic visions for the future. In a rare philosophical moment, he told an audience at the Blaisdell Center in Honolulu that creativity occurs not only in the minds of a few born geniuses but in "processes that operate unobtrusively on all levels." Reflecting on his political tactics, Sparky said, "While conflict at the top grabs the headlines, the creative impulse goes quietly, unceasingly, about its work at the grass roots."

Another time, at a reunion of friends who had long ago played barefoot football on Kaua'i, Sparky said, "I have found that the most successful public servants are the ones who continue to dream, who refuse to become cynical and who have the courage to try to translate their dreams into reality."

During that second term, Sparky worked behind the scenes to see his proposal for a peace institute finally realized and continued to be an outspoken supporter of arms control abroad and gun control at home. He pioneered the way toward joint exploration of space with the Russians and took pleasure in seeing his long-standing call for a poet laureate become a reality. Sparky obtained passage of several bills intended to promote alternative uses of energy — but saw several others fail. Most important, he played a vital part in engineering an apology and redress from the U.S. government to the 120,000 Japanese-American citizens and permanent resident aliens who had been incarcerated in "relocation centers" during World War II. *(See Chapter 10.)*

Sparky defended the volunteer military service, promoted programs for veterans and continued to seek curbs on the power of the President to engage the U.S. in war. He called for equal rights for women, better education, better health care and improved social security, and, as he grew older himself, for assistance to the aging. He took a new interest in foreign trade as chairman of a Finance subcommittee. On the negative side, Sparky found himself more often opposing measures because he disagreed with the proposals of the Republican majority.

He also joked that his life had been complicated by the Japanese government, which named Nobuo Matsunaga to be Tokyo's ambassador in Washington. The two Matsunagas were not related but Sparky repeatedly made the point in speeches in Hawai'i that it was nice to meet an audience that did not take him for a foreigner.

Sparky's love of the parliamentary process and his mastery of detail won him plaudits from both sides of the aisle. He offered amendments for clarity and to close loopholes with an eye to the effect they would have on ordinary people. Senator Robert Dole, the Republican leader, was managing a bill in June 1983 that would revise computations of the census taken every ten years. Sparky offered an amendment that would strike only ten words from the bill, arguing that "there is a hidden danger that it may be misinterpreted by the overenthusiastic." Senator Dole said immediately, "It is a technical amendment. I am prepared to accept the amendment."

That was it. Similarly, in a discussion of a complicated fiscal bill in March 1986, Sparky sought to establish a legislative record in case the law was disputed later. He wanted to know what sort of majority would be required to obtain a waiver. The bill's floor manager, Senator Orrin Hatch, a Republican from Utah, said it would be a majority of those present. Senator Dennis DeConcini, a Democrat from Arizona and an authority on fiscal matters, interrupted to say he thought it important that Sparky had raised the issue. "It is clear to me," DeConcini said, "but it may not be clear to everyone else."

Sparky raised another question, to which DeConcini commented that it was well that Sparky had pointed out the need for precision, "just as the Senator from Hawai'i always does." The colloquy continued, with Sparky raising questions that Hatch answered for the record. Hatch concluded, "I think he (Sparky) has done a real service to everyone here concerned and I compliment the Senator from Hawai'i for it."

Whatever his legislative skills, Sparky continued to win lighthearted applause for his non-political talent. During a lunch with members of Congress in the spring of 1986, Yasuhiro Nakasone, the visiting Prime Minister of Japan, commented on the cherry blossoms around the Tidal Basin (3,000 cherry trees had been the gift in 1912 of Mayor Yukio Ozaki of Tokyo). Sparky stood to recite a *haiku:*

Cherry blossoms bloom.
Washington is beautified.
East and West do meet.

Nakasone, who understood some English, applauded and asked for a copy.

Sparky's talents extended even to the kitchen. In May 1987, he entered a Congressional cooking contest sponsored by *Roll Call*, a newspaper devoted to news of Capitol Hill, and took first prize for his macadamia icebox cake. The judge was Craig Claiborne, *The New York Times's* food critic, and the prize was $1,000 donated to charity.

During these years, the Republicans were on a roll. The "Reagan Revolution" promoted economic reform and military buildup. Reagan was reelected in a landslide in 1984 and was succeeded by Vice President George Bush in 1989. At home, the economy came out of recession and hit a growth rate of 6.8 percent in 1984; inflation was down, employment was up and the stock market rose to new highs.

Even so, 35 million Americans were in poverty in 1983, the highest in 19 years, and the trade deficit hit new records. The President saw two nominations to the Supreme Court, those of Robert Bork and Douglas Ginsburg, turned down by the Senate; Sparky opposed both. Abroad, U.S. relations with Russia were rocky, with Reagan labeling the Soviet Union an "evil empire" in 1983. The President did, however, hold a successful meeting with General Secretary Mikhail Gorbachev in Washington in 1987, when they signed the first treaty intended to reduce nuclear arms. The Iran-Contra scandal was exposed; the U.S. Embassy in Beirut was blown up in 1983, leaving 63 people dead; and 241 marines and soldiers were killed by a suicide bomber at the Beirut airport.

In the Senate, the Republicans held a majority until the elections of 1986 when the Democrats took control, 55–45. Sparky carried on as chief deputy whip for the minority until 1987, then resumed for the majority when Senator Robert Byrd again became Majority Leader. Sparky retained his place on the influential Finance Committee and would have become chairman if Senator Lloyd Bentsen had been elected Vice President as the running mate of Governor Michael Dukakis of Massachusetts in 1988. Above all, Sparky continued to believe that the most important duty of a legislator was to legislate. On some issues, he formed a political alliance with Senator Mark Hatfield, the Republican from Oregon, as they shared an ability to work across the aisle.

In his 1982 campaign, Sparky ran as if both Democrats and Republicans were breathing down his neck even though his opposition was practically nil. He accumulated a campaign fund that eventually totaled $805,000, but needed to spend only half of that. He seemed a tad more feisty than in earlier campaigns, perhaps because he was not confronting a challenger personally, but was verbally shooting at people in faraway Washington. When a reporter asked him why he was running so hard when he had no strong opponent, Sparky replied, "Regardless, I always run as an underdog." He had a campaign videotape made because 35,000 to 45,000 voters had moved into Hawai'i or had come of age since he had been first elected. "They may know there is a Senator Matsunaga," he said, "but they don't know Sparky Matsunaga."

Even though he didn't formally announce his bid for reelection until May of 1982, Sparky started running in January, many times jumping on a plane for Honolulu on Thursday afternoon. More than once he complained to audiences on Friday and Saturday that he suffered from jet lag. "I got to bed shortly before midnight," he said, "and yet at 2:30 this morning, I was wide awake — and you can't imagine how frustrating it is for a politician in an election year to be wide awake and all alone with no one around to shake hands with."

Sparky started jabbing at President Reagan at a banquet of federal managers in Hawai'i, contending that the future was "uncertain" and Reagan's policies "uncomforting." At the Palolo Lions Club, Sparky criticized Reagan's economic policy: "If we don't reverse the present trend, we will find ourselves in a deep depression." The Independent Living Conference heard Sparky say that the government's "strong commitment to the disabled has been eroded under the Reagan administration." On Maui, he told veterans that Reagan's New Federalism, in which power would be returned to the states, "appears to have been proposed to detract attention from serious problems facing our nation that deserve greater priority during this period of economic crisis."

Sparky was a free trader — except when it came to protecting Hawai'i's sugar industry. He criticized Reagan's Caribbean Basin Initiative that would have given to Central American and Caribbean producers of sugar and pineapple preferred access to the U.S. market. Output of those products was, at that time, shrinking but still a vital contributor to Hawai'i's economy. In a talk to the Chamber of Commerce in Honolulu, Sparky asserted, "Now, at the worst possible moment, comes the administration's Caribbean Basin Initiative." He made the same point on the Big Island, saying that in his 20 years in Washington, "I have gained access to all sorts of useful secret passageways in the federal labyrinth but, believe you me, I need all the guns and ammunition I can get in order to defend Hawai'i's interests during these difficult times."

Sparky criticized Reagan for trying to cut veterans' benefits, telling the Veterans of Foreign Wars in Maui, "As a member of the Senate Committee on Veterans Affairs, I will not stand still for such unconscionable cuts in essential veterans' benefits." Before labor leaders in Honolulu, Sparky complained that Reaganomics was "based on the principle of give and take — you take from the poor and give to the rich." He criticized the Republicans for pushing through a tax reform act that restricted tax-qualified pension plans. He even accused the Republicans of taking benefits away from handicapped children.

On the upbeat side, Sparky promoted his energy plans, including the application of sail power in the Pacific and more research into photovoltaic sources of energy. He advocated mining the deep seabed but adamantly opposed dumping nuclear wastes into the ocean. He pushed plans for a peace institute and for joint exploration of space with the Russians. He read three of his wartime poems at a ceremony at Fort DeRussy, next to the beach in Waikīkī, and recited a poem by Walt Whitman about whaling at a gathering in Lahaina, the Maui seaport that, in the 19th Century, had been the center of whaling in the Pacific. Before an audience of engineers, he proposed a Japan-Hawaii Center for High Technology. "As a politician, I am truly grateful to you engineers, for you belong to a profession charged with the responsibility of bringing order out of chaos," he said. "By the same token, you engineers should be grateful to the politicians, for without them there would be no chaos."

All of this contributed to an overwhelming victory, Sparky winning 245,000 votes to Clarence Brown's 52,000.

A couple of days after the election, Sparky analyzed the results at the Pacific Club in Honolulu, noting that the Democrats had picked up 24 seats to increase their control of the House while the Republicans had maintained their 54–46 hold on the Senate. Somewhat subdued despite his big win, Sparky drew four conclusions: "Enough voters were disaffected with the economy to increase the Democratic seats in the House." "The voters were not sufficiently disaffected to end the Republican Senate majority." "Although the President's personal popularity remains high, his policies are being questioned." "The Democrats have not devised a positive program to win voters decisively."

When Sparky returned to Washington for a lame-duck session in December, Senator Robert Byrd sauntered over to say, "Well, Sparky, I see you won by 82 percent." Sparky acknowledged that he had, whereupon Byrd, referring to Sparky's penchant for entertaining his constituents, said, "Well, it seems to me you have yet to take 18 percent of Hawai'i's population for lunch."

Sparky thought his victory entitled him to chide the Senate, noting that the House got more done in a shorter time because it was well run. "I believe that much of our dilemma can be eliminated by putting someone in the chair who has been properly briefed as to the applicable rules and procedures," he contended. "If a Senator refuses to review the rules before he is assigned as acting President Pro Tempore, then he ought not be appointed to preside over the Senate." Both the Majority and Minority Leaders agreed — but not much changed.

Sparky and his staff moved from the older Dirksen Senate Office Building to the plush new Hart Senate Office Building. Many Senators had resisted the move because they feared constituents would see them in surroundings that some termed "palatial." Sparky's press secretary, Elma Henderson, said Sparky had been reluctant but his staff was glad to have the space: "We're virtually sitting on top of each other now."

When members of Congress were called on to disclose their earnings outside of their salaries, Sparky said, "It is with a degree of ambivalence that I so comply since my share of the world's goods tends to pull down the median personal worth of my colleagues. I take solace, however, in the Sermon on the Mount regarding the poor and their eventual inheritance." Sparky reported only $6,000 in speaking fees and $1,279 from interest and dividends. By the next year, he had boosted that to $40,000 but, under Senate rules, could keep only $30,400. The rest went to charity.

A pleasant event was the award of an honorary degree, Doctor of Laws, by the University of Hawai'i in December 1983. At the mid-year graduation ceremony, Sparky reminded each graduate that he or she was "one of the rare two percent of the world's population with a college degree." His remarks centered on three favorite themes — environmental protection, scientific discovery and world peace.

Early in 1984, Sparky suffered his first physical setback, a mild heart attack that kept him in the hospital for ten days and then at home for a couple of weeks. He returned to the Senate with a flourish, having placed on each Senator's desk a fresh pineapple, a copy of a *Washington Post* travel article on Hawai'i, a full-color poster of a pretty girl on a beach, several brochures about Hawai'i and a letter from him saying: "Hawai'i, dear colleague, has made snow obsolete." Sparky claimed that his physical fitness, at the age of 67, had helped him to make a quick comeback. Even so, he stayed home from the Democratic National Convention that summer to rest.

The following month, Sparky was back in feisty form as he railed against a proposal to resume the death penalty for a federal crime. Rising in opposition to a bill introduced by Senator Strom Thurmond, a Republican from South Carolina, Sparky recalled his experience in Hawai'i where he pushed through the Territorial Legislature a ban on the death penalty. "The only justification for the death penalty in a civilized society such as ours is to deter others," Sparky said. "Research in this field suggests that the death penalty does not deter crimes." He concluded, "All life is sacred or no life is sacred at all." That measure died in the House Judiciary Committee.

Persuading Congress to establish an Academy of Peace was among his most cherished proposals. Sparky, who was nothing if not persistent, had introduced legislation to establish the academy in every Congress since his election to the House in 1962. He introduced a bill again in February 1983, with 52 co-sponsors or enough to pass the bill. "The art of peacemaking, the art of settling conflicts without resort to war," Sparky said on the floor, "is what our leaders not only of this nation but of all other nations need. The Peace Academy is an idea whose time has come at long last."

The route to reality was tortuous and the final product was not exactly what Sparky had proposed. Somewhere along the line, the focus of the institution was changed from undergraduate education to scholarly research and grant-making to universities, and it was renamed the United States Institute of Peace, or USIP. The bill went to the Senate Committee on Labor and Human Resources, which referred it to its Subcommittee on Education. That subcommittee held hearings in March and reported the bill back to the parent committee, which approved an amended version in July and reported it to the Senate in September, where it languished.

Sparky went to Republican Senator Hatfield to ask him to introduce the bill as an amendment to another bill, a channel frequently used to bypass blocks. Hatfield agreed and, ironically, proposed it as an amendment to the Defense Authorization Act that was approved by voice vote in June 1984. The only significant change affecting USIP was to reduce the initial capitalization to $7.5 million from $15 million. Operating funds of $6 million for the fiscal year that started in October and for the following year at $10 million remained intact. When the defense bill got hung up in conference between the Senate and the House, Hatfield took to the floor and got an amendment to another bill passed quickly by voice vote to give the institute $4 million in start-up funds. President Reagan finally signed the defense bill later in October, after the fiscal year had started, but was not pleased with the provision for USIP and allowed it to go forward only because it was part of a $291-billion defense authorization.

With Sparky back in Hawai'i in November 1984, the University of Hawai'i threw a reception for him, and 700 people showed up to applaud his efforts on the peace institute. He recalled that 47 years earlier, when he was a student, he had written a paper in which he asserted, "We must replace attitudes favorable to war with attitudes opposed to war."

Obstacles remained as President Reagan procrastinated in nominating the 11 members of USIP's board of directors. In August of 1985, Sparky denounced the President for missing the deadline by three months in seeming violation of the law. "I devoutly hope it will not be necessary to take the President to court for a *writ of mandamus* ordering him to perform his duty under the law," Sparky told the Senate. Reagan made nine appointments four months later, in December 1985, whereupon Sparky rose to "urge President Reagan to expedite his nominations of the two remaining board members so the institute will be able to begin its work with a full complement." They were named the following month.

Nearly two years later, Sparky deplored a 50 percent cut in funding, to $5 million, made by the Appropriations Committee and sought a pledge that no more would be sliced off. Hatfield again backed him. Senator Lawton Chiles, a Democrat from Florida, assured Sparky that the $5 million would be retained by the House-Senate conference. In 1988, Sparky sought to have the funding for the institute made permanent with a proposal that had bipartisan support with 62 co-sponsors. It never got called up for debate so funding remained on a yearly appropriation.

In October 1990, shortly after Sparky had passed away, Senator Inouye proposed an amendment that would establish the Spark M. Matsunaga Medal of Peace to be administered by USIP. It would go to persons "who have contributed in extraordinary ways to peace among the nations and peoples of the world, giving special attention to contributions advancing society's knowledge and skill in peace-making and conflict management." The proposal called for a cash award of $25,000. While not in the same league as the century-old Nobel Peace Prize, the award for which varied from $100,000 to $800,000, the Matsunaga Medal sought to emulate the world-famous honor. The House agreed to the proposal and President Bush signed it into law in November 1990.

Only once has the prize been given, however, a double award in 1993. One went to President Jimmy Carter for enhancing "the cause of human rights by making it a cornerstone of United States foreign policy." The other went to President Ronald Reagan "for his leadership in promoting arms control agreements with the Soviet Union and...advancing the cause of human rights." Although the awards were politically astute, there were touches of irony as Sparky had opposed each of the Presidents on critical issues. He had disagreed with Carter on the need for draft registration and with Reagan on economic policy and arms sales. Both former Presidents gave the cash prizes to their respective presidential libraries. The prize has since lain dormant because, according to USIP officials, a few members of the House Appropriations Committee and their staffs saw no need for the medal and threatened to reduce the USIP budget if the institute continued to award the prize.

As a believer in arms control, Sparky joined losing fights against President Reagan on the so-called Star Wars missile defense system, on the powerful new nuclear-tipped missile known as MX, on arms sales to Jordan and Saudi Arabia, and on aid to the Contras fighting the Sandinistas in Nicaragua. But he was on the winning team led by Senator Kennedy and Senator Hatfield that pushed through a measure intended to freeze nuclear weapons testing.

After President Reagan went on national television in March 1983 to announce that he intended to build a missile defense that came to be known as "Star Wars," Sparky joined a chorus of critics in Congress, former secretaries of defense, senior military officers, civilian strategists, an array of scientists and advocates of arms control to denounce the scheme. "The Buck Rogers system envisioned by the President is naïve and explosively dangerous," Sparky stormed in a late-night session of the Senate. "It could cost the nation hundreds of billions of dollars, and it would leave us less secure from a global cataclysm than at any time since the dawn of the nuclear age." He argued for using the funds and the technical talent required for Star Wars "in a cooperative effort with other nations to elevate the quality of life here on earth."

The Russians were equally vociferous because, if successful, Star Wars would have become a shield to protect the nuclear sword of the U.S. In the end, the threat of Star Wars helped to destroy the Soviet Union without a shot being fired because it caused the Russians to do just what they didn't want to do, which was to spend money to counter it. Those costs helped to strain the Soviet economy into near bankruptcy. Once the Berlin Wall had been breached in 1989, the Warsaw Pact rendered less threatening and the Soviet Union dissolved, the need for Star Wars diminished and the proposal was relegated to research until a similar scheme, the National Missile Defense, was revived by President Bill Clinton and pushed forward, despite much opposition, by President George W. Bush.

Sparky opposed the MX missile, which was part of President Reagan's plan to build up the nation's nuclear triad of intercontinental ballistic missiles (ICBM), long-range bombers and submarines armed with ballistic missiles. Debate over the plan, and MX specifically, was rip-roaring, consuming two months of intense deliberations in Congress and scores of votes on amendments and resolutions in both Houses. When the MX was proposed during the Carter years, Sparky said, "I gave the plan and the missile an initial endorsement with serious reservations." Later, he said, "I withdrew my support of the MX because I was not convinced that it would solve the so-called vulnerability problem of our land-based ICBM forces." Instead, he advocated relying on the submarine-launched Trident D-5 missiles that would have the same capability to destroy well-protected, or hardened, targets.

As Sparky noted, the MX "has a lot of friends in the Reagan administration, in the Congress and in the Pentagon." When Senator Gary Hart, a Democrat from Colorado, proposed an amendment to cut off funds for the MX, Sparky supported it. He argued that the missile would not add to the nation's security, could not be used as a "bargaining chip" in arms control negotiations with the Russians and would not serve as a deterrent. "As a defensive weapon, it is overpriced and of dubious utility," Sparky contended. "As an offensive weapon, it raises a specter that the people of this country have firmly rejected, as evidenced by the polls, and rightly so."

Those arguments failed to persuade a majority and the proposal went down 41-58. Later, the defense authorization bill with a reduced provision for the MX missile went through the Senate, 83-15, and, after the House agreed, was sent to President Reagan for his signature. The battle over MX and the nuclear program went on for several years. In 1985, for instance, Sparky was again on the losing side when the Senate voted 55-45 for funds to continue producing and deploying the missile. In the end, as with Star Wars, MX forced the Soviet Union into military spending it couldn't afford.

When Senators Kennedy and Hatfield introduced a resolution calling for "a mutual and verifiable freeze and reduction in nuclear weapons," Sparky leapt up in support even though the measure would have only political influence, not the force of law. A danger greater than the threat from Nazi Germany or Imperial Japan during World War II had arisen, Sparky contended, from "the ever-increasing possibility of a nuclear conflict between the United States and the Soviet Union as a result of the continued and accelerating nuclear arms race between the two superpowers." He noted the Reagan administration was negotiating an arms reduction agreement with the Soviet Union but argued that a freeze would be "a meaningful alternative to the stalled negotiations in which we have placed our hopes to avoid nuclear war."

Kennedy and Hatfield got the amendment through the Senate by attaching it to a House bill to raise the limit on the national debt that was passed 58-40. Sparky and four other Senators were named to the conference to work out differences with the House, which they did in less than a day. The resolution did not require the President to seek a freeze but it did keep pressure on the administration to pursue an arms agreement with the Russians. Later, Sparky supported the treaty to limit intermediate nuclear forces (INF) that went into effect in May 1988.

A resolution backed by Sparky in 1985 called on President Reagan not to sell arms to Jordan but it never got further than the Senate calendar. Sparky joined 60 other Senators in a joint resolution denying approval of the President's plan to sell $354 million worth of missiles to Saudi Arabia in 1986 because of Saudi Arabia's implacable hostility toward Israel. That measure got through both the Senate and the House but was vetoed by President Reagan. The Senate failed to override the veto by one vote.

Similarly, Sparky backed a proposal to halt payments of $40 million to the Contra insurgents because he saw them as being as no better than the dictatorial Sandinistas in Nicaragua. That measure was defeated, 48-52. He opposed more aid but to no effect until the Iran-Contra scandal blew up in the Reagan administration's face. A White House cabal centered on Marine Lieutenant Colonel Oliver North had sought to sell arms to Iran to get funds that would support the Nicaraguan Contras against the leftist Sandinistas. Senator Inouye played a critical role as chairman of the Senate committee investigating the shenanigans of North and his associates as they ran out of control. That exposure ended the scheme.

When President Reagan launched a bombing raid on Libya in 1986, Sparky was among the few who criticized it. The raid was intended to retaliate for a terrorist bombing in a West Berlin nightclub that was blamed on Libyan terrorists. Sparky demurred: "I doubt that the bombing of Libya will be effective in curbing terrorism and (Libyan leader Muammar) Khadafy's involvement. President Reagan must learn that violence begets violence." Senator Inouye, who said he was privy to intelligence showing that Khadafy was involved, defended the bombing but said the President should have consulted Congress first. Subsequently, Sparky was proven wrong as Libyan terrorism subsided for several years.

After the Soviet Union test-fired two long-range missiles that landed within 600 miles of Hawai'i in October 1987, Sparky joined Senator Inouye and Senator Malcolm Wallop, a Republican from Wyoming, in drafting a vehement protest. It said: "The Congress of the United States condemns the Soviet Union for its actions that demonstrate an utter disdain for civilized and acceptable standards of international behavior." Sparky said that if one missile had not malfunctioned, "it is possible that the first missile could have passed directly over portions of my state, making it the first time any superpower missile had flown over the other's soil." Sparky was the only one to speak as the measure went immediately to a vote and was passed, 96 to 0.

Outside the Senate, Sparky stubbed his toe with a delegation of visiting Canadian politicians in town to discuss trade, telling them, "I think that the sooner your culture and ours can blend, the better it is going to be for both our countries." Evidently failing to note the discomfort of the Canadians, who are fiercely proud of not being Americans, Sparky plunged on: "When we say free trade between Canada and the United States, I would mean the same sort of relationship that exists among the 50 states of the Union." The Canadian press excoriated Sparky, the *Calgary Herald* calling him "Senator Windbag." Sparky, for once, was nearly speechless, telling an American reporter, "It's amazing."

Just before terrorists drove a bomb-laden truck into a U.S. Marine encampment at the Beirut airport in Lebanon in 1983, Sparky sought to have President Reagan abide by the War Powers Act. Senator Charles Mathias, a Republican from Maryland, proposed that the Marine Expeditionary Unit, which had been deployed to maintain an uneasy truce between warring factions in Lebanon, be permitted to stay on. Senator Byrd submitted an amendment requiring that the President report to Congress on the mission of the marines and limit their deployment to another 60 days. Senator John Glenn, the astronaut and former colonel of marines, agreed, saying he had asked the administration four questions about the commitment of troops to Lebanon. "I have yet to receive a satisfactory answer to these questions from anyone," he said.

Sparky chimed in: "It is apparent that the administration is not recognizing the War Powers Act or giving it any standing." He said he would vote against the Mathias measure unless the Byrd amendment was adopted. It was, 55–45, and Sparky voted reluctantly for the Mathias bill, which passed 54–46 on September 29. A few days later, the whole issue became moot when 241 Americans were killed in a suicide bombing and the forces were withdrawn shortly after.

At home, Sparky's views on gun control came into sharp relief during consideration of a bill introduced by Senator James McClure, a Republican from Idaho, to ease restrictions on firearms used by hunters and sportsmen. Sparky, who managed the bill for the Democrats, agreed to vote for the bill so long as it did not loosen restrictions on handguns. Handguns, he said, "are intended for one purpose only; that is to kill other human beings. Whatever controls we can impose upon the sale and distribution of those weapons of death, I say let us go to it." Sparky put into the record a letter from the International Association of Chiefs of Police who urged that any change not jeopardize "law enforcement's ability to respond to the use of handguns in violent crime." The bill passed the Senate, 79–15, and the House and became law in May 1986.

Sparky's interest in space began in 1980 on a visit to the 13,000-foot peak of Mauna Kea on the Big Island. By 1986, nine observatories had been built or were under construction there by Americans, Canadians, French, British, Dutch and Japanese. In a conversation with a French scientist at a lodge three-quarters of the way up the side of the mountain, Sparky wondered if "language, nationalism and political differences can be almost insurmountable barriers even among yourselves." The Frenchman replied, "For politicians, the world is many divided communities. But scientists belong to one community. We all speak the same language — the language of science. And we share the same goals. If an astronomer in Chile or Canada discovers a new star, astronomers everywhere benefit equally."

"At first," Sparky wrote later, "I saw no way to act on those reflections." There was too much to do on budgets, taxes, foreign trade — not to say getting reelected. "Building bridges to a new future in space," he wrote, "seemed beyond the scope of everyday politics, an impossible dream." In addition, he got no encouragement from the Defense Department or from the President's science adviser, George Keyworth. Sparky submitted a resolution in 1982 warning of an arms race in space and urging the President to explore "the possibilities for a weapons-free international space station." That resolution and another like it in March 1983 died in the Foreign Relations Committee.

In yet another display of persistence, Sparky had more success in 1984 when he introduced a measure calling for "cooperative East-West ventures in space as an alternative to a space arms race." The concept was not new, having been started by President Richard Nixon in 1972, which led to the docking of the spaceships *Apollo* and *Soyez*. Space cooperation lapsed in 1982 during the depths of the Cold War. In seeking its revival, Sparky argued in the Senate, "Perhaps more than any other avenue, United States-Soviet space cooperation offers an opportunity to practice the policy of 'hard-headed détente' advocated by President Nixon and others, involving sharply defined activities and limited expectations in the context of an expanded, hopeful vision of the future."

To support his arguments, Sparky appended letters from world-class scientists, including Carl Sagan of Cornell, J.A. Van Allen of the University of Iowa, Tobias Owen (then of the State University of New York and later of the University of Hawaii) and Thomas M. Donahue of the University of Michigan. More backing came from Donald Slayton, who had commanded the *Apollo* mission, and Christopher Kraft, director of the Johnson Space Center during the *Apollo* mission. Still more came from novelists Herman Wouk and James Michener. Arthur C. Clarke, author of books entitled *2001* and *2010,* endorsed Sparky's proposal. The proposal plodded its way through Senate and House committees until October, when it was passed in the Senate on October 10, passed in the House on October 11 and had minor differences worked out in conference the same day. The bill was on the President's desk on October 19, was signed and became law on October 30.

Meanwhile, Sparky invited a staff aide, Harvey Meyerson, for coffee one day in the spring of 1982 to ask him to do a comprehensive study on cooperation in space. Sparky told Meyerson, "This issue is important. I want you to take all the time you need to do it." Meyerson said the words remained vivid in his mind because "Congressional staffers are rarely told to take all the time they need on anything." Sparky further told Meyerson to come back with realistic, workable ideas.

Out of that came a book, *The Mars Project: Journeys Beyond the Cold War,* that was finished in 1985 and published in 1986. In it, Sparky laid out his vision for the peaceful exploration of space based on Meyerson's research and his own readings of Wernher von Braun, the German rocket pioneer; Robert Goddard, the father of American rocketry; Giovanni Schiaparelli, an Italian astronomer who discovered canals on Mars; and Konstatin Tsiolkovsky, a Russian scientist. Sparky said that even though ancient civilizations had seen Mars as the god of war, Mars to him "meant interplanetary exploration and settlement on a time and scale such as never before had been attempted." An attempt to reach Mars would have technological spin-offs but the real purpose would be "to understand the meaning of the Space Age — how vast it really was and how best to exploit the unique opportunities it offered."

While the research was underway, Sparky went to the Senate floor on Inauguration Day, 1985, to introduce a resolution calling on President Reagan to direct the National Aeronautics and Space Administration (NASA) to explore opportunities for cooperating with the Soviet Union on missions to Mars. Addressing a sparsely filled chamber, Sparky noted the pressures on the Senate but said, "I believe we also have a duty to try to see beyond the cascading issues that engulf us daily, even while we are considering them." Sparky got a mild show of support from 11 other Senators, including Senator Albert Gore, a Democrat from Tennessee and later Vice President, but the resolution was referred to the Foreign Relations Committee where it was ignored.

Undeterred, Sparky plunged ahead, noting that the Mars project "needed broad-based intermediary objectives that would immediately mobilize governments and the world public and set the stage for Mars." He persuaded the organizers of a scientific conference to set the date for July 17, which would be the tenth anniversary of the *Apollo-Soyuz* venture, and to invite the American astronauts and Russian cosmonauts to take part. After a conversation with John Simpson, a scientist from the University of Chicago, Sparky thought an International Space Year (ISY) might be the way to drum up support for his Mars project. He knew the Russians were planning a space shot for 1992, which would be the 75th anniversary of the Russian Revolution. "Meantime," he wrote, "we would be commemorating the discovery of America with ceremonies featuring replicas of the *Nina, Pinta,* and *Santa Maria* and actors in fifteenth century costumes. The contrast would be embarrassing."

The Mars conference was moved up to July 16 to avoid a conflict with another conference, and Sparky was asked to give an address. "The Mars conference speech was a pleasure to draft," Sparky said. "At last, I wasn't arguing against anything." He listed possibilities for cooperative ventures into space, including a lunar mission and coordination on space stations similar to that among the Antarctic stations of 14 nations. "I did not include an international manned Mars mission on the ISY list because that would be expecting too much too soon," Sparky said.

The next day, Sparky treated the American and Russian astronauts to lunch in the Senate dining room and took them to the Senate gallery while he introduced a resolution calling on the President to endorse the concept of an International Space Year in 1992 and to direct NASA to initiate discussions on missions of international character. "An International Space Year won't change the world," Sparky said, "but at the minimum, these activities help remind all peoples of their common humanity and their shared destiny aboard this beautiful spaceship we call Earth."

Finally, Sparky brought the American and Russian astronauts to a reception room just off the floor where Senators could slip out to meet them. Sparky got Senator Jake Garn, the Republican from Utah who was the first member of Congress to journey into space, on the shuttle *Discovery* in 1985, to co-sponsor the resolution. It sat in various committees until November, when Representative Don Fuqua, the Democrat from Florida and Sparky's old ally in the House, incorporated it into the NASA budget bill of 1986, which became law in December. The ISY was held seven years later and accomplished much, though not all, of what Sparky advocated.

Sparky, like everyone else in America, was stunned and saddened by the explosion that destroyed the space shuttle *Challenger* shortly after liftoff in January 1986. During memorial addresses in the Senate, he noted that the nation was in mourning from Concord, New Hampshire, home of schoolteacher Christa McAuliffe, to Kealakekua, Hawai'i, the home of Air Force Lieutenant Colonel Ellison Onizuka, a Japanese-American. "As the shuttle drew on our diversity in recruiting its crew, so does this national tragedy bring us together in mourning its loss," Sparky said. "As one who views space exploration as a key to our world's continued search for peace, I join with all who mourn the tragic loss of the brave crew who sacrificed their all in a mission of peace."

Despite the tragedy of *Challenger*, Sparky continued to advocate the peaceful exploration of space and occasionally got a pat on the back from colleagues. Senator Paul Simon, a Democrat from Illinois, praised Sparky's book on Mars, saying, "Sometimes we do not see the obvious because it makes too much sense." Senator Claiborne Pell, a Democrat from Rhode Island, applauded Sparky and noted that "we are beset with questions about the wisdom — or lack of it — in deploying weapons in space, mindful of the terrible *Challenger* disaster, as seized with the problems inherent in the deteriorated relationship with the Soviet Union."

Senator George Mitchell, a Democrat from Maine, noted that Sparky had generated bipartisan support for his proposal to send a manned mission to Mars: "A joint mission to Mars also represents a more prudent investment that the Reagan administration's strategic defense initiative." Senator Charles "Mac" Mathias, the Republican from Maryland, commended Sparky for having "vigorously pursued an imaginative strategy to improve East-West relations and expand our understanding of the universe."

President Reagan eventually backed the ISY proposal in a cover letter to a NASA report required by the ISY legislation. In 1989, Senator Gore said he had come across Sparky's book while sorting out his office: "We are always exposed to so much information and argument over policy that we sometimes forget the moment when even quite important ideas become part of our own conception. Holding Spark's book in my hand, I was reminded of how important his thoughts were to become a part of my own thinking."

Sparky was equally persistent in persuading Congress to establish the position of poet laureate modeled on that in Britain where John Dryden was the first poet laureate, appointed in 1668. Alfred, Lord Tennyson held it from 1850 to 1896 while John Masefield was poet laureate from 1930 to 1967. Sparky, who had introduced a bill on the poet laureate's position in every Congress in which he served, finally got it passed in 1985, but through the back door. He threw his bill into the hopper in January and it was promptly referred to the Committee on Labor and Human Resources where it gathered dust. In October, Sparky was asked to offer an amendment that would combine the Office of Poetry Consultant in the Library of Congress with his proposed poet laureate. Ever the practical, compromising politician when it came to tactics, Sparky agreed, saying he hoped the post would reflect America's ethnic, racial and cultural diversity. The measure was passed by voice vote and a parallel measure authorized the meager sum of $10,000 to set up the office.

Early in the following year, Robert Penn Warren was chosen to be the first poet laureate after having won three Pulitzer Prizes. The first was in 1947 for *All the King's Men,* a novel based on the political life of Louisiana's autocratic governor, Huey P. Long. The second was for *Promises: Poems 1954–1956,* which was awarded in 1957, and the third was for *Now and Then: Poems 1976–1978.* The poet laureate was then 80 years old and a bit less than gracious on learning of his appointment: "The people who create these posts don't give a damn about poetry." Nonetheless, Sparky professed to be pleased with the choice, reading into the Record a tribute from a former student of Warren named James Shannon.

Years later, the Library of Congress noted on its Web site that each poet laureate has brought a different emphasis to the position: "Joseph Brodsky initiated the idea of providing poetry in airports, supermarkets and hotel rooms. Maxine Kumin started a popular series of poetry workshops for women at the Library of Congress. Gwendolyn Brooks met with elementary school students to encourage them to write poetry. Rita Dove, an African-American, brought together writers to explore the African diaspora through the eyes of its artists. She also championed children's poetry and jazz with poetry events. Robert Hass organized the 'Watershed' conference that brought together noted novelists, poets and storytellers to talk about writing, nature and community."

Robert Pinsky, who was named poet laureate in 1997, sought to bring poetry to the Internet and to get political leaders and private citizens to include more poetry in their public appearances. Stanley Kunitz was named poet laureate in 2000 at the age of 95 after having published ten volumes of poetry. Billy Collins, a professor of English and winner of many literary prizes, became the poet laureate in 2001. The annual stipend has been raised to $35,000.

On mundane issues, Sparky struggled for legislation to stimulate new forms of energy but most of his pleas fell on deaf ears in the mid-1980s. The energy crises of the 1970s had passed, relieving the pressure to find new sources of energy. During his second term, he sought to have the federal government finance research into hydrogen as a form of energy and eagerly pushed renewable energy bills, with no success on the first and only limited on the second. Sparky argued that "hydrogen is the most abundant element in the universe and is readily available on Earth.

Three quarters of the world's surface is covered with water, the feedstock of hydrogen." It is the lightest of the elements and could replace jet fuel on aircraft. It could substitute for electricity, Sparky asserted, could be conveniently stored and cost less than electricity to transport through pipelines.

"Hydrogen is indeed very much the ultimate, natural and cleanest fuel," he said in 1983. His proposals got shot down one after the other over the next six years. Two decades later, Sparky would have been shown to have been visionary as General Motors prepared to bring to market, probably in 2004, an automobile powered by a fuel cell. As *The Economist* said in 2000: "It looks increasingly likely that the eventual replacement for the internal combustion engine in motor vehicles will be the fuel cell." It should prove to be four times more efficient than the best gasoline-driven engines.

Similarly, Sparky pleaded for tax incentives for renewable sources of energy, such as wind, geothermal, hydroelectric and solar. "Unless we establish ourselves as an energy self-sufficient nation, we will never be able, fully and effectively, to control our own economic destiny. This imperative, in turn, requires us to exploit our renewable energy resources." That, too, was ignored, although the cry for less dependence on oil from the Middle East could be heard again after the assaults in New York and Washington mounted by Arab terrorists on September 11, 2001. Despite the lack of interest in the 1980s, Sparky's advocacy made his office a gathering place for energy activists who were surprised to find a Senator interested in what they had to say. When he could, Sparky would invite them in for informal discussions during which he picked their brains for information that might prove useful.

Sparky, who had always been an admirer of those who had served in the armed forces, fought hard in his second term as a co-sponsor of a bill that would extend educational benefits to military veterans as a way of attracting top-quality recruits. That G.I. Bill would provide varying amounts for college education depending on the length and hardship of service. It was a bipartisan bill backed by Sparky and Senators William Armstrong, a Republican from Colorado; William Cohen, a Republican from Maine and later Secretary of Defense in the second Clinton administration; Ernest Hollings, a Democrat from South Carolina; and Alan Cranston, the Democrat from California. The opponents of the measure were mostly Southerners of both parties who sought to discredit the volunteer force in favor of a return to conscription because they still felt the volunteer force had recruited too many African-Americans. Senator Cohen, in a testy exchange with Senator John Tower, a Republican from Texas and chairman of the Armed Services

Committee, asserted that opponents of the volunteer force said "we have too many poor, too many blacks, too many minorities, too many such people in the Army."

Senator Armstrong, saying that Sparky had shown "a great deal of leadership and perspicacity in dealing with this issue," called on him to enter the fray. Sparky noted the bipartisan support for the measure and especially that a Southerner, Senator Hollings, who favored a return to the draft, had come out for it. "Unfortunately," Sparky said, "there are signs that the Armed Services Committee and the President have forgotten the lessons of only a few short years ago," when military benefits lagged so far behind that recruiting fell off. Even with proposed raises, Sparky argued, military pay would fall further behind the private sector.

The main focus of his argument was on a period four or five years down the road. "What we are asking the Congress to do in establishing a peacetime G.I. Bill is to anticipate rather than react to a future recruiting crisis in the All-Volunteer Force," Sparky said. "In 1980, the Congress reacted sharply, but belatedly, to the severe recruiting and retention shortfalls experienced by the military services. The damage had already been done to the combat readiness of our military forces. We foresee a recruiting crisis which could be exacerbated by a swiftly improving economy, the failure to keep military pay competitive, and forced adherence to recruit quality standards. We are convinced that the answer is putting a G.I. Bill on the books for fiscal 1987 so that we are prepared for the recruiting shortfalls which are sure to come."

The measure drew support from Senators Robert Dole and Edward Kennedy but was ruled out of order by the chair on a technicality. The sponsors were back again the next year, with Senator Armstrong again applauding Sparky: "When Spark Matsunaga signs on to get something done, he is ready to carry the battle forward." Sparky repeated his earlier argument: "We need this G.I. Bill in place now to head off what will inevitably be serious recruiting problems in the near future and improving economic conditions combined with the shrinking pool of eligible recruits to create a highly competitive recruiting market."

Again they were turned away because opponents argued that recruiting had not gone sour. By 1985, the tide had changed as signs could be foreseen of recruiting problems. Representative Sonny Montgomery, a Democrat from Mississippi and longtime member of the Committee on Veterans Affairs, led a charge to reestablish the G.I Bill. Two years later, Senator Cranston was back with a bill to make the G.I Bill permanent, with Sparky's enthusiastic support. It went through the Senate, 89–0, and the House, 401–2.

The G.I. Bill was a benefit for the man or woman leaving the service and becoming a veteran, another cause to which Sparky gave high priority. He was pleased to be appointed to the Committee on Veterans Affairs in 1985, which gave him more standing when he argued for veterans' benefits. He was co-sponsor of a bill in 1987 that expanded the job counseling services of the Veterans Administration, or VA, but lost a debate later that year on mandatory drug testing for doctors, nurses and other members of VA staffs. Sparky argued that the testing at that time was unreliable and "could well result in unjust, adverse effects on careers, high testing costs and a decline in the VA's ability to deliver adequate health care." The measure was approved by voice vote. He got no action on a bill he introduced that would have provided for studies of psychological problems among Asian-American veterans of the war in Vietnam. Sparky supported, with success, a bill that permitted judicial review of claims submitted by veterans.

In 1988, a bipartisan group sought to have the VA raised to the level of a department with representation in the President's cabinet. Sparky agreed with the thrust of the bill but queried Senator Glenn, chairman of the Committee on Government Affairs who was shepherding the bill on the floor: "I see no mention of any provisions in this important legislation that specifically addresses the concerns of minority veterans." Glenn reassured Sparky that those concerns had been addressed but not in the text of the legislation itself.

Sparky said, "It is extremely important that we build into the new Department of Veterans Affairs a mechanism that will deal automatically with minority concerns." He said he would not propose an amendment to the bill that might jeopardize its passage but would accept Glenn's suggestion that the issue be taken up with the new Secretary of Veterans' Affairs. Sparky strongly supported a measure to provide extra benefits to veterans who had been exposed to the defoliant known as "Agent Orange" in the Vietnam War.

Toward the end of his second term in the Senate, Sparky sided with Senator Daniel Patrick Moynihan, the Democrat from New York, to impose restrictions on billboards along the nation's highways. Sparky noted that he had drafted a bill passed by the Territorial Legislature in Hawai'i that banned billboards, giving tourists the opportunity to be "looking at the landscape unblemished by billboards." On the mainland, he argued with *haiku* poetry:

Welcome winter snow
Covers Nature's blemishes.
Man-made ones remain.

Senator Wendell Ford, a Democrat from Kentucky and a proponent of billboards, drew a laugh when he said of Hawai'i: "Once you get on the island, you cannot get off, so you do not need billboards." To which Sparky drew another laugh when he responded, "I am glad the Senator has been there because now…he knows what Heaven looks like. And if on Judgment Day he is directed to go the other way, at least he will have had that satisfaction." Ford went on to assert that the billboard ban would put people out of business, and his argument won the day.

Back home, Sparky was instrumental in having returned to their rightful owners some wartime diaries of soldiers in the 442nd Regimental Combat Team. Each of the 300 journals had been kept during the soldiers' first days in the Army, then collected while they were aboard the *S.S. Lurline* being transported to the mainland. The diaries had nothing of military value in them, only jottings about bad food, hard work and whether their girlfriends would be waiting when they got home. The *nisei* saw the confiscation as more evidence that they were not trusted.

The journals sat in boxes for 40 years until a researcher, Chester Tanaka, found that they had been stored in the Federal Records Center in San Bruno, California. The U.S. Customs Service didn't want to let them go but Sparky intervened, arguing that the seizure had been an "unwarranted invasion of privacy." The diaries were returned to the owners or their families at a ceremony in the clubhouse of the 442nd RCT in Honolulu in August 1987.

Three years earlier, Sparky had marked the 25th anniversary of statehood for Hawai'i by returning to two favorite themes as he addressed the Senate: Democracy and racial equality. "The people of Hawai'i have risen to meet the challenges of a young and growing state, non-contiguous to the North American continent, yet firmly bound to its sister states by the ideals of American democracy," he said. Sparky claimed that Hawai'i had contributed to the nation in "ethnic equity for all our peoples and the consequent domestic tranquillity we have gained. The racial harmony of Hawai'i's multiethnic people — while not attaining an ideal state — nevertheless represents a model of integration and a standard of neighborliness that have left a lasting impression on millions of American tourists over the years and, indeed, on our visitors from foreign shores." ❖

10

Redress
1987–1988

The culminating achievement in Sparky's political career was his vital role in obtaining redress for Americans of Japanese ancestry who had been torn from their homes, deprived of their property and incarcerated in ramshackle camps in desolate regions in the West during World War II.

This endeavor illuminated Sparky's sense of equity, his dreams and vision, his persistence and art of persuasion, and his abhorrence of discrimination even though his family and relatively few Japanese-Americans from Hawai'i had been affected. Moreover, the years of Sparky's toil on redress brought out the manner in which his fundamental American nature was flavored with the culture of Japan. On his American side, he and his allies were motivated by the deepest American traditions and sense of fair play, and they applied time-tested American lobbying tactics to advance their cause. On his Japanese side, Sparky's own tactics resembled the *nemawashi*, loosely translated to mean "thorough preparation," of his forefathers. Behind the scenes, he sought out all 99 of his colleagues in the Senate to persuade them one by one to vote for his proposal either on its merits or out of friendship or favors due him. Much of his success in this issue could be attributed to the personal relations he had cultivated over the years.

Redress, however, was more than seeking an apology and compensation for a comparatively small number of people who had been treated unjustly. The issue went to the very heart of American democracy, of the due process that is the constitutional birthright of all Americans, of the sense of justice without which America would not be America. Certainly Sparky saw the issue in its broadest terms, contending that the essence of the civil rights of all Americans had been profoundly violated. What happened to the Japanese-Americans, he argued, could happen to anyone if things were not set right. Representative Norman Mineta, Sparky's friend in the House, summed it up: "Redress was not a Japanese-American issue to Spark. It was not an Asian-American issue. It was an American issue, which is how he wished the lessons of the internment to be remembered."

Leslie T. Hatamiya, among the more articulate Japanese-Americans on this issue, argued in her 1993 book, *Righting a Wrong: Japanese-Americans and the Passage of the Civil Liberties Act of 1988:* "It was a matter of constitutional rights and justice, of setting the historical, political, and moral record straight. It was not only about vindicating a small minority group, but about clearing the conscience." Hatamiya, a young *sansei*, or third-generation Japanese-American whose grandparents and parents had been interned, continued: "The issue was 'all-American,' touching the fundamental pillars of the U.S. Constitution, notably the Fifth Amendment guarantee of due process."

The campaign for redress comprised four separate and sometimes competitive courses of action:

- Legislation through Congress, favored by the Japanese-American Citizens League, or JACL, and by Japanese-American members of Congress. This required educating Congress, the executive branch and the public about the injustices experienced by the AJAs, then asking for an apology and compensation. It was eventually successful.

- The National Coalition for Redress/Reparations sought to mobilize support for redress through a grassroots letter-writing campaign, getting the attention of the press, and having legislation that demanded redress introduced in a frontal assault on Congress. It was unsuccessful.

- The National Council for Japanese-American Redress, of which William Hohri of Chicago was the leader, brought to court a class-action suit naming 22 causes of action and demanded a total of $27 billion in redress. It was ultimately dismissed by the U.S. Supreme Court.

- Minoru Yasui, Gordon Hirabayashi and Fred Korematsu, who had been convicted of violating regulations of the evacuation, filed lawsuits. After years of legal wrangling, Yasui's case became moot when he died, while the convictions of Hirabayashi and Korematsu were vacated by the courts but without recompense.

These rival courses of action divided the Japanese-American community. A further split opened between Japanese-Americans who sought redress and those who opposed the endeavor. By the 1970s, opponents were pointing to the progress made by Japanese-Americans in politics, business and especially in rebuilding their lives. "To some," said a passage in *The Asian American Almanac,* "accomplishments such as these were clear evidence of the wisdom of putting aside the past. Others felt that nothing could compensate them for their suffering; there was concern expressed that many of the *issei* (first generation), who perhaps had suffered the most, had already died or were too elderly to want or need to undertake such a quest. Still others felt it was a form of welfare. For many, discussion of redress reopened old wounds." Among the outspoken opponents was former Senator S.I. Hayakawa, the Republican from California, who said the proposal for redress was "appallingly humiliating" to Japanese-Americans.

Sparky's proposal for redress was based on the recommendations of a national commission and included an apology from the United States and the payment of $20,000 to each survivor. He spearheaded the campaign in the Senate while Norman Mineta, the California Democrat who had been detained in a camp as a child, led the way in the House. Mineta, in turn, persuaded the Majority Leader, Representative Thomas Foley of Washington, to give the campaign a push by introducing a critical piece of legislation. He arranged to have the bill numbered H.R. 442, which recalled the 442nd Regimental Combat Team that had fought with such distinction in World War II.

Outside of the Congress, the labors of JACL in support of redress by legislation, were led by Mike Masaoka, who had been a soldier in the 442nd RCT and was later a prominent lobbyist in Washington, D.C. JACL obtained support from political, civic and religious groups. Jewish organizations were particularly supportive, the plight of Japanese-Americans echoing the Holocaust in Europe even if the hardships of the detention centers did not approach the horrors visited upon the Jews by the Nazi Germans. Moreover, *nisei* units had been among the first of the U.S. Army to reach the concentration camps in Europe and to rescue Jewish survivors at the end of World War II. Nathan Perlmutter, the national director of the Anti-Defamation League of B'nai B'rith, wrote to a JACL committee in 1980: "You can, therefore, count on our complete support in your efforts to rectify this past injustice."

The obstacles were formidable. Opponents of redress, led by Senator Jesse Helms, the powerful Republican from North Carolina, argued that President Franklin Delano Roosevelt had been right in authorizing the Army to round up AJAs, about two-thirds of whom were American citizens. The rest were legal resident aliens who had not been permitted to apply for American citizenship because of the Oriental exclusion laws. The exigencies of war, the opponents argued, justified the violation of constitutional rights. Others asserted that the cost of redress, estimated to total $1.3 billion, was excessive when the federal budget was plunging into deficit. Still others contended that an apology for the admittedly unjust detention of AJAs for nearly four years would be appropriate but that attaching money to such an apology would be demeaning.

In addition, opponents pointed to a 1948 Japanese-American Claims Act in which $147 million had been paid to *nisei* who could prove they had lost property.

They argued that President Gerald Ford had, in effect, apologized in 1976 when he rescinded President Roosevelt's Executive Order 9066 authorizing the detention. Several opponents contended that redress for Japanese-Americans would set a precedent under which African-Americans could seek redress for slavery, American Indians for having been driven off their land and other hyphenated Americans for other wrongs allegedly perpetrated by the United States. Lillian Baker, a historian whose husband had been killed in the Pacific, contended that the incarceration had been justified and the camps a pleasant haven for Japanese-Americans.

President Reagan, who had come to office in January 1981, was opposed to redress and threatened to veto it. Richard K. Willard, the assistant attorney general heading the Civil Division in the Department of Justice, submitted a brief to Congress in which he asserted: "We question the wisdom and, indeed, the propriety, of accusing leaders of the United States government during World War II, both civilian and military, of dishonorable behavior." Willard said the Justice Department opposed "paying additional reparations to individuals" after having settled claims under the 1948 act. He complained that the restitution would "impose heavy administrative burdens on the Attorney General." He opposed the definition of who would be eligible for payments, contending that "the term 'living' is imprecise." The Justice Department also opposed a provision for payments to the 900 Aleuts of Alaska, American citizens who had been uprooted from the Aleutian Islands and sent to miserable camps in southeast Alaska, supposedly to prevent them from being captured by Japanese soldiers who occupied several islands in the Aleutian chain during the war.

Lastly, the vast majority of American voters and taxpayers didn't know much about the incarceration of the Japanese-Americans and the few who did might have felt that most Americans suffered during World War II and none should be expected to be recompensed. Nor were many Americans comfortable with the accusation that President Roosevelt and his advisers had been dishonorable in their treatment of the Japanese-Americans — and besides, it was easy to be critical in hindsight. It was also a time of "Japan bashing," when the U.S. was locked in economic disputes with Japan; many Americans had a hard time distinguishing between the Japanese and Japanese-Americans who were American citizens. Even the prominent newspaper, *The New York Times,* repeatedly referred to Japanese-Americans as Japanese.

The plea for redress started long after detention had ended in 1946. About 1970, a few Japanese-Americans began contemplating redress. From the beginning, divisions among them caused the movement to sputter until 1976, when Michiko

Nishiura Weglyn published an extensively researched book entitled *Years of Infamy: The Untold Story of America's Concentration Camps*. Weglyn had been detained in a camp in Arizona for two years, had been forced to drop out of Mount Holyoke College because she had contracted tuberculosis and later had married a survivor of the Holocaust in Europe, Walter Weglyn. She spent eight years poring over documents and interviewing Japanese-Americans to expose what had happened.

Weglyn's book appears to have been catalytic. She wrote: "Persuaded that the enormity of a bygone injustice has been only partially perceived, I have taken upon myself the task of piecing together what might be called the 'forgotten' — or ignored parts of the tapestry of those years." Weglyn was supported by best-selling author James Michener, whose third wife, Mari Yoriko Sabusawa, was Japanese-American. Noting that he had spent 33 years dealing with the moral issues of the 1942 evacuation, Michener contended in the book's introduction: "We struck out blindly, stupidly, to our eternal discredit."

The JACL national convention in Salt Lake City in July 1978 adopted a resolution calling for a $25,000 payment to each person who had been detained. Few Japanese-Americans knew how to go about obtaining redress as they lacked experience in political maneuvering in Washington. A delegation from JACL met in Washington in February 1979, with four Japanese-American members of Congress — Sparky, Senator Inouye, and Representatives Mineta and Robert Matsui, another California Democrat. Led by Dan Inouye, the members of Congress argued that first priority should be given to getting a public acknowledgment that Japanese-Americans had been wronged. He suggested a national commission to bring the facts to public attention.

Senator Inouye introduced a bill in August 1979 that provided for a national commission to investigate the incarceration of the Japanese-Americans. "Many Americans," he said when the bill reached the floor in May 1980, "do not know about this event in which due process and equal protection of the law as guaranteed under our Constitution was denied for up to 4-1/2 years for some citizens."

Sparky, in support, said, "It remains the single most traumatic and disturbing event in the lives of many *nisei*. More importantly, their children have started to ask questions about the internment camps: Why did not their parents and grandparents protest? Did they commit some crime that they were ashamed of?" He concluded: "The proposed study would finally make all the facts known and would allow Congress to decide whether any further action should be taken to compensate victims of the wartime relocation policy." A year later, President Carter signed the law establishing the Commission on Wartime Relocation and Internment of

Civilians. "We want to prevent," the President said, "any recurrence of this abuse of the basic human rights of American citizens."

The commission of nine, with three each named by the President, the Senate and the House, was comprised of prominent citizens who represented a cross section of America. It was led by Joan Z. Bernstein, a Washington attorney who was later named general counsel of the Department of Health and Human Services. The commission included Arthur J. Goldberg, the former Supreme Court Justice; Edward W. Brooke, a Republican from Massachusetts and the first African-American Senator elected by popular vote; and Arthur S. Flemming, the former chairman of the Civil Rights Commission. In addition, there were Representative Daniel E. Lungren, a Republican from California, the state in which the majority of the detained Japanese-Americans had lived; Hugh B. Mitchell, a Democratic State Senator from Washington, another state that had been home for many interned Japanese-Americans; and the Rev. Robert Drinan, a Jesuit priest and authority on civil rights who had been a Democratic member of Congress from Massachusetts. The commission was rounded out with Judge William M. Marutani of Pennsylvania, a Japanese-American who later successfully argued in the Supreme Court against the Virginia law prohibiting interracial marriage; and the Rev. Ishmael V. Gromoff of Alaska, a Russian Orthodox priest who had been interned with the Aleuts.

Meantime, the Seattle chapter of JACL dissented from the commission approach and persuaded Representative Michael Lowry, a Democrat from Washington, to introduce a bill in November 1979 that called on the federal government to pay each person detained a sum of $15,000 plus $15 a day for each day they had been interned. Payments for deceased persons would go to their families. The bill was referred to a committee and disappeared.

In 1981, the national commission said it "held 20 days of hearings in cities across the country, particularly on the West Coast, hearing testimony from more than 750 witnesses: evacuees, former government officials, public figures, interested citizens, and historians and other professionals who have studied the subjects of Commission inquiry. An extensive effort was made to locate and to review the records of government action and to analyze other sources of information including contemporary writings, personal accounts and historical analyses." The commission spent another year analyzing documents and deliberating over what its report should say. The findings were issued in December 1982, in a 467-page report, *Personal Justice Denied*, that concluded: "Executive Order 9066 was not justified by military necessity, and the decisions that followed from it — exclusion, detention, the ending of detention and the ending of exclusion — were not founded upon military considerations. The broad historical causes that shaped these decisions were race prejudice, war hysteria, and a failure of political leadership."

As Hatamiya pointed out, "The establishment of the commission turned out to be the most prudent political move that the effort for redress could have made." It provided a basis for legislation, it educated Congress and the public, and it got wide press coverage. The commission's report took the issue beyond a single special interest and made it "easier for the four Japanese-American members of Congress to come out in full support of the redress legislation," Hatamiya wrote. Sparky applauded the commission for "its thorough and unbiased examination" of the internment. "If there is a lingering belief that there must have been a good reason for the evacuation and detention of the Japanese-Americans, this report will surely dispel it forever."

The commission issued the second part of its report in June 1983, recommending that the U.S. government apologize to the Japanese-Americans for the violation of their constitutional rights and award each surviving person $20,000. Issuing the findings in December and recommendations six months later was a shrewd move, doubling the attention received from Congress and the public.

The redress movement then stalled because of Congressional inertia, the opposition of the Reagan administration and the dissent of Daniel Lungren, the Republican Congressman from California who disagreed with the provision for $20,000 payments. Later that year, the Democratic Majority Leader, Representative James Wright of Texas, introduced a measure with 106 co-sponsors, or about one-quarter of the House, calling for acceptance of the national commission's recommendations. Sparky submitted a companion bill with 19 sponsors. Both died in committee.

Over the next year, Senators expressed their objections or noncommittal views. Senator Strom Thurmond, the Republican from South Carolina and chairman of the influential Judiciary Committee, wrote to Peter Okada, an AJA from Seattle: "I am not convinced that the proposed relief appropriately compensates those who were harmed by this governmental action, nor am I convinced that a reopening of this issue after four decades will serve the public interest." Senator Matt Mattingly, a Republican from Georgia and a member of the Appropriations Committee that would vote on any funds, was direct with Mrs. Julia Hunter in Atlanta: "I do not favor the compensatory payment." Senator Barry Goldwater, the Republican from Arizona and onetime presidential candidate, said in an exchange with Roland Ingraham of Mesa: "Frankly, I don't think the reparation legislation stands a chance in the present form of making payments to specific individuals."

Senator Paula Hawkins, a Republican from Florida, told Mrs. Ida Hayataka, a Japanese-American in Jacksonville: "World War II created great hardships for all Americans. No monetary compensation would overcome this suffering." Senator Lowell Weicker, the Republican from Connecticut, was sympathetic but noncommittal in a letter to Mrs. Don Hibino, an AJA in Portland, Connecticut: "I believe that these Americans and their descendants deserve just compensation for the suffering they endured. It is very important, however, to allow Congress to consider the extent and type of restitution the government will offer."

Senator Charles Mathias, the Republican from Maryland, was equally noncommittal in a letter to Ms. Katherine Kumamoto, a Japanese-American in Riverside, California: "I will review such legislation when it comes before the full Senate." Similarly, Senator Paul Laxalt, the Republican from Nevada, wrote to Takeshi Kubota, a Japanese-American in Reno, that a Senate subcommittee had asked for comment from several government agencies: "Before I take a stand on this issue, I would like to review these responses in order to get some of the effects of S. 2116 [Sparky's bill] on the respective agencies."

On the other side, Senator Slade Gorton, a Republican from Washington, wrote Tim Otani, an AJA in Seattle, that he would support the proposal. Senator Edward Kennedy, the Democrat from Massachusetts, was among the few who openly came out for redress, telling Ms. Elyse Kaneda, a Japanese-American in Cambridge: "We cannot erase this mistake, but we can reaffirm our commitment to civil liberties and our commitment to reject future pressures to abandon our sense of decency."

When the 99th Congress convened in January 1985, Majority Leader Wright was back with a proposal similar to an earlier measure and with 143 co-sponsors. Sparky brought in the same bill some weeks later with 28 co-sponsors in the Senate. Still nothing happened. In July, JACL called a "summit meeting" with three other Japanese-American committees but, as the book *Japanese-American History*, edited by Brian Niiya, succinctly recounts: "Good will is promoted; little else is agreed upon."

Even so, support was stirring outside of Congress. Tim Gojio of JACL reported to Elma Henderson of Sparky's staff that resolutions supporting redress had been adopted by the United Methodist Church, Trinity Episcopal Church, Ecumenical Ministries of Oregon and the Congregation Neveh Shalom. More support had come from Jewish civic groups. The 34th Infantry Division, with which the 100th Infantry Battalion had served, and other veterans' associations said they backed redress.

In the Senate, Senator Mark Hatfield, the Oregon Republican, said in a 1986 letter to Marvin Stern of Seattle: "This is a time for healing. As this issue is considered by the Senate, I will be guided by that belief." Senator John Glenn wrote to Frank Titus in Dayton that "this action was a grave injustice unsupported by military necessity." Howard Metzenbaum, the other Democratic Senator from Ohio, wrote to Ms. Sachi Kajiwara, an AJA from Dayton: "I believe the United States owes Japanese-Americans both an apology and restitution for the injustices committed against them during World War II." Senator Carl Levin, a Democrat from Michigan, told Emo Honzaki, an AJA in Ypsilanti: "We must never again in the name of national security inflict injustice on our citizens, and we must find a way legislatively to acknowledge the mistake and compensate for the suffering."

The tide was moving but had not yet turned. As the 100th Congress opened in January 1987, President Reagan was still in the White House but the Democrats had won control of the Senate, 55–45, to go along with their control of the House, 258–177. This meant that Senator Robert Byrd, Sparky's friend, became Majority Leader again, and Senator Alan Cranston of California, who was sympathetic to redress, returned as majority whip. In addition, Senator Glenn, a supporter of redress, replaced Senator William Roth, a Republican from Delaware and an opponent of redress, as chairman of the Governmental Affairs Committee that would have jurisdiction over bills concerning redress.

In the House, Representative Thomas P. (Tip) O'Neill retired as Speaker and was replaced by Representative Wright, a supporter of redress. Representative Thomas Foley of Washington became Majority Leader and he, too, supported redress. Representative Norman Mineta drew up the strategy for getting redress before the House, and his office became an operations center just as Sparky's office took the lead in the Senate. Like Sparky, Mineta spoke with many of his colleagues one-on-one. Further, Mineta had been in the camps as a child and could speak from personal experience, which carried considerable weight with his colleagues.

At the beginning of the session, Sparky geared up a campaign with Elma Henderson of his staff, instructing her to keep her finger on the pulse of the Senate, to stay in almost daily touch with the staffs of uncommitted and opposing Senators, and to feed information to him as he made his rounds. Sparky was eager to have co-sponsors because that meant a Senator favored the bill even before it was debated. He took to the floor to recall the plight of the Japanese-Americans in 1942 and to note that 42 Senators from both parties had agreed to co-sponsor the bill that he would soon reintroduce. "As we celebrate the bicentennial of the U.S. Constitution this year," he said, "it would be most appropriate for us to act to remove once and for all this singular blot on that greatest of all human-written documents, and to solemnly resolve that such a mass denial of protection guaranteed by the Constitution shall never occur again in the United States of America."

For the next couple of months, Sparky concentrated on *nemawashi* to line up supporters. Elma Henderson reported by memo on February 13th that Senator Pete Wilson, a Republican from California who had been dubious about redress, had addressed a meeting of *nisei* farmers in Fresno and "came within a hair's breadth of saying he would co-sponsor the bill." Henderson said she spoke with David Wetmore on Wilson's staff and found that Wetmore had recommended to the Senator that he sign on.

Henderson told Sparky the Denver chapter of JACL had written to Senator William Armstrong, a Republican, asking him to co-sponsor. Armstrong's legislative director, Brian Waidman, said he would talk to the Senator. She found the staff of Senator Dave Durenberger, a Republican from Minnesota, had enough information about the bill and expected the Senator to make a decision shortly. Henderson talked with Kevin Quigley, legislative director for Senator John Heinz, a Republican from Pennsylvania, and Quigley was surprised that Heinz had not signed on yet. He said he would talk with his Senator and hoped he would be a co-sponsor.

Henderson called Robert Lallett, who handled bills in the Government Affairs Committee for Senator Lloyd Bentsen, the Democrat from Texas, and reminded him of the 442nd RCT's sacrifices in rescuing the "Lost Battalion" of Texans who had been nearly captured by the Germans in World War II. Mallett said he hadn't known that and would include it in a memo to Senator Bentsen.

Two days later, Henderson reported to Sparky that Susan Schwab, legislative director for Senator John Danforth, a Republican from Missouri, was "very encouraging." She spoke with Martha Pope and Bob Corolla on the staff of Senator George Mitchell, the Democrat from Maine, and "they were also very encouraging." Senator David Pryor, a Democrat from Arkansas, declined to be a co-sponsor but his staff said he was sympathetic and would support it on the floor.

Sparky struck out, however, with Senator John McCain. Henderson said Chris Cook, McCain's legislative assistant, said "no" so quickly that "I am just not sure he actually checked with Sen. McCain," the Arizona Republican who sought his party's presidential nomination in 2000. Sparky noted in a memo to his staff that he had gone to the Republican cloakroom just outside the Senate chamber to speak with Senator Heinz, who said he was opposed.

Henderson gave Sparky a rundown on a meeting of representatives from civic organizations that had pledged to support redress. "The Leadership

Conference on Civil Rights, which is composed of about 100 separate civil rights groups, is going to send a letter to all the Senators who have not co-sponsored the bill," she reported. "The Friends Committee on National Legislation is going to take the lead with church groups." Mike Lewis of the International Longshoremen's & Warehousemen's Union "is preparing a letter to all Senators who have not co-sponsored for signature by ILWU's international president," she said.

Henderson ticked off a list of Senators who would be approached by the American Civil Liberties Union. Wade Henderson of the ILWU, Elma Henderson wrote, "said the photographs of camp life and Japanese-American children being herded into detention camps are very effective and urged that we use them as much as possible." Staff members of the Anti-Defamation League, a Jewish civic organization, said they had many members in Florida who would speak to the Senators from Florida as well as to Senators Robert Kasten, a Republican from Wisconsin, and Senator Heinz. AFL-CIO said it would put its effective lobbying organization to work for redress. Grace Uyehara of JACL said the governor of Utah had written to Senators Jake Garn and Orrin Hatch, both Republicans, urging them to become co-sponsors. The group believed, Henderson concluded, that they had no way of winning support from Republican Senators Jesse Helms of North Carolina, Donald Nickles of Oklahoma, Mitch McConnell of Kentucky, John Warner of Virginia and Dan Quayle of Indiana, who later became Vice President.

It went on like this for two months. When Sparky rose on Friday, April 10, to introduce his bill on accepting the findings and recommendations of the Commission on Wartime Relocation, his measure had 70 co-sponsors, compared with 42 only two months before. Sparky addressed a Senate chamber that was almost empty, most Senators having left for the Easter holiday, but delivered his address as if he were in a packed Roman Coliseum. He related a particularly tragic story to underline the hardships of those interned. One summer evening in broad daylight, Sparky said, a grandfather and grandson were playing catch in one of the camps. The grandfather missed the ball and ran toward the fence, which the inmates were not allowed to go near. The guard in the watchtower yelled at the old man, "Go back!" The grandfather responded, "Oh, I am just going after the ball!" The guard then fired his machine gun and killed the old man on the spot.

"Perhaps the most traumatic experience," Sparky said, "the one thing that has haunted Americans of Japanese ancestry for 45 years, was the stigma of being cast as disloyal to their own beloved country, the United States of America. One elderly internee, an American veteran of World War I, committed suicide rather than bear the brand of disloyalty to his country." He said Japanese-Americans welcomed the study by the national commission because it showed what they already knew — that the camps were not justified.

The lobbying continued. To the 70 co-sponsors, six more were added in succeeding months — but five withdrew for a net of 71 co-sponsors. The responses to Sparky's entreaties ranged all over the lot. Senator Alan Simpson, a Republican from Wyoming and the Republican whip, wrote a note to thank Sparky for sending a box of chocolate-covered macadamia nuts for which Hawai'i is famous but said his measure "will not go on the statute books without controversy." He added: "The Heart Mountain Relocation Center was located just 14 miles from my home in Cody, Wyoming, and I remember the pain and confusion of it all quite vividly."

Senator Paul Trible, a Republican from Virginia, wrote: "I am strongly sympathetic to the goals of this legislation, and I applaud your persistence in seeking its passage." Then came the *but*: "Nevertheless, I am concerned about the potential costs of a reparations bill....For that reason, I am reluctant to co-sponsor your bill at this time." On the other hand, Senator Patrick Leahy, a Democrat from Vermont, wrote to say he was proud to be an "original co-sponsor" of the legislation and to thank Sparky for sending the chocolate macadamia nuts as "I must admit they are a favorite of mine."

In one case, Sparky's tenacity didn't work. He ran into an unnamed colleague who told him he couldn't vote for redress because large numbers of his constituents were opposed to it and would not reelect him if he supported it. Sparky said he understood but asked for a minute of the other Senator's time. The colleague said, "No, if I give you a minute, I'll change my mind and I won't be back here next year."

In the House, Majority Leader Foley introduced H.R. 442 in January 1987. Norman Mineta said later, "I am proud that this legislation was written in my office, put together by a brilliant legislative director I had at that time, Glenn Roberts." Sparky and Senator Inouye trooped over to the other side of Capitol Hill to testify before a House subcommittee, with Sparky reiterating much of what he had said in the Senate. Copies of letters from civic organizations and private citizens to Representatives asking for support for H.R. 442 poured into Mineta's office. The National Education Association said it concurred with the recommendations of the national commission.

Paul Yzaguirre, president of the National Council of La Raza, a Hispanic-American civic group, wrote that "the denial of civil rights to one group of Americans constitutes an affront to all Americans." The United Church of Christ wrote that H.R. 442 "will help to reassert the fundamental principle that a free society judges by individual acts, not by ancestry." The Friends Committee on National

Legislation, a Quaker civic group, said: "By the rules of equity that govern this country, compensation is due to those who were so seriously wronged." The Leadership Conference on Civil Rights urged Representatives to vote for H.R. 442 because "Americans of Japanese Ancestry suffered the personal stigma of suspect disloyalty and removal from the mainstream of American life." The Jewish War Veterans wrote to each Representative saying: "H.R. 442 will help to reassert the fundamental principle that a free society guarantees equal rights to all people without regard to their ancestry." Just before the bill came up in the House, the American Bar Association, which carries special weight since so many members of Congress are lawyers, urged that it be passed "without weakening amendments."

When H.R. 442 was called up for debate on September 17, 1987, Representative Lungren proposed to strike the $20,000 payments. That amendment was voted down 162-237. Representative Norman Shumway, another California Republican, proposed to limit payments of $20,000 to those who had spent at least three years in the camps and $18 a day to those who had been interned for less than three years. Children would get $1 a day times their age. It failed by voice vote. Later that day, H.R. 442 was passed by the whole House, 243-141. Mineta, in a speech in 1992, said the sentence in the law "that means more to me than perhaps any other in law" was: "For these fundamental violations of the basic civil liberties and constitutional rights of these individuals of Japanese ancestry, the Congress apologizes on behalf of the nation."

That passage was most encouraging for Sparky. Good news came on another front, which was acceptance of redress by the Reagan administration. Grant Ujifusa, a senior official of JACL, was a friend of Richard Wirthlin, a political strategist and pollster for President Reagan. In July 1987, Ujifusa enlisted Wirthlin in an effort to reverse the administration's opposition. Wirthlin wrote Ujifusa a note saying, "I have already discussed with the White House the issue we spoke about. Apparently I have a sympathetic ear in Howard Baker and Tom Griscom, but on this one I would also be willing to speak directly with the President." Baker was the former Republican Senator from Tennessee who became President Reagan's chief of staff and ambassador to Japan in the George W. Bush administration. Griscom was a skilled communications strategist in the White House.

Wirthlin went on: "As always, timing is everything. Please keep me informed of the status of the bill and tell me when it gets to the critical point at which my discussing it with the President would have the most value. I would also reinforce it with the chief of staff at that time."

Ujifusa called Elma Henderson in Sparky's office to elaborate, telling her that when he started to explain redress to Wirthlin, Wirthlin said, "You don't have to explain it to me." When Wirthlin was a boy, some of his schoolmates in California had been taken away to the detention camps. In her memo to Sparky, Henderson said, "He is also interested in it because of the political ramifications in California and other West Coast states where Japanese-Americans and other Asian-Americans are the swing votes in close elections." She recommended that Wirthlin talk with the President before H.R. 442 reached the floor of the House. Sparky agreed.

About the same time, the Justice Department backed away from its opposition. Richard Williard, the assistant attorney general who had presented the brief against redress, told Ujifusa that Justice would no longer actively oppose the bill, for reasons unclear.

In the Senate, Sparky's bill, S. 1009, had been referred to the Committee on Government Affairs, chaired by Senator Glenn, who moved the measure along rather than let it be shunted aside. The committee held hearings and reported out Sparky's bill with amendments in October 1987. Sparky picked up a couple more co-sponsors, one being Senator Pryor, the Arkansas Democrat who had said he would not co-sponsor the bill while it was in committee. Another was Senator Quayle, who Sparky's staff had written off as an impossible convert.

After the passage of H.R. 442, movement toward redress again stalled. Sparky's staff discovered that eight Republican Senators had put a "hold" on his bill, an informal practice in which Senators tell their party's floor leader they oppose voting on the bill. It is sometimes a warning a filibuster would be mounted if the bill came to the floor. Senator Byrd, the Democratic Majority Leader, told Sparky he hesitated to bring up the bill while it was threatened with a filibuster. Moreover, despite the word from the Justice Department, Sparky feared that President Reagan would veto the measure. In public, Sparky kept plugging redress, inviting Senators to the opening of an exhibit in the Smithsonian Institution's National Museum of American History: "For a More Perfect Union: Japanese-Americans and the U.S. Constitution." The exhibit featured pictures of Japanese-American children behind barbed wire. "I am sure," Sparky told the Senate, "it will shock their sense of liberty, justice and fair play which we take for granted."

Behind the scenes, there was confusion and anxiety. Elma Henderson laid it out for Sparky in a memo at 2:45 p.m. on October 18, 1987, just before Sparky was to meet with Mike Masaoka, Grant Ujifusa and Grace Uyehara of JACL to map out the next tactical moves. Henderson noted that the Democratic Policy Committee had still not agreed on when to bring Sparky's bill to the floor. "At some point," she said, "SMM [Sparky] needs to decide whether or not to try to bring the bill up even without a time agreement." Such an agreement would be negotiated among leaders of the two parties to facilitate consideration of a bill. "We could get more than 60 votes in favor of cloture," she said, referring to the votes needed to end a filibuster.

Henderson said they had heard rumors that Senator Helms had put a hold on the bill. Andrew Hartsfield, a member of Helm's staff, had said Helms opposed the payments, feared redress would set a precedent and "is opposed to the whole concept of the bill." Henderson told Sparky that Masaoka and Ujifusa were worried the President would veto the bill. They were trying to arrange for supporters of the bill to meet with President Reagan and Chief of Staff Baker. She concluded, "There will be enough votes in the Senate to override a veto; however, it is uncertain whether or not the House could also override." H.R. 442 had been passed by the House with 243 votes and it would take 290 to override it.

Later that day, Henderson wrote another memo to recapitulate the meeting. Sparky had said he would hold up the bill until the stock market stabilized on the off chance that it would be affected by the call for redress; the market had suffered sharp declines in the October "Crash of '87." This would give JACL more time to work on the White House to prevent a veto. Sparky said Senator Byrd had agreed to bring up the bill whenever Sparky was sure they had the votes to invoke cloture. Sparky said he would talk with Helms to see if he might convince him to allow a vote on the bill. He further agreed to call Howard Baker in the White House to seek his support and to speak to the President about it.

Ujifusa said that Governor Thomas Kean of New Jersey, a Republican on good terms with the President, had talked with the President for 35 minutes on the issue, that the President was familiar with it, recounted anecdotes about his efforts to help Japanese-Americans find jobs after the war and recalled that he had used his radio program to urge that they be welcomed back to California. But President Reagan was aware of former Senator Hayakawa's opposition and thought Hayakawa, a fellow Californian, spoke for the Japanese-American community. JACL was therefore looking for people who could tell the President that Hayakawa did not speak for all Japanese-Americans. They would try to talk to White House staff members Kenneth Duberstein and Tom Griscom, both believed to oppose redress.

A couple of weeks later, Sparky ran into Baker in a Senate elevator and urged him to ask the President not to veto the redress bill. Baker replied that if he was still a Senator, he would co-sponsor the bill. When Sparky told Baker that members of his staff were advising a veto, Baker seemed surprised and said he would check into it. He thought the Office of Management and Budget, which oversees government spending, might be the culprit. At the appropriate time, Baker said, he would advise the President to sign the redress bill. When this news was relayed to Ujifusa, he said he knew James Miller, the director of OMB, and would try to talk with him. Meantime, Sparky spoke with Helms and asked him to reconsider as a personal favor to him. Helms continued to object to paying $20,000 to "Japanese." Sparky reminded him that no Japanese were involved, only Americans of Japanese ancestry. Helms said he would think it over. Sparky wanted to bring the bill up before Thanksgiving to avoid the December 7 anniversary of the Japanese attack on Pearl Harbor and the forthcoming summit meeting between President Reagan and the Soviet leader, Mikhail Gorbachev.

In mid-November, Elma Henderson reported to Sparky on the status of the White House lobbying. Deputy Chief of Staff Kenneth Duberstein had changed his mind and agreed to support the bill. Tom Griscom "has shut up." Vice President George Bush said he would urge the President to sign the bill. Governor Kean of New Jersey had sent President Reagan a letter and packet of material backing the bill. Grayce Uehara, the JACL activist, and Representative Mineta had appeared on NBC's "Today" show in favorable interviews, and Sparky talked about the bill on CNN. Henderson also reported "there is some evidence of a semi-organized letter-writing campaign against the bill." JACL would counter with letters to co-sponsors of the bill and would ask members to write to President Reagan. Sparky scribbled a note to the staff: "The time may have arrived to schedule it for floor action, as soon as the budget reconciliation bill, now under negotiation, is passed."

That time slipped by because two filibusters still threatened. Sparky had talked six of the eight Republicans, led by Helms, out of a filibuster but Senator Malcolm Wallop, a conservative Republican from Wyoming, and Senator John Chafee, a moderate Republican from Rhode Island, held out. For that reason, Sparky said, the Majority Leader "will not bring the measure up on the floor this year, but has promised consideration early in the second session," opening in January 1988. Henderson said she had run into Ralph Neas of the Leadership Conference on Civil Rights and had told him of the two threatened filibusters. Neas, noting that another civil rights bill had been kept off the floor since June, urged Sparky to hold Senator Byrd to his promise of bringing up the redress bill early in the 1988 session and to invoke cloture if necessary. From Ujifusa, Henderson learned the disturbing news that one of Wallop's objections was that "we may have to do that kind of thing again in the event of a national emergency."

After the New Year holiday, consideration of Sparky's bill was postponed once more while more efforts were made to remove the threat of filibuster. In early February 1988, Sparky met again with Mike Masaoka, Grace Uyehara and Grant Ujifusa of JACL; they agreed that things were set as far as the President was concerned. Henderson reported that the President had asked Duberstein to review the bill once again. A former senior staff member of the National Security Council said the legislation came to the NSC staff three times and was sent back each time with the comment that this was a domestic issue.

Two months later, the Justice Department sent a memo to leaders of the Senate saying the administration would support Sparky's bill if amendments were made to exclude people who escaped from the U.S. to Japan or were not living in the U.S. when the war began. The Justice Department further asked that the bill provide that payments made under the bill would constitute "full settlement" of claims against the U.S. and that the payment period be extended to ten years from five years. Sparky agreed to all of those requests but balked at removing provisions pertaining to the Alaskan Aleuts, which the Justice Department argued were not warranted because they had been removed from a war zone for their own safety. For Sparky to have agreed with that would have been to break faith with Senator Stevens of Alaska and a strong ally of redress. Sparky penciled onto the fax that came into his office: "No."

Finally, on April 19, 1988, deliberations on Sparky's redress bill began. Senator Glenn, whose committee had prepared the bill, ran through its provisions. Sparky, Glenn said, "deserves full credit for the success of this legislation. I do not believe that, in the 13 years I have been in the Senate, I have ever seen anyone pursue a particular piece of legislation, buttonhole Senators more effectively, call on them in their office, make certain he had their support for a particular piece of legislation and do that job as well as Spark Matsunaga has done on S. 1009. He has been a real bird dog on this one."

Sparky thanked Glenn and others, then launched into a sweeping history of the incarceration down to the findings of the national commission. He reviewed the provisions of the bill and noted up front that the proposed payment of $20,000 to each living internee was controversial. He said a firm called ICF, Inc. had come up with that number after losses of income and property had been estimated. The estimate did not take into account losses in education and experience nor for pain and suffering. Sparky defended the proposed payments: "Those who contend that token payments are an inappropriate way to redress this injustice overlook the basic fact that compensatory remedies are deeply rooted in American jurisprudence. It has long been considered proper for our courts to award monetary damages to individuals who have been unjustifiably injured."

Sparky noted that opponents were concerned about the precedent that redress might set, and argued: "Payments are to be made only to those living individuals who were victims of the federal government's wartime policy. No payments are made to the heirs or descendants of former internees. S. 1009 would therefore not open the door for claims by descendants of former slaves or the descendants of Native American victims of the federal government's 19th-Century policies with respect to American Indians." Sparky further said he was often asked about compensation to Americans captured by the Japanese during World War II or North Korea during the Korean War or North Vietnam during the war in Vietnam, all of whom were compensated for the time they were imprisoned. "Like the Japanese-Americans, these Americans suffered a loss of liberty," Sparky said. "The difference is that Japanese-Americans were deprived of their freedom through the actions of their own government — the United States of America — not the enemy."

Over the rest of that day and the following day, the Senate debated Sparky's bill with intensity despite the overwhelming support with which it had come to the floor. In Congress, nothing is ever considered settled until the final vote has been taken — and even then there are often attempts to reopen an issue. Sparky had staunch allies, including some who had personally seen the injustice done to Japanese-Americans in 1942. Senator Paul Simon, a Democrat from Illinois, recalled that as a boy in Oregon, his father was a Lutheran minister who had gone on a radio program to denounce the detention. "I remember some of my friends shunning me," Simon confessed. "I remember being embarrassed, wishing my father had not done it." Simon said one sentence in the bill stood out: "On behalf of the nation, the Congress apologizes." That, he said, "is a powerful sentence and it is a sentence that we owe to Japanese-Americans." Further, he asserted, "I want to pass this so we send a signal to future administrations and Supreme Courts of the nation. At no time should we ever perpetuate this kind of an injustice to a people."

Senator Stevens of Alaska painted a grim picture of the 900 Aleuts who "were taken from their island homes and placed in squalid relocation camps in southeastern Alaska. The evacuation and relocation were a logistical nightmare. Housing, eating and sanitation conditions were totally deplorable." The abandoned camps were not insulated and were not intended for habitation during the winter. Stevens continued, "There were repeated epidemics; disease ran rampant. Medical care was entirely inadequate and nearly ten percent of the Aleut people died during their internment." He pointed to the commission's conclusion: "This treatment clearly failed to meet the government's responsibility to those under its care."

Senator Frank Murkowski, a Republican from Alaska, supported the bill for the same reasons.

More support came from Senator Brock Adams, a Democrat from Washington, who recalled that a third of his classmates from Broadway High School in Seattle had vanished in 1942. "We were all playing basketball one day and the next day they were gone," he said. He recounted tales of neighbors being forced to sell even their children's toys for pennies on the dollar and of "Mrs. Yasushi Ichikawa and her family of seven children as she watched her minister husband led from their home on Jackson Street in central Seattle by the FBI to a military prison in Crystal City, Texas, not knowing if she would ever see him again." Adams said, "Not all of my constituents are in agreement with the position I take today, but I think the position is right and those of us who were there in the 1940s and came back at the end of World War II feel that way. I think it is important that we say so."

A surprise came from Senator Cranston who told the Senate he had opposed detention from the very beginning when he was assigned to the Office of War Information shortly after the attack on Pearl Harbor. "There I worked closely with Eleanor Roosevelt and Archibald MacLeish trying to dissuade President Roosevelt from forcefully evacuating Japanese-Americans from the West Coast and interning them in so-called relocation camps." Eleanor Roosevelt was the President's wife, MacLeish a Pulitzer Prize-winning poet and Librarian of Congress during the war. Cranston said he visited the camps at Tule Lake in California and Heart Mountain, Wyoming, where he met with friends who were distressed at the racial prejudice behind their internment. "It was ironic," Cranston said, "to see American *nisei* soldiers, home on furlough and clad in uniform, wandering around inside a fenced-in camp." Cranston concluded, "This act is a just and fair redress to those individuals who were excluded and/or interned without justification in gross violation of their civil liberties as American citizens and residents."

Sparky was amazed: "I did not know of the Senator's experience during the early period of the war and his efforts to convince President Roosevelt that he not issue Executive Order 9066."

Relieved that the debate had gotten off to a favorable start, Sparky said late in the afternoon, "I am pleased that we have had no one speak against the measure all day today." He spoke too soon. Senator Ernest Hollings, the Democrat from South Carolina, rose to oppose the bill. "To attach a price to the Japanese-American suffering — as I see it — would have the unintended effect of demeaning and cheapening their tragic experience," he argued. "If we establish a precedent with S.

1009, where do we draw the line against reparations to the countless other groups of Americans who have suffered because of actions of the U.S. government?" Hollings thought an apology would suffice, all the more so because "the government is broke."

The next day, opponents launched a full-scale assault on the bill on principle, on cost and on the precedent they feared it would set. At one point early in the debate, Sparky's feelings got the better of him as he reiterated the incident in which a guard had shot and killed a grandfather chasing a ball. "I myself become overly emotional when I think about it even today," he said. Senator Stevens came to his rescue: "I sort of interrupted my friend, but he was choking up, as I am wont to do in this debate once in awhile, and I wanted him to know that I share his emotions." Sparky recovered to say, "I thank the Senator from Alaska for coming to my relief and for his major role in bringing about the passage of the bill."

In the attack on redress, Senator Chic Hecht, a Republican from Nevada, was first up with an amendment that would preserve the apology but eliminate the $20,000 payments. "With this huge federal deficit," Hecht said, "how can we in good conscience now approve a bill with a price tag of $1.3 billion — $1.3 billion in new money — money that this nation just does not have to spend?"

Senator Inouye immediately countered. "While it is true that all people of this nation suffer during wartime," he said, "the Japanese-American experience is unprecedented in the history of American civil rights deprivation." He pointed to a finding of the commission that in 1942, "the government and society at large refused to recognize the distinction between the Japanese who bombed Pearl Harbor and Japanese-Americans and resident aliens of Japanese ancestry."

Senator Stevens opposed the Hecht amendment: "It says that, as a nation, let us apologize but let us ignore all of the losses, all of our failures, to compensate the victims." Senator Pete Wilson, who earlier had been noncommittal, said the question was whether "we are required to make adequate compensation. The answer is that we are." Wilson delivered an impassioned plea by recalling the Holocaust against the Jews in Europe. "As we must never forget the Holocaust and what the indifference and the timidity of good and decent people permitted to occur in Europe throughout the duration of World War II, so we must recognize that good and decent people had a lapse of judgment and, very candidly, a lapse of the mind, of spiritual courage." He concluded, "We should pay this debt. We should acknowledge this injustice. We should right this wrong."

The Hecht amendment was voted down, 67 to 30.

Shortly after, Senator Helms rose to renew the assault. He offered an amendment that no payments to Japanese-Americans would be made unless the federal budget, then running a huge deficit, was balanced. Helms argued that payment had already been made in 1948, that President Roosevelt had "acted on the best information available to him" and that the U.S. "cannot afford to spend $1.3 billion for this purpose now."

An ally, Senator John Warner, a Republican from Virginia, objected to the bill for its criticism of wartime leaders: "What we are doing is trying to judge the actions of our predecessors." Warner said he conceded that wrongs had been done but was obligated to "defend members of this chamber, members of the executive branch and to a certain extent the members of the judicial branch who at that time, in light of the facts, felt they were rendering the best judgment they could on behalf of the nation."

Senator Malcolm Wallop, the Republican from Wyoming, was another hard-charging opponent. He argued that "what seems incomprehensible today was the frightening reality of national security at the height of World War II." He asserted the proposed payments were "a repugnant and an offensive idea — that a clear conscience is to be had for a mere $20,000 a head." The act, he maintained, "demeans the Congress, demeans the United States and demeans the recipients." He contended that redress for Japanese-Americans would set a bad precedent. "Perhaps we owe some monetary apology," he said, "to the descendants of slaves, to the Cherokee Indians who endured the Trail of Tears or to the Chinese-Americans who were pressed into virtual servitude."

Despite those arguments, the Helms amendment was voted down 61 to 35.

Helms was soon back with another amendment that infuriated Sparky, Stevens and perhaps others because it sought to connect two unrelated events. "No funds shall be appropriated under this title," the amendment said, "until the Government of Japan has fairly compensated the families of the men and women who were killed as a result of the Japanese bombing of Pearl Harbor on December 7, 1941." Declaring his respect and admiration for Matsunaga and Inouye, Helms said, his amendment was "a way of emphasizing the horror, the terror, the grave apprehension that motivated the then President."

Sparky, in cold fury, said, "This amendment is totally unacceptable...The amendment presumes that we Americans of Japanese ancestry had something to do with the bombing of Pearl Harbor. That is absolutely false, as the Senator from North Carolina will readily concede. Japanese-Americans had nothing to do with that act. In this bill, we are trying to distinguish between Japanese-Americans and

Japanese. The amendment of the Senator from North Carolina would obscure this distinction by denying compensation to Americans for what the Japanese did at Pearl Harbor."

Helms backtracked: "I made that distinction. I will be glad to make it again, of course."

Sparky, still seething, replied, "If the Senator from North Carolina wishes to preserve that distinction, I respectfully suggest that he withdraw this amendment." Helms insisted on a vote. His amendment went down, 91 to 4, as even opponents of the bill were turned off by the illogic of Helms's proposal.

Even with the defeat of three amendments that would have gutted the bill, the opponents pressed on. Senator Charles Grassley, a Republican from Iowa, regretted what had happened to Japanese-Americans but argued "we were in a desperate war of national survival." He denounced what he saw as hindsight: "We need to place ourselves in the minds of those who made the decision at the time." Senator Strom Thurmond, the Republican from South Carolina, asserted, "As commendable as the objectives of this legislation are, this bill is unnecessary and too costly." Senator Steven Symms, a Republican from Idaho, said, "I am very much opposed to attaching price tags to personal freedoms in an attempt to atone ourselves for the internment of the Japanese-Americans."

Finally, undaunted, Helms attacked the bill itself. He argued that the issue should be subject to a statute of limitations as the wrongdoing had taken place far in the past. He cited Japanese-Americans who opposed redress, including Senator Hayakawa. He contended it was not the place of Congress "to adjudicate the private claims for a specific class of citizens." He questioned "the wisdom and propriety of accusing leaders of the U.S. government during World War II, both civilian and military, of dishonorable behavior." He asserted that conditions in the camps were not so bad as depicted. He opposed the manner in which individual payments would be made and brushed off "grave injustices" as the product of war. Helms cited the opposition of Representative Lungren and finally asserted: "I fear the potentially grave consequences of extending the principle of restitution contained in the bill...It is not too difficult to think of arguments concerning the need for restitution (for African-Americans) for the period before the 1954 decision in Brown versus Board of Education." In that case, perhaps the most far-reaching in the history of civil rights, the Supreme Court ruled that separate schools were inherently unequal.

In response, from Sparky's side came an outpouring of support. Senator

Harry Reid, a Democrat from Nevada, emphatically disagreed with his fellow Nevadan, Senator Hecht. "From time to time," Reid said, "there arise issues which test not only the conscience of a man but that of mankind. They deal, almost always, those great questions, with the rights of an unpopular minority." Senator James Exon, the Democrat from Nebraska who had seen what he called a "dump of an internment camp" during his military service in World War II, asserted that the relatively small amount of money over which they were debating was not worth the quibble. Senator Daniel Evans, a Republican from Washington, was forceful: "Opponents of this legislation choose to ignore raw racial prejudice woven into what was supposed to be legitimate national security justification for internment." Evans continued, "What is perhaps most alarming about the Japanese internment is that it took place in the United States of America."

Another drawing on his personal experience was Senator Alan Simpson, the Republican from Wyoming. As a boy of 12, Simpson recalled, he had been puzzled when the scoutmaster of his Boy Scout troop announced that they planned to go out to Heart Mountain to meet with Boy Scouts there. Simpson asked if there were any Boy Scouts in what was known as the "Jap camp," only to have the scoutmaster say, "Yes, yes, these are American citizens." He remembered meeting Norman Mineta, then a scout. Simpson was concerned about the payments to Japanese-Americans but said, "The conflict of the actual money appropriation is overcome in the final analysis by the humanity of what happened." Simpson paid tribute to Sparky: "It is an emotional and extraordinarily charged issue which has been conducted beautifully by our friend from Hawai'i, my friend, Senator Sparky Matsunaga. Without the respect and affection we hold for him, this debate would have ranged into other fields, and he kept it from that."

Philosophical support came from Senator Pete Domenici, a Republican from New Mexico, who asserted, "Our future strength as a nation depends greatly on our commitment to the founding principles of the United States, and our willingness to make restitution when we have departed from those principles." In a similar vein, Senator Robert Dole, the Republican Minority Leader from Kansas, said, "It is a tragic irony that, at the very moment I and millions of others were fighting for America's ideals, America itself — our country — was engaging in one of the most terrible acts of injustice in our entire history." Senator Robert Packwood, a Republican from Oregon, said, "Governing officials in democracies as well as dictatorships may find it more convenient to bend to transitory, popular prejudices that would trammel, or even extinguish, our individual liberties for the alleged common good."

Senator Dennis DeConcini applauded Sparky for "his diligent and dogged efforts to protect the civil rights of all Americans." Senator Timothy Wirth, a Democrat from Colorado, said, "The Congress and the President have an obligation to correct an intolerable injustice." Senator Nancy Kassebaum, a Republican from Kansas, believed that an apology was due but said, "I just do not believe that money can buy atonement." Despite mixed emotions, she said she would vote for the bill. Senator Carl Levin, the Democrat from Michigan, said redress "should also serve as a reminder to this proud nation that we should always have the strength to resist the racial hysteria and prejudice that plagued us during these particular years of World War II."

After the debate had concluded, Sparky pulled off a slick parliamentary maneuver. He brought up H.R. 442, asked the Senate to strike out all after the enacting clause, meaning the substance of the bill, and to substitute the text of S. 1009 in its place. He thus got the number 442, magic to Japanese-Americans, instead of the nondescript S.1009 attached to the legislation. He hoped this might ease the bill's way through a conference that would follow between the House and the Senate to resolve differences in the two bills.

Sparky called for a vote and the bill passed, 69 to 27.

At one time, Sparky had 77 co-sponsors, counting himself, but lost seven along the way and another in the voting. Three of the four absent Senators would have voted for the bill, all of which was intended to show President Reagan that the Senate, at least, had the votes to override a veto.

Work on redress was not over. Sparky and four other Senators met with five Representatives in June to resolve three critical differences that might have brought the measure down. The House version called for payments over ten years; the Senate had no time limit. They agreed on ten years. The House would have allowed vested rights of payments; if a former internee was alive on the day the bill became law but died before payment, his or her heirs would get the money. In the Senate version, only those living at the time of payment would be paid. The House prevailed and recipients were vested. Lastly, the Aleuts were in the Senate version but not in that of the House. The Senate prevailed and the Aleuts were included.

On July 27, the Senate brought up the conference report and Sparky asked for its passage, saying, "It is most gratifying to me personally to see this long battle for personal justice come to an end at last…all Americans can take great pride in the fact that this long overdue legislation will have set right a most grievous wrong." The Senate adopted the bill by voice vote. A week later, the House did the same by a vote of 257-156. On August 10, 1988, President Reagan signed it into law.

There was a hitch. H.R. 442 had been adopted without funds being appropriated. Senator Inouye, a senior member of the Appropriations Committee, took the lead in getting funds allotted for redress and was supported by Sparky, Mineta and Matsui. As Leslie Hatamiya wrote in *Righting a Wrong*: "It was Inouye's loyalty and dedication to his fellow veterans that persuaded him to propose to the Senate that redress should be made an entitlement program." That way, there would not be an annual debate over the funds. Senator Helms was once again a major obstacle but Inouye outmaneuvered him and the House agreed.

In a ceremony at the Justice Department on October 9, 1990, the first payment of $20,000 was made to a 107-year-old survivor of the camps, the Reverend Mamoru Eto of Los Angeles. Five others ranging down to 101 years were also given their checks that day. During the following year, a letter of apology from President Bush went to each of the 25,000 Japanese-Americans who received their funds. From then until August 8, 1998, when the program ended, 81,970 Japanese-Americans received checks for redress.

Unhappily, Sparky did not live to see any of it. ❖

11
Legacy
1988–1990 and Beyond

Even before he filed for reelection in 1988 for a third term in the Senate, Sparky knew he was gravely ill. He had suffered the symptoms of prostate cancer, such as lower back pain and difficulty in urinating, and Helene had urged him to see a doctor. Sparky put it off until the pain became unbearable, then went to a military hospital to be checked, as was his right as a member of Congress. When the results came back showing that he, indeed, had cancer, his son Matt said, "I think part of him was in denial or disbelief. He had been through much worse and he was known as Senator Stamina for the long hours he put in. He thought he could beat it but I'm not sure it fully sank in."

Sparky told Helene first, then the children one by one as he began chemotherapy treatments. Little by little, he informed his political confidants of his illness but did not make it public. The question quickly arose: Should he retire from the Senate or should he run again when he was not sure he would be physically able to be a full-time Senator? Matt said Sparky had "blunt conversations" with his family, friends and advisers and decided to run. Because of his seniority, he stood a good chance of becoming chairman of the influential Finance Committee if Senator Lloyd Bentsen, the Democrat from Texas, was elected Vice President as the running mate of Governor Michael Dukakis of Massachusetts, the party's presidential nominee. Even so, Sparky again did not attend the Democratic National Convention that year.

The Washington of 1989, at the beginning of Sparky's third term, saw the White House still in Republican hands, President George H.W. Bush having succeeded President Reagan. The Democrats controlled the Senate but Sparky's close friend, Senator Robert Byrd, resigned as Majority Leader to become chairman of the Committee on Appropriations, where he thought he could do more for his home state of West Virginia. Senator George Mitchell of Maine became Majority Leader and Sparky stepped down as chief deputy whip. As a legislator, Sparky seemed to have lost some of his verve, partly due to his health, perhaps, and partly due to fatigue from the long crusade to obtain redress. He introduced little legislation and seemed content just to support others.

His whimsical sense of humor, however, did not desert him. On March 17, 1989, Sparky addressed the Senate: "This being St. Patrick's Day, as you can plainly see I am wearing a green tie, and I do that because I am really one-quarter Irish. People look at my face and say, 'How can you be?' Well, I have a grandson who is half Irish. I made him half Japanese by descendancy and he made me a quarter Irish by ascendancy." Sparky yielded the floor to Senator Byrd, who commented, "I thank my friend, the happy Irishman whose name is Sparky Patrick Matsunaga."

Sparky started talking about running for a third term long before his second term was to end. In March 1987, he told a news conference in Honolulu: "I have made no secret about it. There is so much to be accomplished." With questions about his health cropping up, the Republicans thought Sparky might be vulnerable. Senator Rudy Boschwitz of Minnesota, the chairman of the Republican Senatorial Campaign Committee, stopped in Hawai'i in January 1988, on the way back from Asia, to tell the press: "Look, Minnesota is a very Democratic state and now we have two Republican Senators," the other being Senator David Durenberger. "If we have a good, strong candidate, we could win." Sparky, appearing to take no notice, registered with the authorities in Honolulu in June 1988 that he intended to be a candidate that fall. He said he wanted to push ahead with proposals for alternative sources of energy, space cooperation with the Russians and improving the funding for the Institute of Peace.

That summer, the press in Hawai'i began to speculate that Sparky would become chairman of the Finance Committee if Bentsen was elected Vice President. Sparky relished the idea, saying, "I've always felt, since my days at Harvard, that the tax code should be used to engineer social goals. So I've been a champion of tax incentives." When some in the Washington press questioned his ability to lead the powerful committee, Sparky shot back: "They don't understand committee work. Much of it is done behind closed doors." Senator Bentsen backed Sparky: "He's an able man. He'll do fine."

Sparky had little difficulty in brushing off a challenge in the Democratic primary in September 1988 from Robert Zimmerman, a writer and management consultant, winning with another 82 percent of the vote. On his return to Washington, Sparky was teased again by Byrd, who said in the Senate, "I have a little tinge of sympathy for him in view of the fact that he only got 82 percent of the vote in Hawai'i's primary last week. I am sure he wondered what happened to the other 18 percent."

Sparky thanked the Majority Leader, then moved on to deliver a statement supporting a bill that would establish the United States-Canada Free Trade Agreement, especially because it would increase trade in energy. "While energy trade between our two countries now moves virtually without restriction, the provisions of the free trade agreement will establish as a certainty based in law assured access to the massive energy resources of this bountiful continent." It was passed by the Senate that day and, having already been voted by the House, was signed into law by President Reagan later that month.

In the general election in November, Sparky coasted home even though he had again spent little time campaigning. This time, he drubbed Maria Hustace, a rancher from the island of Moloka'i, taking 77 percent of the vote. Questions about his health persisted, including speculation that he would retire before the end of his term. Sparky's rebuttal: "There's no such possibility. So long as I am in good health and able to carry on the work, I will be in office." The defeat of Dukakis and Bentsen ended Sparky's chance of becoming chairman of the Finance Committee because Bentsen retained his seat in the Senate and his place as chairman. Sparky acknowledged he was "very much disappointed" but, as the senior majority member of the committee after the chairman, he would become chairman of the Subcommittee on Taxation. He was also named to the Congressional Joint Committee on Taxation.

Sparky's bad luck in health continued as he fell down the stairs to the basement of his home and broke his leg and two ribs in January 1989. Later he suffered from shingles, a virus that attacks nerve endings, and the flu, plus an accident in which he broke his right arm in January 1990. The Congressional Quarterly reported that Sparky, after years of compiling a record for being present for Senate votes, had missed more votes during 1989 than any other Senator due to his illnesses and accidents. That put his office on the defensive in asserting that he would finish out his term.

Even though newly elected President Bush was a Republican, Sparky spoke highly of him early in the 101st Congress. Pointing to Bush's service in Congress, Sparky said, "He knows our responsibilities as well as his own as President. I think it will make all the difference in the world in how the American people are served by their government over the next four years."

As chairman of the Finance Subcommittee on Taxation, Sparky was dubious that Bush could promise no new taxes and balance the budget. Sparky supported most of the President's cabinet nominations, such as James Baker for Secretary of State, retired Admiral James Watkins for Secretary of Energy and Elizabeth Dole, the wife of Senator Robert Dole, as Secretary of Labor. He followed the lead of Senator Sam Nunn, the Georgia Democrat who chaired the Armed Services Committee, in announcing that he would vote against John Tower, the Republican Senator from Texas who was former chairman of Armed Services, for Secretary of Defense. Nunn was critical of Tower's drinking habits, his alleged womanizing and the appearance of a conflict of interest in consulting with defense contractors. Sparky agreed: "We must hold the defense secretary to the same personal standards that we require of line command officers even of the most junior rank." Left unsaid in public was that Tower, who was killed in a plane crash in 1991, had made enemies with what were perceived to be mean-spirited relations with his colleagues.

In legislation, Sparky concentrated on bills related to energy and veterans, with moderate success. He introduced a bill calling for a five-year research effort intended to bring a hydrogen fuel onto the market. Another bill called for developing fuel cell technology as an alternate form of energy. Sparky supported a measure introduced by Senator Inouye that established within the Smithsonian Institution in Washington a museum to exhibit objects related to American Indians. Similarly, he introduced a bill to reestablish an advisory committee to the Department of Veterans Affairs on Native American veterans. He supported what he called a "test pilot's dream," the development of the X-30 supersonic aircraft that would fly from New York to San Francisco in one hour — and to Hawai'i in two hours — even though he had opposed the supersonic passenger plane called SST while in the House. He supported the Veterans Benefits and Health Care Act of 1989 that would improve medical care, educational benefits, compensation and loans for veterans.

A bill that required the Attorney General to compile hate crime statistics drew Sparky's support. He persuaded the Senate to exempt Hawai'i and Alaska from a law intended to prevent motorists from crossing state lines to buy cheaper gasoline. "This objective," Sparky told the Senate, "is not relevant to Alaska, Hawai'i, and the U.S. territories and commonwealths." He urged passage of the Vocational Educational Act Amendments of 1989 that would provide funds for American Indians and native Hawaiians. He incurred the wrath of voters back home by declaring that he would vote in favor of a pay raise for members of Congress, to $135,000 from $89,500 a year. Senator Inouye and Representatives Daniel Akaka, a Democrat, and Patricia Saiki, a Republican, said they would vote against it because of the large federal deficit.

Sparky was not successful in getting adopted a bill that would require the Department of Veterans Affairs to conduct a comprehensive study of psychological problems experienced by Vietnam veterans of Asian, Pacific Island, native American and native Alaskan descent. Another unsuccessful bill would have improved other capabilities of the Department of Veterans Affairs. A third bill, with 27 co-sponsors, would permit disabled veterans who were retired members of the armed forces to receive both disability pay and a portion of their retired pay and not be penalized for taking either one or the other. A proposal to establish a strategic petroleum reserve in Hawai'i never got out of committee. Neither did a bill that Sparky co-sponsored to require a waiting period before a handgun could be sold or transferred. A measure that would have benefited Vietnam veterans who became ill from exposure to Agent Orange, a defoliant, passed the Senate but died in a House committee.

After Chinese soldiers killed several hundred demonstrators around Tiananmen Square in Beijing in June 1989, Sparky joined in passing a unanimous resolution condemning the "use of force by the People's Republic of China against unarmed advocates of democracy and human rights in China." On the floor, Sparky was forceful: "China's aging, reactionary leaders have clearly demonstrated that their lust for power and privilege outweighs their concern for the welfare of the people they govern." Continuing, he said, "I am pleased with the President's response to the crisis thus far, including the suspension of military sales and a halt to high-level military contacts; we should not be in the business of arming a government which is responsible for killing its own citizens."

Two weeks later, Sparky joined a third of the Senate in signing a letter to President Bush to commend him for permitting Fang Lizhi, a leading Chinese astrophysicist and dissident, to seek refuge in the American embassy in Beijing. "In the name of freedom and democracy," the letter said, "we call on you never to bow to the demands of the Chinese government by turning Fang Lizhi over to the brutal regime that is now in control in Beijing." Fang and his wife, Li Shuxian, were there for a year before being allowed to leave for Britain. The signers ranged from Senators Jesse Helms and Strom Thurmond on the right to Senators Edward Kennedy and Joseph Lieberman on the left.

One of Sparky's early habits, personal and direct correspondence with his constituents, had long since vanished, with a few exceptions, because the volume of mail had become overwhelming. In its place were thick loose-leaf notebooks filled with stock answers to comments or inquiries, with paragraphs that a staff aide could lift out and fit together to fashion a coherent reply to voters back home. "I have urged Japan to open further its markets," he said at the height of the "Japan bashing" in trade disputes. "I share your opposition to the use of American troops to overthrow Noriega," he said in reference to the Panamanian dictator; Noriega was captured by

American troops the following year. When a constituent wrote that the U.S. should abrogate the treaties that Sparky had helped to approve a decade before, Sparky slid off the question: "I will keep your thoughts in mind as Congress addresses the question." In reply to a question as to whether he could use campaign funds for personal use, Sparky replied, "Senate rules prohibit Senators (retiring or active) from converting campaign funds to personal use."

Over that summer of 1989, Sparky's health continued to deteriorate. Finally, he was forced to end the dissembling and to admit, in January of 1990, that he had prostate cancer. That, of course, immediately fueled the question as to whether he should continue in office, a decision that Sparky deferred. "This is a judgment call and others may disagree," Sparky said. "Certainly, I deeply regret the fact that 1989 marred my 27-year record in Congress for roll-call voting attendance, and if it appears that my attendance in the second session of the 101st Congress does not show marked improvement over the record of the first session, I will reassess my present intention of fulfilling my term of office." Sparky showed up in the Senate several days later to take part in the debate and voting.

Six weeks later, Sparky reported that the cancer had spread to his bones. He was confined to a wheelchair in which he struggled to reach the Senate for votes. His son Matt said his father "was really a shell of his former self." His voice had weakened to the point where he could barely talk, perhaps the most frustrating aspect of the illness for a man who loved the spoken word. A specialist on the Japanese therapy called *shiatsu*, in which finger pressure applied to key points is intended to relieve pain, began treating Sparky. Helene was at his side constantly and Merle, his daughter, arrived in mid-March to help with the care.

Back home, a political wrangle broke out between those who thought Sparky should resign, including some newspaper editorial writers and writers of letters to the editor, and those who urged him to stay. Dallas McLaren, a longtime friend and political supporter wrote: "I know that thousands of your friends in Hawai'i and in many other places are pulling and praying for you. Personally, I am glad to note that you are exhibiting the fighting spirit that has characterized all of your life." Sparky wrote back: "I want you to know that your note lifted my spirits greatly — and that's half the battle, I understand." Senator Inouye defended Sparky: "After 40 years of public service, I think he's entitled to some sick leave."

In an unusual move, Senator Howard Metzenbaum, the Ohio Democrat who had been Sparky's ally in several political fights, circulated a letter addressed to Inouye that was signed by the other 98 Senators calling on people in Hawai'i to cease their calls for Sparky's resignation. "We view this development with great dismay and hope you will relay our strong views in this regard to the good people of Hawaii," the letter said. "For so many years, we have known him to work into the long hours of the night on behalf of his constituents. There is no more vigorous or effective advocate of his state's concerns than Sparky." Inouye himself commented: "My colleagues said, 'I thought you were supposed to be the aloha state. Where's that aloha you speak of?'"

Even with those shows of support, a poll at the end of March 1990, reported that 52 percent of the people in Hawai'i thought Sparky should resign while 37 percent said no and 11 percent said they were not sure. In that same poll, 60 percent said they had a favorable opinion about Sparky while 19 percent said they were neutral, 11 percent said they had an unfavorable opinion and four percent said they didn't recognize his name — even though he had represented them in Congress for 28 years.

Despite the increasing pain and knowing that he was dying, Sparky spent the last weeks of his public service trying to move his favored causes along. His body was failing but his spirit and courage were not. In late February, he told the Committee on Veterans Affairs that the proposed 1991 veterans budget "still falls short." In typical Sparky fashion, he succinctly ticked off the reasons, one by one. Early in March, he told the Committee on Energy and Natural Resources that an amendment to the Hawaiian Homes Commission Act of 1920 would make it easier for the commission "to obtain federal and private loans for the development of housing and related roads, sewers, development of water resources, and other needed improvements."

On Thursday afternoon, March 29, 1990, Senator Byrd sought to have adopted an amendment to the Clean Air Act that would establish a $500-million fund for coal miners who might lose their jobs under provisions of the law. The amendment was politically vital for the Senator from a state that was a leading coal producer and Byrd thought he had enough votes to win, although it would be close. Sparky knew this and had himself hauled onto the Senate floor where he voted for Byrd's measure. It lost 49 to 50, Byrd said nine years later in a telephone interview, when two Senators switched sides at the last minute; Byrd did not name them.

After the vote, he took the floor to pay tribute to Sparky: "He could easily have avoided this vote. He gave this vote out of his dedication to a belief in what is just, and he made the same strong fight for justice when he was talking to all of us many months ago about the Japanese-Americans who had been wrongly treated by this country in World War II...Today, he did what he wanted to do, and at some inconvenience and cost to himself." Nine years later, Byrd was still emotional, lamenting in an interview about the change in votes by the two Senators and praising Sparky for his loyalty.

The next day, Sparky submitted testimony for the bill he had introduced to establish a national hydrogen research and development program, asserting, "The case of hydrogen is overwhelming, and in the race for a hydrogen economy, the rest of the world is already out of the starting gate while we in the United States are hardly pawing the ground. This technology is too important to get away from us." The bill was eventually passed.

Sparky returned to the Senate in a wheelchair on Tuesday, April 3, to vote for the Clear Air bill itself, so weak that he could not speak but signaled his vote with a thumbs up. It was his last vote in the United States Senate, and many Senators seemed to sense that as they gathered around Sparky to shake his hand or pat him on the shoulder before he was wheeled out of the chamber.

Two days later, on Thursday, April 5, Sparky presented a written statement to the Committee on Energy and Natural Resources urging the Senate to adopt a national energy policy that would reduce the effects of global warning. "The pace of climatic change may be debatable," Sparky said, "but the indicators of it are not." That bill got through the Senate but languished in the House.

Several days afterward, Helene, Merle and the *shiatsu* specialist, Newman Shim, drove Sparky in a van to a private clinic in Toronto, a grueling eight-hour trip that was a last-ditch effort to save him. There, Dr. Rudy Falk experimented with alternative ways to treat cancer. It was a desperate move, and to no avail. Sparky was transferred from the clinic to Toronto General Hospital on Saturday, April 14, when his condition deteriorated even further. There he died early in the morning on April 15, Easter Sunday.

Helene; Merle; Keene, who had flown to Toronto from California; and Matt, who had arrived from Honolulu just after his father expired, took Sparky back to Washington where they were joined by the other children, Karen and Diane, as he lay briefly in state in the Capitol Rotunda on Monday. On Tuesday morning, they escorted Sparky to Andrews Air Force Base where they boarded one of the six airplanes in the President's fleet designated Air Force One when the President is aboard, and took off at 6:00 a.m. After a quick stop at Travis Air Force Base outside of San Francisco, they arrived in Honolulu shortly after noon, having picked up six hours in time changes along the way. An honor guard from the 100th Infantry Battalion, by then a reserve unit stationed in Hawai'i, met the group for a brief ceremony. A motorcade then took Sparky to the State Capitol, where he lay in state for 24 hours in a coffin covered with an American flag and lit with spotlights under a white canopy.

The Reverend Abraham Akaka rendered a brief benediction: "May the blessing of God and our aloha, like the gentle *kilihune* rain, kiss you through the holy hours of today and tomorrow." An honor guard stood watch while several thousand people filed by to pay their final respects. Tony Kinoshita, Sparky's friend from the war and political confidant, said simply, "It's going to take a long time before we find another guy like that." A Honolulu newspaper reported that a man in a windbreaker and fishing cap approached the casket, took off his hat and bowed three times. He straightened up, heaved his shoulders back in a deep sigh, took two steps back, turned, put his cap back on and strode out into the bright sunlight. No one got his name or his connection with Sparky.

The political, business, labor, academic and civic leaders of Hawai'i, led by Governor John Waihee and Senator Inouye — and hundreds of ordinary folks — turned out for Sparky's funeral the next afternoon at Central Union Church. Many of Sparky's aging comrades-in-arms from the 100th Battalion were there. Thousands more watched on live television. From Washington came Sparky's friend and former Majority Leader, Senator Robert Byrd, Majority Leader Senator George Mitchell of Maine and Republican Senator Mark Hatfield of Oregon, who had been Sparky's ally in more than one debate in the Senate. All flew 4,500 miles each way to be there. So did Senators Ted Stevens of Alaska, Dennis DeConcini of Arizona, Christopher Dodd of Connecticut and Jeff Bingaman of New Mexico. From the House came Norman Mineta of California as well as Danny Akaka and Patricia Saiki, both of Hawai'i and soon to compete for Sparky's seat in the Senate.

In the eulogy, Byrd said, "To me, Sparky represents fidelity, loyalty, dedication, integrity. His word was his bond." Hatfield recalled that Sparky got things done through quiet persistence. "His life was a testament...to the unmatched strength of dignity." Mitchell summed it up: "Most of all, Sparky Matsunaga loved his country enough to make it right when it was wrong," referring to Sparky's leadership in obtaining redress for those incarcerated during World War II. It was not all solemn. Governor Waihee remembered that he had once, as lieutenant governor, visited Sparky in Washington to discuss renewable energy. "And all the time I was thinking: 'Will Sparky invite me to lunch?'" Sparky did, just as he had with nearly every other visitor from home.

Sparky's remains were cremated the next day at Hosoi Garden Mortuary in Honolulu. The family held a private service, then took his urn to Punchbowl, site of the National Memorial Cemetery of the Pacific. This crater of an extinct volcano is the sacred and serene resting place of American warriors from World War II, the Korean War and the war in Vietnam. Among those buried there are famed WWII war correspondent Ernie Pyle and Colonel Ellison Onizuka, the astronaut who died in the explosion of the space shuttle *Challenger*. For a burial site, the Matsunaga family had two options and choose a place tucked away in a corner up a slope. A plain slab embedded in the ground, like every other marker at Punchbowl, marks Sparky's grave near those of Staff Sergeant Floyd Brown and Private First Class James Ogata. The inscription is simple: "Spark Masayuki Matsunaga, United States Senator, Oct. 8, 1916–Apr. 15, 1990: Beloved Son of Hawaii."

Meanwhile, in Washington, there was a remarkable outpouring of respect for Sparky in the Senate and House. Both houses went into recess on the day of Sparky's funeral, which was usual, but over the next three weeks, 54 Senators rose to pay tribute to Sparky, including many who had opposed him on one issue or another. Most briefly recited the highlights of his childhood in poverty, his military service, and his accomplishments in the House and Senate. Even taking into account the flowery hyperbole of the Senate, the affection for Sparky was striking. Almost every speaker focused on Sparky the man, a kind and gentle person who was universally liked and evidently did not have a single enemy in a town where the knives are always out and where political combat can be personally vicious. Both his friend and fellow Democrat, Senator Byrd, and a sometime opponent and a Republican, Senator John Heinz from Pennsylvania, quoted from Shakespeare: "His life was gentle, and the elements so mix'd in him that Nature might stand up and say to all the world, 'This was a man!'" After Byrd finished, he paused and added, "Whence comes another?"

Senator Christopher Dodd, the Democrat from Connecticut, paid Sparky perhaps the highest compliment in suggesting that Senators be more like him. "There are many ways, of course, to memorialize a fallen colleague," Dodd said. "I would suggest that we can pay no higher tribute to Sparky Matsunaga as Senators and as a Senate than to be more like him, to listen to one another more carefully, to be more patient with one another, to be more understanding, to work for the common good, and maybe most important of all, to be better friends to one another. In all the years I served with Spark Matsunaga, ten years here in the Senate, two or three years in the House of Representatives, I never heard Spark Matsunaga ever say an unkind word about another human being, colleague, official or anyone."

Senator Mitchell, having just returned from Sparky's funeral, told the Senate, "In the mysterious but uplifting way in which democracy works, his personality reflected perfectly the state he represented and loved so much: Open, sunny, full of life." The Republican floor leader, Senator Dole, inserted into the record what he called an appropriate editorial from *Roll Call,* the paper that reported on Capitol Hill: "He served in the Senate with tenacity, intelligence, and distinction...He was a thoughtful, sweet, engaging man — one of our favorite people on the Hill." Senator James Exon, the Democrat from Nebraska: "Above all else, Sparky Matsunaga was a keeper of the faith, a truly loving and caring person, the likes of which the U.S. Senate may never have seen before and may never see again."

Senator Sam Nunn, the Georgia Democrat with whom Sparky repeatedly clashed over the volunteer armed force, added, "Spark served this nation bravely and honorably in war and sought to instruct it in the gentler art of peace, with a poet's graceful touch. His life exemplified his belief that the best way to achieve a goal was not through coercion but friendly persuasion." Senator Rudy Boschwitz, the Republican from Minnesota who sought Sparky's defeat in 1988, brought a light touch, recalling that he had told Sparky, "I want to recruit somebody to run against you and I am going to talk to some people."

Sparky, taking Boschwitz seriously, asked, "Who are you going to talk to?"

Boschwitz answered, "If you would give me a list of those people you have not taken out to lunch in the Senate dining room, I will start with them." Sparky thought it was hilarious, Boschwitz said.

Another with whom Sparky had clashed, over redress, was Senator Strom Thurmond, the Republican from South Carolina, who said, "We all saw firsthand the dedication he exhibited in his courageous fight against cancer when he cast his final vote as a Senator from a wheelchair." Senator David Pryor, the Democrat from Arkansas: "I have always maintained that Sparky was the sort who represented the conscience of the U.S. Senate. I never heard him speak ill of any individual Senator nor any individual human being." Senator Paul Sarbanes, a Maryland Democrat, echoed that: "I never knew him to say a mean word. He always sought you out with a warm comment, with a happy demeanor."

Senator Brock Adams, the Democrat from Washington, recalled Sparky's final days: "Though his body was ravaged, his mind was clear, his sense of humor was intact and his commitment to serve the citizens of Hawai'i was undiminished." Senator Patrick Leahy, the Democrat from Vermont, said Sparky had discovered that Leahy's mother spoke Italian. When she came to visit, Leahy said, "We were walking through the halls and ran into Senator Matsunaga who immediately ignored me and started speaking in rapid-fire Italian to my mother. I think today of the smile that came across her face." (Sparky had picked up a bit of Italian during his service in Italy in World War II.)

Senator Mark Hatfield said he wanted to repeat some of the things he had said at Sparky's funeral in Honolulu: "There are those who briefly capture our attention with loud pronouncements and angry confrontations — and there are those who touch our lives forever with quiet strength and gentle compassion. Sparky Matsunaga was not a loud man, although his voice was heard loud and clear. And he was not an angry man, although his fierce tenacity gave birth to several landmark pieces of legislation...Spark brought Hawai'i — and its gentle calm — to Washington."

Senator Lloyd Bentsen, the Democrat from Texas, recalled a poem Sparky had written after he had been wounded in Italy, asking "what lasting imprints, good or ill, have I for future mortals wrought?" Bentsen answered, "Few Americans have left more of a lasting imprint." Senator Orrin Hatch, the Republican from Utah, noted, "In the nomenclature voiced in D.C., Sparky Matsunaga was probably low profile, but he was effective as a junior Senator and he accomplished a great deal of things that never made the front pages." Even Senator Malcolm Wallop, the Wyoming Republican who had opposed Sparky on redress, spoke briefly: "His fierce determination and pride for his home state of Hawai'i made him a formidable legislator who knew well the subtle art of compromise."

On it went with frequent tributes to Sparky's tenacity and with repeated acknowledgments from Senators who said they voted Sparky's way on many issues just because he was a friend who asked them to. Senator Howard Metzenbaum, the Democrat from Ohio, voiced a view repeated by others: "Sparky Matsunaga had no enemies in the U.S. Senate."

Senator Dale Bumpers, a Democrat from Arkansas who was considered to be among the more thoughtful of Senators, waited until the end, saying he wanted to speak "extemporaneously from the heart and not from prepared script." Bumpers said, "I have sat endless hours listening to him tell me how much he loved poetry, letting him read some of his poetry, which was not topflight. He was a lot better Senator than he was a poet." On redress, Bumpers said, "I heard a lot of people I never dreamed would co-sponsor that bill say, 'I did it for Spark.'...I do not know that anybody else could have ever gotten it done."

Bumpers recalled that he had risen in a Democratic conference after the 1988 elections, when it had become apparent that Sparky had been ill but had returned looking fit, to say, "How pleasing and gratifying it was to see Spark back and in good health. The applause was just instantaneous and deafening because everybody thought that whatever had been wrong with him, he was well and we were all so pleased." The Senator concluded, "I sometimes wonder, in this body, does anybody really care about what you do? I want the world to know that I cared about what he did, and I want Helene and his children to know that he was a great man in the eyes of everybody in this body I have ever talked to about him."

In the House, those who spoke about Sparky were mostly old-timers who had served with him there. Representative Mineta started. "Mr. Speaker," he began, "there are a great many words etched in stone in Washington. Binding these words together is a special resolve: To seek the unique voices among us for the decency and determination to better ourselves and our nation. Senator Spark Matsunaga — our great friend and colleague from the state of Hawai'i — was such a voice. Spark drew his strength from people — and he responded with warmth, persistence and inspired public service....His ideals will continue to live in us so long as there are wrongs to right, people in need of justice and a world in need of peace."

Representative Dante Fascell, a Democrat from Florida, compared Sparky with Will Rogers, the Oklahoma humorist in the early 20th Century who once said he had never met man he didn't like. "It is fair to say," Fascell said, "that Will Rogers and Spark Matsunaga would have enjoyed each other's company." Representative John Moakley, a Democrat from Massachusetts, spoke with admiration of his years on the Rules Committee with Sparky. "He understood that even though you may have the political advantage, it was usually wise not to push that advantage in order to work for the greater good of the body and the country. That is not to say that he hesitated to use his knowledge of the House on the rare occasions when it came to the vital interests of his constituents."

One of the 12 remaining members of the House who voted to admit Hawai'i to the Union, Representative Neal Smith, a Democrat from Iowa, said, "In his work in the House, Spark would zero in on an objective and keep after it with unfailing good humor but unbelievable tenacity." Representative Robert Matsui, the California Democrat, brought up a footnote to Japanese-American history. After he had won the primary in 1978, Matsui went to Washington to thank Sparky and others for their help. He met Sparky in a lobby just off the Senate floor and had chatted for a couple of minutes when Sparky said, "I'll be right back." In a few minutes, Sparky came back with Senator Hayakawa, the California Republican, in tow. Sparky introduced Matsui to Hayakawa, then with a twinkle in his eye, said to Hayakawa, "Sam, you are going to have to promise me one thing....I don't want you campaigning against this fine young man." Hayakawa replied, "That's fine, Spark." And, Matsui said, "Hayakawa did not come out and campaign for my opponent that year."

Representative Jake Pickle, a Democrat from Texas, reminded the House that he had been elected in 1963, the year of the 88th Congress and the same year as Sparky. "We elected Spark Matsunaga as president of the 88th Congress and he has remained our president ever since, even after he was elected to the Senate."

Representative James Quillen, a Republican from Tennessee, was another elected in 1963. "Even though we were members of different political parties," he said, "I found that he was friendly, knowledgeable, and hardworking…I think in part because of him, those of us who were first elected in the 88th Congress have maintained an unusually strong group identification." Representative Romano Mazzolia, a Democrat from Kentucky, closed the proceedings: "Mr. Speaker, Spark Matsunaga possessed many talents which made him an outstanding Representative, statesman, poet and friend."

In the ensuing months and years, other honors came to Sparky, some playful, such as having the center table in the Senate dining room named for him, and others distinguished, such as being decorated by the Emperor of Japan. The American Civil Liberties Union of Hawai'i had chosen Sparky to receive the annual Allan F. Saunders Award for "his legendary defense of liberty" and had to redo its program between Sparky's death on April 15 and the awards dinner on April 22. ACLU managed to include a tribute to Sparky in its program.

About 200 veterans of the 100th Infantry Battalion gathered at their clubhouse on April 24 to "talk story" in remembrance of Sparky. "There is no greater bond than friendship made in combat," said Mike Tokunaga. "We all spilled blood together." A conference of space scientists in Japan paused in May to remember Sparky for his "vision, his appreciation of space science and applications, and his support for international cooperation." The Pacific Peace Institute at the University of Hawai'i was renamed the Spark M. Matsunaga Institute for Peace. Ruth Ono, a regent of the university, said, "To think of Sparky is to think of peace."

Back in Washington, a memorial service in St. Joseph's Church on Capitol Hill drew 300 relatives, friends and colleagues in May to hear the chaplain of the Senate, the Rev. Richard C. Halverson, say, "He was an uncommon man." The following month, Sparky was honored at a military memorial service in Arlington National Cemetery. The bill Sparky had introduced that called for a program of research and development of hydrogen as an alternate fuel was named for him and President Bush signed it into law in November 1990. In 1999, the U.S. Treasury, in a new series of savings bonds, issued a $10,000 bond named for Sparky.

The distinguished decoration Sparky received from Japan was the Order of the Rising Sun, First Class. Immediately after Sparky's death, the Japanese government had set the wheels in motion to make the award, an honor he had quietly declined during his lifetime because he did not want to be too closely associated with Japan in the public eye, especially during the long struggle for redress. The decoration, signed by Emperor Akihito, recognized Sparky's pride in being Japanese-American, his efforts to lift the status of Japanese-Americans, and his endeavors to improve relations between America and Japan. Ordinarily, said informed Japanese officials, the Tokyo government considers such awards for many months but this one went through swiftly.

During his service on the Senate Veterans Committee, Sparky had tried to have a hospital built for the 110,000 veterans living in Hawai'i. He once said that a daylong hearing in Honolulu "confirmed the long-known fact that extremely serious deficiencies exist in the extent and quality of health care provided Hawai'i veterans, many of which can be attributed to the lack of a VA hospital." But his proposal died in committee.

After his death, the idea was revived and a modern, well-equipped clinic was built in a revamped wing of the Army's Tripler Medical Center in Honolulu. Senator Daniel Akaka, who had won Sparky's seat, proposed that the veterans medical center be named for Sparky. That proposal easily passed the Senate by voice vote. Akaka had placed in the record letters of support from the American Legion Post in Hilo, the Non-Commissioned Officers Association, the 100th Infantry Battalion veterans and other veterans associations. Only the Hawai'i Chapter of the American Ex-Prisoners of War dissented, saying they preferred "it being named in honor of a Hawai'i-born veteran," a letter that presumably would have amused a Kaua'i boy like Sparky. A month later, Akaka advocated adoption of the measure on the floor, saying, "His support never wavered on the G.I. Bill or any other issue of importance to veterans." It passed the House by voice vote. After much delay in construction, the medical center was dedicated on May 31, 2000, and named for Sparky.

Senator Inouye explained how Sparky would have liked it. During a quiet moment on the Senate floor toward the end of Sparky's life, they had a private conversation that turned into a philosophical discussion. In it, Senator Inouye said he asked Sparky how he would like to be remembered. Sparky ticked off several ways he wanted to be remembered, including: "I want to be remembered as a friend of the peacemakers." Equally high on his list was: "I want to be remembered as a friend of the veterans, because if not for them, we would not be enjoying the fruits of democracy."

After an adult lifetime of public service, Sparky left behind a legacy as a warrior and a peacemaker, as a patriot and a poet. Most of all, the quality of Spark Masayuki Matsunaga that stands out was his civility to high and low, to friend and foe, in the corridors and chambers of Congress, and before an audience of working men and women in Hawai'i. Civility was rare during his time in public life and even more rare today.

In the Senate's remembrances, Senator Nancy Kassebaum, the Republican from Kansas, said it best: "Spark's tactics and skill in achieving his goal were the mark of the man. His persistent prodding, his thoughtful questions, and his straightforward, common-sense remarks caused me and many others to enlist in the cause." Senator Kassebaum's credentials for assessing another politician were impressive — at the time she had served 12 years in the Senate and she was the daughter of Alf Landon, the onetime governor of Kansas and 1936 Republican presidential candidate.

Of Sparky's civility, she said: "Spark was a man who believed that reconciliation was more important than confrontation, that friendship should moderate partisanship, that reason should balance appeals to emotion. He not only believed in these high ideals, he lived by them. In doing so, he assured that his own life and his long, productive career of public service would always stand as his most eloquent and lasting tribute." ❖

Acknowledgments

Akamine, Bernard. Interview, March 1997, served in 100th Infantry Battalion

Ariyoshi, George R. Interview, March 1997, former governor of Hawai'i

Baker, Richard. Interview, Washington, D.C., July 1999, Historian of U.S. Senate

Benz, David. Interview, September 1996, publisher, labor leader

Boylan, Dan. Interview, September 1997, political columnist

Brandt, Gladys. Interview, September 1996, educator

Burns, Hon. James. Interview, July 1998, John A. Burns's son, appellate judge

Byrd, Hon. Robert. Interview, Washington, D.C., July 1999. Senator (D-W. Va), Sparky's
ally in Senate

Case, Ed. Interview, March 1999, Sparky's staff aide in Washington, later legislator in Hawai'i

Chaplin, George. Interview, October 1996, former editor of *The Honolulu Advertiser*

Chapman, Ellen. Archivist, Matsunaga Collection, Hamilton Library, University of Hawai'i,
pointed out many pertinent materials

Collins, Katherine. Archivist, 442nd RCT Club, found pertinent materials

Dole, Hon. Robert. Interview, Washington, D.C., July 1999, former Senator (R-Kan.) and
Majority Leader

Fenig, David. Interview, Washington D.C., May 1997, Sparky's staff aide

Foley, Hon. Thomas. Interview, Honolulu, September 1998, former Speaker of the House (D-Wash.)

Frenzel, Hon. William, Interview, Washington D.C., May 1997, former Representative (R-Minn.)

Fuqua, Hon. Don. Interview, Washington, D.C., May 1997, former Representative (D.-Fla.),
friend of Sparky's

Gill, Hon. Thomas. Interview, September 1997, former Democratic Representative from Hawai'i

Hashimoto, Margo. Librarian, Kauai High School, found 1933 yearbook and other materials

Hooper, Paul. Interview January 1997, scholar in American Studies, University of Hawai'i

Inouye, Hon. Daniel K. Interview, August 1997, senior Senator (D) from Hawai'i

Kawakami, Keiji. Interview, August 1996, grew up in Sparky's hometown, served in 442nd RCT

Kinoshita, Tony. Interview, March 1997, political supporter of Sparky, friend from 100th Battalion

Klass, Tim. Kauai Historical Society, pointed out relevant materials

Kono, Hideto. Interview, January 1997, served in Military Intelligence Service, community leader in Hawai'i

Lovell, James. Interview, February 1998, executive officer, 100th Infantry Battalion

Matano, Cherry. Interview, August 1996, Sparky's longtime executive assistant

Matsunaga, Andrew. Interview April 1998, Sparky's younger brother

Matsunaga, Helene. Several interviews, Washington, D.C., and Honolulu, Sparky's widow

Matsunaga, Keene. Correspondence, Sparky's son

Matsunaga, Matthew. Several interviews, Sparky's son

Matsunaga, Merle. Correspondence, Sparky's daughter

Meyerson, Harvey. Several interviews, Washington, D.C., Sparky's staff aide.

Midkiff, Marjorie Carter. Interview. January 1997, friend of Sparky at University of Hawai'i drama society

Mineta, Hon. Norman. Interview, Washington, D.C., May 1997, former Representative (D-Calif.), in House with Sparky

Mink, Hon. Patsy. Interview, Washington, D.C., May 1997, Democratic Representative from Hawaii

Mukaida, Sam. Interview, February 1997, lived in Okumura Home with Sparky, knew him at University of Hawai'i

Okamura, Satoru. Interview, September 1997, served in National Guard with Sparky

Oki, Albert. Interview, June 1997, knew Sparky at University of Hawai'i

Oki, Eiichi. Several interviews 1997–1998, Sparky's law partner

Oshiro, Robert. Interview, August 1997, Democratic party leader in Hawai'i

Otagaki, Hon. Kenneth. Several interviews, 1997–1999, medical company, 100th Infantry Battalion, scholar and civic leader

Quinn, Hon. William. Interview, August 1997, first elected governor of Hawai'i (1959–1963)

Ritchie, Donald. Interview, Washington, D.C., July 1999. Associate Historian of U.S. Senate

Santoki, Mark, ed., *Hawai'i Herald*, furnished clippings and other materials

Senda, Kazuo. Interview, Kauai, March 1997, grew up in Kaua'i, lived in Okumura Home, served in 100th Battalion

Smyser, A.A. Interview, March 1997, former editor, *Honolulu Star-Bulletin*

Solymon, Bronwen. Librarian, University of Hawai'i, assisted in finding materials

Suzuki, Mabel. Librarian, University of Hawai'i, government records, assisted in finding documents

Tanaka, Drusilla. Several interviews, executive director, 100th Infantry Battalion Veterans Association (Club 100), Honolulu

Tateishi, Margaret. Several interviews, furnished pertinent materials, relative of Matsunaga family

Tohara, Martin. Several interviews beginning January 1997. First sergeant, D Company, 100th Battalion

Tolchin, Martin. Several interviews, Washington, D.C., former Congressional correspondent, *The New York Times*

Tsukayama, Conrad. Several interviews, beginning January 1997, member D Company, 100th Battalion

Tsukiyama, Ted. Interview, April 1999, knew Sparky from University of Hawai'i and throughout his political career

Yamamoto, Cora. Interview, Washington, D.C., May 1998, former staff aide to Sparky

Bibliography

Allen, Gwenfread E. *Hawaii's War Years 1941–1945*, Pacific Monograph, Kailua, HI, 1999

Allen, Gwenfread E. *Men and Women of Hawaii*, a biographical directory, *Honolulu Star-Bulletin*, 1966

Ariyoshi, George R. *With Obligation to All*, Ariyoshi Foundation, Honolulu, 1997

Baker, Ross K. Friend & Foe in the U.S. Senate, Copley Edition, 1999

Berry, Thomas Elliott. *The Biographer's Craft*, Odyssey Press, New York, 1967

Boylan, Dan & T. Michael Holmes. *John A. Burns: The Man and His Times*, University of Hawai'i Press, Honolulu, 2000

Broder, David. *Changing of the Guard: Power and Leadership in America*, Simon & Schuster, New York, 1980

Burns, Hon. John. *Reflections*, former governor of Hawai'i, unpublished transcript of oral history

Chang, Thelma. *I Can Never Forget: Men of the 100th/442nd*, SIGI Productions, Honolulu, 1991

Chinen, Kathleen, ed. *Japanese Eyes, American Heart: Personal Reflections of Hawaii's World War II Nisei Soldiers*, Tendai Educational Foundation, Honolulu, 1998

Congressional Record 1963–1991

Cook, Chris. *Kauai: The Garden Island, A Pictorial History*, The Conning Company, Virginia Beach, VA 1999

Cooper, George & Gavan Daws. *Land and Power in Hawaii*, University of Hawai'i Press, Honolulu, 1985

Crost, Lyn. *Honor by Fire: Japanese Americans at War in Europe and the Pacific*, Pacific Press, Novato, CA, 1994

Daniels, Roger and Sandra Taylor and Harry Kitano, eds. *Japanese Americans: From Relocation to Redress*, Revised edition, University of Washington Press, 1991

Daws, Gavan. *Shoal of Time: A History of the Hawaiian Islands*, University of Hawai'i Press, 1968

Duus, Masayo Umezawa. *Unlikely Liberators: The Men of the 100th and 442nd*, University of Hawai'i Press, 1983

Fuchs, Lawrence H. *Hawaii Pono: A Social History*, Harcourt, Brace, and World, Inc., New York, 1961

Gall, Susan, Managing Editor. *The Asian American Almanac*, Gale Research Inc., Detroit, 1995

The Garden Island (Kauai newspaper) 1937

Glazer, Sarah Jane. Spark M. Matsunaga, "Democratic Representative from Hawaii," Nader Congress Project, Grossman Publishers, Washington, D.C., 1972

Hatamiya, Leslie. *Righting a Wrong: Japanese Americans and the Passage of the Civil Liberties Act of 1988*, Stanford University Press, 1993

Hawai'i Herald (newspaper) 1962 & 1976

Hawaii Hochi, (newspaper) 1962 & 1976 (in Japanese)

Hawaii State Data Book

Hazama, Dorothy Ochiai and Jane Okamoto Komeiji. *Okagesama de: The Japanese in Hawaii 1885–1985*, Bess Press, Honolulu, 1986

Hohri, William Minoru. *Repairing America: An Account of the Movement for Japanese-American Redress*, Washington State University Press, 1988

Honolulu Star-Bulletin. 1941–1991 (newspaper)

Hosokawa, Bill. *JACL in Quest of Justice*, William Morrow, New York, 1982

Hosokawa, Bill. *Nisei: The Quiet Americans*, William Morrow, New York, 1969

Inouye, Daniel K. Journey to Washington, Prentice-Hall, Englewood Cliffs, New Jersey, 1969

Ke Kuhaiu, Kauai High School yearbook, 1933

Kimura, Yukiko. *Issei: Japanese Immigrants in Hawaii*, University of Hawai'i Press, 1988

Kotani, Roland. "The Japanese in Hawaii: A Century of Struggle", *Hawaii Hochi*, 1985

Krauss, Bob. *Our Hawaii; The Best of Bob Krauss*, Island Heritage Publishing, Honolulu, 1990

Lum, Arlene, ed. *Sailing for the Sun: The Chinese in Hawaii 1789–1989*, Three Heroes (publishers), Honolulu, 1988

Lyman, Richard Ka'ilihiwa. *Mea ho'omana'o, Thoughts, Estate of Richard Lyman*, Honolulu, 1995

Matloff, Maurice, general ed. *American Military History*, Office of the Chief of Military History, Washington, DC, 1973

Matsunaga, Spark M. & Ping Chen. *Rulemakers of the House*, University of Illinois Press, Urbana, 1978

Matsunaga, Spark M. *The Mars Project: Journeys Beyond the Cold War*, Hill and Wang, New York, 1986

Murphy, Thomas. *Ambassadors in Arms: The Story of Hawaii's 100th Battalion*, University of Hawai'i Press, 1955

Newton, L.C., ed. *Who's Who in the Counties of Kauai and Maui*, Territory of Hawaii 1939, Maui Publishing, Wailuku.

Niiya, Brian, ed. "Japanese American History, Facts on File", New York, 1993

Ogawa, Dennis M. *Kodomo no tame ni: For the sake of the children, the Japanese American Experience in Hawaii*, University of Hawai'i Press, 1978

Oie, Harold. "Military Intelligence Service", self-published, undated

Okihiro, Gary. *Cane Fires: The Anti-Japanese Movement in Hawaii 1965–1945*, Temple University Press, Philadelphia, 1991

O'Reilly, John Boyle. *Songs from the Southern Seas*, in James Jeffrey Roche, *John Boyle O'Reilly, His Life, Poems, and Speeches*, Cassell Publishing, New York, 1991

Robeson, Barbara. Research coordinator, Kauai Historical Society, pointed out pertinent materials

Roth, Randall W., ed. *The Price of Paradise*, Mutual Publishing, Honolulu, 1993

Takabuki, Matsuo. *An Unlikely Revolutionary: Matsuo Takabuki and the Making of Modern Hawaii*, University of Hawai'i Press, 1998

Tamashiro, Ben. *Remembrances: 100th Infantry Battalion*, Sons and Daughters of the 100th Infantry Battalion, Honolulu, 1997

Tanaka, Chester. *Go for Broke: A Pictorial History*, Go for Broke Inc, Richmond, CA, 1982

The Honolulu Advertiser. 1941–1991 (newspaper)

The New York Times, 1963–1990

The Washington Post, 1963–1990

United States Senate. "Spark M. Matsunaga, Late a Senator from Hawaii", Memorial Addresses Delivered in Congress, Government Printing Office, Washington, D.C., 1992

University of Hawai'i Yearbook 1941

War Department. *Salerno*, Historical Division, Washington, D.C., 1944

War Department. *Volturno 6 Oct.–15 Nov. 1943*, Military Intelligence Division, Washington, D.C., undated

Weglyn, Michiko Nishiura. *Years of Infamy: The Untold Story of America's Concentration Camps*, William Morrow, New York, 1976

Index

About the Author

Richard Halloran is a newspaperman who writes "The Rising East," a weekly column about Asia and America's relations with Asia. He has written for *The Washington Post* and *Business Week* and was with *The New York Times* for 20 years, serving as a foreign correspondent in Asia and a military correspondent in Washington, D.C. He has also been Director of Communications and Journalism at the East-West Center in Honolulu and editorial director of the *Honolulu Star-Bulletin*.

Halloran graduated from Dartmouth College, earned an M.A. in Asian studies at the University of Michigan, and studied at Columbia University's East Asia Institute on a Ford Foundation Fellowship. As a paratrooper in the U.S. Army, he saw duty in Korea, Japan, Taiwan and Vietnam. He has won the George Polk Award for National Reporting and the Gerald R. Ford Prize for Distinguished Reporting on National Defense. He has also been awarded Japan's Order of the Sacred Treasure, Gold Rays with Rosette, given a Lifetime Achievement Award by the Pacific and Asian Affairs Council of Hawaii, and is an honorary member of the 100th Infantry Battalion Veterans Association. Halloran is married to Fumiko Mori Halloran, an author who writes about America for a Japanese audience. The couple lives in Honolulu.

Other books by Richard Halloran are:

Japan: Images and Realities
Conflict and Compromise: The Dynamics of American Foreign Policy
To Arm a Nation: Rebuilding America's Endangered Defenses
Serving America: Prospects for the Volunteer Force